THE VAMPIRE NEXT DOOR

THE VAMPIRE NEXT DOOR

The True Story of the Vampire Rapist

J.T. HUNTER

Pedialaw Press

Copyright

Contents

Preface

This is a work of non-fiction. The story that follows was pulled together from extensive interviews of the people who lived it, court filings and transcripts, police files, prison records, news articles, FBI records, and letters and other documents prepared by the individuals involved in the relevant events. Nonetheless, as most historians will attest, any work attempting to piece together the past must overcome the lack of direct evidence that inevitably leaves holes in the puzzle. As the author Julian Barnes observed, "[h]istory is that certainty produced at the point where the imperfections of memory meet the inadequacies of documentation." In other words, not everything that occurred in the past was recorded or remembered in reliable detail. By necessity, then, some parts of this story were produced by using the best available evidence of how those events unfolded. Most prominent in this regard is the fact that, other than the fortunate young woman who managed to escape from a living nightmare, no other victims of the Vampire Rapist survived to tell their tale. Out of respect for her request for privacy, the sole survivor's name has been changed, as have the names of other individuals who agreed to speak with the author on the condition that their real names not be used.

The Dead
Under the pure light of the stars
The dead sleep
Wrapped about in a silence unutterable
The ages come and go, like a tale that is told
Time stretches out to the golden unbarred gate
Of eternity,
But the dead sleep on, sleep on.

- J.A. Edgerton

Part I

THE MISSING AND THE DEAD

ONE

Hungry like the wolf

The hunger was eternal, and once again, the hunger had returned. Just as it always had, just as it always would. It was a beast that could never be banished, a shadowy creature that hounded him and demanded gratification. He could not escape it and he knew that it would never relent. There was only one way to satisfy it. He had to hunt again.

The hunger had begun as an unexplainable emptiness, an indescribable yearning for something more. It had been with him for as long as he could remember, his constant companion since childhood, and as he grew the hunger grew with him. It came to him now as an irresistible need to strangle, to constrict the carotid arteries, block off the jugular veins, or slowly compress the windpipe until his victims passed out from lack of oxygen to the brain. It excited him to see the panic in their eyes as their faces turned alternating shades of purple and blue. It invigorated him to see the pupils of their eyes as they faded away, as the very spark of life, that inner glint illuminating the window to the soul, flickered and began to fade, until at last the eye went dim and dull. Watching a young woman gasping desperately for breath gave him an intense sexual high, but it was more than a chemical cocktail of oxytocin and endorphins that drove him to kill. While there was a sexual component to the addiction, the hunger went deeper than that. The power and control he felt was what provided an unparalleled sense of pleasure, a state of ecstasy far exceeding any orgasm.

He discovered early on that he only felt truly alive when watching another human being die. The only times he truly lived were those all too transitory moments when he killed. Like some exiled demon from the underworld, he celebrated life in the shadow of its obliteration. Each victim served as a sacrificial lamb, temporarily pacifying the dark creature that so often controlled him.

He did not enjoy the act of killing in and of itself. What he needed went beyond that. It was the feeling of total control, the knowledge that he had the power to grant life swiftly or steal it away, that he savored. He had a pathological need to exercise absolute power over his victims by physically possessing them, much like he might possess a motorcycle or car. To satisfy his need, his victims were systematically stripped of their humanity and reduced to objects. They were no longer human beings. They were merely toys for his amusement.

The first time he killed was almost an accident. He had become so aroused and excited by the fear in the woman's eyes as she struggled for air that he squeezed too hard for too long. She had fallen unconscious before during prior sexual forays, but she had always revived. This time, however, she never came back.

It was a simple procedure really. So simple, but so deadly. Ten to twenty seconds in a choke hold compressing the carotid artery worked every time. But this time he could not stop himself. The usual ten to twenty seconds of pressure had surged past a minute, and still he did not stop. It was if some unseen force had taken control of his mind and taken command of his body. He was no longer aware of the passage of time. He had seen the warning signs as the carbon dioxide levels in her blood rapidly escalated to the point of hypercarbia. He felt her pulse quicken as her blood pressure surged higher, but he kept squeezing even when the convulsions began, triggered by her unoxygenated and hypercarbic brain. He looked on excitedly as her body's unconscious efforts to breathe became weaker, as her lungs' feeble attempts to inhale slowly faded away. Then her heartbeat became increasingly irregular, steadily decreasing in force and frequency, continually slowing until it finally stopped.

When he realized that she was gone, his excitement and euphoria gave way to exasperation and anger. He was not upset over the fact that he had killed her. Really, he thought nothing more of the act of killing a human being than he did of brushing his teeth. Indeed, the notion of a remorseful conscience was an alien concept to him. He experienced no feelings of guilt, suffered no moral or spiritual crisis. Rather, his displeasure was aimed at his own lack of discipline and loss of self-control. More than that, he was annoyed at the lifeless girl for ruining his fun.

At first, he could not decide what to do with her. He knew that he needed to get rid of the body, but not having killed before, he did not know how. As he analyzed his options, he remembered news reports that he had seen over the years about unidentified bodies found partially buried in wooded areas or discovered in shallow graves in remote fields. He knew of many such places. It had not been hard to find a suitable location for her, especially with the aid of darkness.

He had always felt most relaxed at night. The night never failed to welcome or aid him. It embraced him with understanding arms, caressing his face with gentle fingers, comforting him with tender, nurturing hands. Even as a child, anxious and alone, the night had reassured and restored him, a surrogate mother who always knew how to make things right.

———————

Even though it had not been entirely purposeful, that first time had whetted his appetite. Something in him yearned for more, like a wolf fresh off its first kill. He developed an irrepressible urge to do it again. If you asked him why he had enjoyed it so much, he would not be able to tell you, but the inability to explain his feelings would not bother him. The simple fact that he enjoyed it was enough. While he knew it was considered to be wrong, he also knew that he could not stop himself from doing it again.

The next time the hunger came, he was better prepared. He rehearsed the events in his mind multiple times, over and over again. He had taken the time to refine his methods and he was initially pleased with the results. He succeeded in keeping the second girl alive for much longer, enjoying his control over her, reveling in the power he felt as she pleaded for him to let her go. But reality once again failed to measure up to fantasy, and when he had taken his fill of her, one final squeeze of frustration finished it.

The third time was not the charm. Indeed, his next victim had been problematic, causing him considerable trouble with the police. He made a mistake in targeting someone he knew, a mistake that nearly proved too costly, as the police came close to gathering sufficient evidence to support an arrest. An alibi manufactured after-the-fact had helped to muddy the waters, and some well-timed allegations of police misconduct had stopped the investigation in its tracks, but he knew that he had been lucky to get away with it. It had been a hard lesson to learn, but he would not make the same mistake twice.

He was well down the darkened path when he developed a taste for blood. It was a nurse who shared his interest in the occult

and experimental sex that first introduced him to the erotic pleasure of drinking human blood. Well versed in the act of bloodletting, she taught him the most effective tools and techniques, and he
took advantage of having a willing partner with which to practice
and perfect his methods. He found the crimson color of the liquid
alluring and he quickly took to its salty taste. Now he knew
another way to feed the hunger. With strangulation the appetizer,
blood and sex served as the main dish. Death was the sweet
dessert.

When it came time to find his next victim, he indulged the new
dimension to his appetite. As the helpless woman lay bound before
him, he did not just violate her body, he violated her very being by
taking her blood, the essential element of life, feeding on it,
devouring and digesting it, subordinating it to his own bodily
essence. He did not just feed on her blood. He fed off her fear as
well. Unable to experience any genuine feelings himself, the intensity of her abject terror momentarily masked his own inner anguish.

Once satiated, simply taking a little more blood finished the job.
He watched as she began to hyperventilate, her body attempting to
saturate its decreasing volume of blood with as much oxygen as
possible. He felt her fear as her heart rate skyrocketed in a desperate
attempt to make up for her body's rapidly falling blood pressure. As
her coronary arteries received less circulating blood, her pulse rate
plummeted, she lost consciousness, ceased breathing, and her
exhausted, oxygenstarved heart shuddered, slowed, and then
stopped. Yet, as always, her suffering only temporarily alleviated
the emptiness inside him.

Aside from being cheated by the transitory nature of his relief,
he had always been amused and intrigued by his victims' reactions
to what was happening to them. Like a clinical psychologist
studying the effect of self-awareness of one's impending death, he
had observed first-hand his victims' many faces of fear. It fascinated
him how they all seemed so different on the outside, yet death never

failed to function as the great equalizer. Every death illuminated the truth that, at our innermost core, we are all essentially the same.

Some of them had whimpered silently to themselves in the dark, crying quietly as if they had already seen how it would end, the basic compulsion of self-preservation having long since been drowned by fear, the survival instinct having been short-circuited by an irrepressible hopelessness. Some sobbed loudly, pleading hysterically, promising anything in a desperate attempt to barter for their lives. Some had shrieked uncontrollably, their sheer horror so intense that their very eyes seemed to scream out in terror. Even those who might have had the will to fight back did not realize the dire truth of their situation until they had been rendered incapable of resisting. Only one of them had surprised him. Her fear had transcended itself, eclipsing its initial state, transforming into a beautiful, primordial anger, blossoming into the purist, uncompromising rage. He had been transfixed by the raw power of her emotion, its sheer psychic energy, as she spent her final moments fighting back the only way possible, using her last breath to curse him as he strangled her into oblivion before finally draining her life away.

She had been the exception. The vast majority had ultimately pleaded through their tears, trying to appeal to him with the same pointless refrain.

"Please let me go, mister. Please, I promise I won't tell anyone."

He always knew that they were lying, that they would say anything to try to preserve their flickering, fading, pathetically fragile, lives. Of course, even if true, their desperate promises meant nothing to him. He lacked any trace of empathy, and guilt was an alien concept that he did not have the capacity to experience. In the end, all of his prey had shared the same fate, succumbing to the finality of death by asphyxiation as he stared excitedly into their eyes, or experiencing the shock of heart failure caused by excessive loss of blood as he bled them into black oblivion.

Physically unassuming, he used his nonthreatening appearance to his advantage; his frail frame and handsome face allowed him to catch his victims off-guard and his friendly disposition and polished charm invited their trust, rendering them readily receptive to his deception. Over the years, he had polished and perfected his hunting style, stalking and capturing his prey in equally efficient ways. Some he had lured into his car with the offer of a ride. Others had been receptive to promises of cash for sexual favors. Sometimes he pulled out a pistol from under his seat and forced his victim to put on handcuffs. Other times, he had one end of the cuffs already secured to the car so that he could immobilize his chosen victim with a quick click on the wrist.

In refining his craft, he learned to appreciate the element of surprise. He had grown fond of strangling from behind to ensure the least resistance. A victim who could not see the attack coming could not flee or prepare to fight back until the chances of successfully doing either had drastically diminished. And no matter how they were initially subdued, all of the girls ended up bound or hand-cuffed so that he could keep them under control, ensuring that he could manipulate them without resistance.

He often wondered how much longer he could get away with it. *How could one do the things that he had done and not be locked up?* The lack of any adverse consequences for his actions continued to embolden him. It affirmed his belief that he was not subject to society's rules. It reinforced his conviction that he rightfully oper-ated beyond the community's artificial boundaries. As a boy, he had learned about right and wrong, and he had been taught about good and evil. He had repeatedly witnessed the rituals of the Episcopalian Church, experienced all of the incantations and incense, parroted the formalistic prayers, and recited the penitent petitions. He had been made to mimic them, but they never spoke to him spiritually, never brought him closer to God. Now the impunity with which he acted crystallized his belief. *After all, how could there be a just God when he continued to walk free, working unhindered and unchallenged, unpunished after contemptuously violating so many of His commandments?* Irrespective of the explanation for his behavior, he could not stop now even if he wished to do so. He had to obey the call to hunt. He had to feed the ravenous beast.

He remembered with much vexation the time when the police had too easily identified one of his victims, how their investigation had come too close. In refining his methods, he learned through trial and error that a simple bathtub worked best both for immobilizing his victims and disposing of their bodies. The sharp, metal teeth of his hacksaw cut through their tendons and bone like a knife through butter, and the blood flowed easily into the drain. But the work had still been harder, more physically grueling, than he imagined it would be. Not to mention much messier.

By the time he had cut enough of the leg bone, he was drenched in sweat and blood. Although the neck severed without much effort, the blood spewed and spattered, saturating his shirt and seeping down the wall. He felt no disgust or repugnance for the fruits of his handiwork, but he was aggravated by the thought of having to do more cleaning. Nonetheless, a short car ride later and the disposal was done.

He kept the head as his prize. He already had a special place picked out for storing it.

And yet, the emptiness still remained. As always, the thrill of the kill too quickly diminished, the temporary rush already fading away. Within days, he was planning the next one, thinking how to make it better, more satisfying, closer to what he needed. He rehearsed the fantasy over and over again in his mind before staging the next performance, each time needing escalating levels of stimulation to get the same gratification. Each time reality returned all too quickly, exposing the illusion, leaving him in need of more. As always, the insatiable hunger did not diminish. As always, the dark creature demanded more.

It was time to hunt anew.

On November 21, 1985, he found his latest victim.

TWO

You were a vampire

Nineteen-year-old Christina Almah was still a virgin, and a bit naïve when it came to matters of sex, but like most teenaged girls on the verge of womanhood, she enjoyed receiving attention from good looking, romantically inclined men. Yet, even she was surprised when, after a handsome, slightly older man took an interest in her, she found herself traveling all the way across the country to see him again.

Christina first met twenty-two-year-old Carl Von Bane several months earlier while he was visiting a friend near her hometown of Westminster, California. She immediately noticed him when he walked into the Drug Emporium where she had been working for the past year as a clerk, and they had quickly hit it off. His rugged, bad boy looks, and confident disposition combined to render her fully smitten. But the budding romance had barely begun before "Von" returned home to Florida. Their brief time together had passed much too quickly for the love-struck Miss Almah.

Since Von's departure, they had continued their blossoming relationship by telephone racking up steep long-distance bills. All the while, Christina had meticulously saved her meager Drug

Emporium pay so that she could afford to purchase a plane ticket to visit him. When Von had called her a few weeks before, Christina hinted at wanting to see him again by casually mentioning that she had some vacation time that needed to be used. When he suggested that she catch a flight to Florida to visit him, she had immediately agreed. After all, this was not some fly by night infatuation. She thought that she might be in love.

Christina had been counting the days until this trip—a weeklong vacation certain to be a memorable one if for no other reason than the fact that it would be the first time she had ever traveled alone. She booked a direct flight on Eastern Airlines from Los Angeles to Orlando International Airport, and Von had picked her up there nearly a week before. Since then, she had been staying with Von in his mother's mobile home at Lot 12 of the Enchanted Lakes Mobile Home Park on Malabar Road, near the eastern edge of the City of Palm Bay in southern Brevard County.

Named for the lush palm trees that lined the bay at the mouth of Turkey Creek, the nearly 100-square-mile Palm Bay had experienced a period of rapid growth in recent years fueled by an influx of retirees, northern transplants, and space industry workers. As part of the "Space Coast," Palm Bay benefited from its proximity to Cape Canaveral, home to the National Aeronautics and Space Administration's space shuttle program. To the west of Palm Bay, just past Interstate 95, a vast expanse of swamps and marsh grass stretched beyond the horizon, home to an endless assortment of flora and fauna. Under the blinding gaze of the eternal Florida sun, cold-blooded creatures swam silent and unseen as they had for ages past, ancient predators stalking their unsuspecting prey.

Immediately to the east of Palm Bay sits the Town of Malabar, a small, quiet community only thirteen square miles in size. Its eastern edge meets the Intracoastal Waterway in a subtropical paradise of palm trees, sailboats, and spectacular sunsets. The area's abundant seafood, perennial sunshine, and constant sea breeze

reminded Christina of her favorite parts of California. That famil-
iarity was reassuring. It felt comfortable. She felt safe.

A petite girl standing about five feet, four inches tall and
weighing a little less than 110 pounds, Christina was not a beauty
queen, but she was not unattractive either. Indeed, her green eyes
and brown hair combined in an inviting way that most men found
sensual and appealing, and she had enjoyed her fair share of suitors.
Although she had shared a few intimate moments with boys in high
school, she had never found one with whom she felt comfortable
enough to sacrifice her virtue. Still sexually inexperienced, she had
the classic Libra traits of compassion, innate gentleness, and a
genuine caring for others, traits that were sometimes misconstrued
by men. Still, it never dawned on her that Von's testosterone-driven
brain would expect something more than a kiss hello, or that he
would interpret her willingness to fly across the country to visit him
as a green light for sleeping together. Von had tried to take that next
step during her first night in Florida, and when she told him that she
was not ready, he had reluctantly played the part of the understanding boyfriend, but he could not wholly hide his irritation and
mounting frustration.

Von worked at Gator Chrysler in nearby Melbourne, and he had
to leave Christina alone for much of the day. That had been the
routine for most of the week, and the excitement of staying with
someone in another state had long since faded away. On this particular morning, she passed some time by listening to a worn down
cassette tape of Madonna's "Like a Virgin" album, popping it into
the cherry red Sony Walkman that Von had given her. She played
several songs, rewound the tape, and played them again, but after a
while she tired of listening to the provocative singer purr about
being "touched for the very first time." She tried watching television after that, but quickly lost interest in the mindless game shows
and melodramatic soap operas that dominated the channels.
Growing bored, she decided to walk to Melbourne a few miles away

to visit several friends that she had met through Von. She would be flying back to California the next morning and wanted to say her good-byes and make the most of her final day of vacation. Wearing blue jeans, sandals, and a black t-shirt with a Harley Davidson insignia splashed across the front, she left the trailer shorty after 1:00 p.m. It was the twenty-first day of November 1985.

As she walked out of the entrance of the mobile home park, a light rain began to fall. She could see dark clouds gathering in the distance and a westerly wind promised that they would soon be present. Somewhere beyond the visible horizon, thunder rumbled ominous and angry, its source hidden behind an approaching wall of grey and black clouds.

Christina turned left and started walking faster as the rain increased, heading east on Malabar Road toward U.S. 1 and the Intracoastal. She planned to stop at the Jiffy Mart at the corner of Malabar Road and U.S. 1 to buy a pack of cigarettes before walking north into Melbourne. She had not gone far when a small, light-colored car pulled up beside her.

Behind the wheel of the two-door automobile sat a clean-shaven man wearing a stylish, navy-blue sports coat, a black-and-white striped tie, and a nice pair of dress slacks, not the cheap K-Mart kind, but the higher quality cloth and cut of a more fashionable men's store. The man looked to be in his late twenties or early thirties. He had loafer style shoes, but he was not wearing them while he drove. Christine thought it slightly odd that the well-dressed man's bare foot operated the gas and brake pedals, but she gave it no more than a fleeting thought. She had certainly seen much stranger things during her time in Florida. The man's eyes were concealed behind darkly tinted sunglasses and his face was framed by a mane of medium-length, dirty blonde hair. He had a thin build, and though slightly pale in complexion, his handsome facial features held an undeniable allure. She could not help feeling an attraction to him.

Flashing a broad, inviting smile, he leaned over, rolled down the passenger door window, and greeted her in a friendly, reassuring voice.

"It's a bit wet today for a walk, isn't it?" he asked with a wry, disarming smile. "Can I give you a lift?"

Although Christina was initially wary of his invitation, he looked harmless enough and it was the middle of the day in broad daylight in a public place, so she did not wait long before responding.

"Well," she said, deliberately drawing out her reply as she decided how much to trust the seemingly friendly stranger. "I'm on my way to Melbourne to meet some friends. Are you going anywhere near there?"

"Sure, I have to go that way to get to my office. I just need to stop by my house real quick to pick up a notebook for work, but it'll only take a minute or two. Go ahead and hop in."

She hesitated for just a moment, studied her Good Samaritan one last time, and then grabbed the passenger side door handle of the car. As she opened the door, she heard Sting's new song, "Russians," playing on the car's radio.

The country had long since fallen into the depths of the Cold War, and the perpetual threat of nuclear holocaust loomed in the back of most people's minds like some amorphous boogieman lurking in the shadows. As Christine pulled the door closed, Sting's voice flowed out of the car's speakers, echoing what seemed to be the universal mood in America and Western Europe, the growing fear of a nuclear attack by the Russian-controlled Union of Soviet Socialist Republics. The song sought to appeal to the good in what President Reagan dubbed the "Evil Empire," expressing a desperate hope that the Russian leaders loved their children enough to avoid the horror of a nuclear holocaust.

Suffering from the same state of uneasiness expressed in the song, Christina found herself captivated by the sense of calm that seemed to radiate from the man behind the wheel. They drove for a little while making small talk. While they chatted, she caught a glimpse of the man's eyes behind his sunglasses. Their azure shade of blue added to the aura of assuredness he projected, and it seemed to Christina that the man's eyes had the power to peer into her very soul, not in any unsettling way, but in an understanding, comforting manner that disarmed her naturally cautious disposition. He seemed genuinely interested in learning about her, and she was impressed with how articulately he expressed himself. He was charming, witty, and exuded self-confidence, and Christine felt relieved that he seemed to be normal. Some of Von's friends that she had met were more than a little on the odd side.

After about five minutes, the man turned his car onto a bumpy, dirt road, and then continued on for a few minutes more before exiting onto a gravel driveway obscured by a tall row of hedges. Planted across the inner edge of the yard, the hedges had grown high enough to block a clear view of whatever was behind them. As the car continued down the driveway, a well-kept lawn, dotted sporadically with pine and oak trees, came into view. At the far end of the lawn stood a redbrick, Colonial style house with four white columns framing a large front door painted the same shade of white as the columns.

The gravel driveway ended at a double-length carport on the left side of the house. The man pulled into the carport and parked. Two motorcycles stood at the opposite end of the parking area.

"I'll be right back," the man told her as he took the key out of the ignition and slipped on his shoes.

He stepped out of the car and walked to the side door of the house, where he paused and glanced back at her. "Hey, you want to come inside for a drink?" She smiled politely.

"Oh, no thanks, my friends are expecting me and I don't want them to worry."

"Suit yourself," he said, before unlocking the door and disappearing into the building.

After a few minutes, the man emerged and announced with an embarrassed laugh that the notebook was not in the house after all.

"It must be in the back of the car," he said, an amused smile spreading across his face as if he had just remembered an irresistibly funny joke.

He walked to the passenger side of the car and opened the door, flashing her the same smug alligator smile. He crawled into the back seat and began looking around, grinning all the while.

Suddenly, the back of Christina's seat shot forward, slamming her violently against the dashboard. Stunned by the force of the impact and shocked by the unexpected attack, she was barely able to register the sound of something rustling behind her.

Then something brushed against her forehead. Before she could react, her neck jerked back painfully, and she began to choke. Frantically, she reached for her purse, attempting to grab something – anything – to try to defend herself. Her fingers brushed against the top of a can of OFF insect repellant. Desperate, she thought that if she could spray her attacker in his eyes, she might be able to blind him long enough to get away.

But as her fingers closed around the spray can, the man's voice, angry and powerful, startled her into submission.

"Stop it or I'll kill you!"

As her initial impulse of self-defense gave way to a paralyzing feeling of despair, her hand retreated out of her purse and her arm fell numbly to her side.

Then the rope tightened and everything went black.

When Christina opened her eyes, she found herself lying on her back on a raised countertop about four feet off of the floor in the middle of a kitchen. She assumed that the nameless man had taken her into his house. Both of her hands were tied tightly over her head with a white nylon rope, and her legs were similarly bound at the ankles on the other end of the counter. She was stretched out in a spread eagle position.

A peculiar smell drifted in the air. It was a heavy, smoky smell, but not the comforting aroma one might enjoy emanating from a fireplace. Instead, the unpleasant odor of brimstone billowed from a bronze bowl of sulfuric incense, permeating the room, penetrating her nostrils, and suppressing any other smell.

A lone light bulb dangling from the ceiling served as the sole source of illumination. On the far side of the dimly lit room, she could see a black video camera mounted on a silver tripod standing in the darkness. A red light on the side of the camera blinked on and off as the camera stared at her.

The thin, pale man stood over her, naked except for a silver necklace that had a starburst-shaped black and silver pendant attached at the end. When the man noticed that she was awake, he grinned wickedly and yanked on a rope that had been shaped into a noose around her neck. Still holding the rope, the man leaned over her and whispered in her ear.

"Do you want me to take your shirt off?"

The warmth of his breath against her ear caused Christine to recoil reflexively.

"No," she said faintly, nearly too frightened to speak.

Fixing her with an icy stare, he reached down and slowly pulled her t-shirt up over her chest. He watched her with wolfen eyes, visibly excited that she was not wearing a bra, her milky-white breasts were now wholly exposed, firm and fully bared for him. He pulled on the rope again while running his tongue up each one, pausing to bite hungrily at each fleshy knob.

Still leering lustfully at her, the lurid figure spoke again.

"Should I take off your pants?" he asked with a twisted grin, growing more noticeably aroused.

"Please, don't," she murmured faintly, her whole body trembling. "Please just let me go."

Ignoring her pleas, the man pushed the legs of her jeans across the silky flesh of her thighs, careful to caress their soft recesses, before pulling the jeans down to her ankles. He untied the rope that gripped her left leg, slid her underwear over the ends of her left foot, and then retied her leg. He repeated the process with the right leg and piled her jeans and panties on the floor. As she lay stretched naked before him, her legs spread wide, the man gazed at Christina through demonic eyes.

She turned her head to look away and again saw the video camera.

It continued recording from the edge of darkness.

The man noticed her watching the camera.

"That's to help me remember you," he said abruptly. "But don't worry, I keep them for myself."

Before Christine could think about what he meant, he tugged lightly on the rope around her neck, using just enough force to make it difficult for her to breathe without cutting off her air supply completely.

He leaned over her and slowly ran his tongue along the inside of her thighs, pausing occasionally and gently biting her, lightly nibbling at her exposed flesh before resuming his tongue's lustful journey. When he finished, he climbed onto the countertop and mounted her, positioning his hard crotch between the soft warmth of her legs. As he pushed himself into her, she felt a momentary pressure, and then winced in pain as he fully penetrated her. She closed her eyes as tight as she could, trying to block out what was happening, desperately hoping that she would wake up from what had to be a terrible dream.

Once inside of her, the man began to thrust, slowly at first, but then faster and more forcibly. She bit her lip to take her mind off the pain as he thrust into her again and again, pounding against her harder and harder.

As the intensity of the thrusts increased, the rope around her neck tightened. Unable to resist or run away, she retreated into the shelter of her mind to try to escape the pain. As her senses faded away, she welcomed the relief of feeling nothing at all.

When she regained consciousness, the man was still lying on top of her, but the violent thrusting had stopped. She could feel his heart racing as his rapid breathing began to slow.

After a few moments, the man climbed off of her, stepped over to another table, and then returned with a roll of masking tape. He placed a piece of tape over each of her eyes, careful not to press too firmly. She struggled to see out of the corners of the tape, but she could only make out blurred shapes.

She felt the man's cold fingers pressing against the inside of her right arm, and she heard something moving beside her. Suddenly, she winced in pain. She felt a sharp prick where the man had been pressing, as if a doctor was giving her a shot. She began to wonder whether the man was drugging her, but within a few seconds, she felt another prick next to the same spot. Although each piercing sensation hurt her, she was too scared to move. She stayed completely still, fearful that her assailant would be angered if she struggled. After a few moments, she felt the painful sensation again, but this time on her left arm.

Then a strange noise broke the frightening silence, a noise that sounded like an infant sucking at its mother's breast. As the disconcerting sound continued, she became aware of an odd feeling on her right arm where she had previously suffered the two painful pricks.

Her heart pounded in terror. She wanted to scream, but the

THREE

A view to a kill

Michael Roberts liked to think of himself as a savvy businessman who had seen it all. He was a seasoned real estate investor with a good sense of where to buy and when to sell. He took pride in outworking the other guy, doing the research and legwork to discover diamonds in the rough, hidden gems overlooked by other investors. He knew that luck had been partly responsible for his success as well, but you would be hard-pressed to get him to admit it.

On January 17, 1985, his nose for finding promising property led him to a rural section of Palm Bay just south of Malabar Road, a couple of miles west of Interstate 95. The weather was nice so he decided to inspect a piece of property on an undeveloped section of Savery Road. Although development in the surrounding area had stalled in recent years, he believed that the region was ripe for significant commercial and residential growth.

As he walked the parcel's boundaries evaluating its potential, he noticed something sticking out from underneath a dense area of saw palmettos. Moving closer, he saw part of what appeared to be a towel or shirt decorated with pink and green flowers. His interest piqued, he pulled on the exposed portion of the cloth, and with considerable effort, he managed to free it from the overgrowth covering it. Now that the material was fully visible, he could see that it was a pink-bordered blanket, and that it seemed to be wrapped around something. Curious to see what it concealed, he lifted the blanket, and its ends came unraveled.

"Jesus Christ!" he gasped, jumping back as if he had seen a snake.

He stared in shock at the pile of human bones that had spilled out at his feet. Dropping the rest of the blanket to the ground, he hurried back to his car and sped away to find the nearest pay phone.

Shortly after receiving Roberts's call, investigators from the Palm Bay Police Department responded to the scene and secured the area. An examination of the bones that Roberts found wrapped in the blanket confirmed that they were parts of a human leg, spinal column, and ribcage. Using weed-eaters and machetes to clear an area encompassing approximately 5000 square feet, investigators scoured the property and found more skeletal remains, including two teeth partially buried in the dirt, just behind the tree line at the northwest corner of the lot. Despite the extensive search, the body's skull and jaw bone were nowhere to be found.

A few days later, June Kavinski contacted the police to report that she had discarded a skull just before Christmas the month before. A resident of Palm Bay, Kavinski explained that she had noticed her dog gnawing on something in the yard that December day, and when she walked closer, she saw that he was chewing on a grimy, faded skull, the whiteness of which had been weathered by the elements and turned brownish grey. At the time, she assumed that the skull had come from some type of large animal. Disgusted, she grabbed the skull and threw it in the trash, thinking nothing more about it until she saw a recent television news report about a human skeleton being discovered nearby without a head.

Homicide investigators initially speculated that the Savery Road skeletal remains were those of an elderly man who had gone missing months earlier. However, on Valentine's Day, the remains were sent to Dr. R.C. Daily, a forensic scientist at Florida State University, for his assistance in identifying the body. On February 21, Dr. Daily completed his forensic examination, concluding that the remains were those of a white female, thirty to forty-seven years of age, approximately five feet, three inches in height, and weighing about 100 pounds. Daily opined that the victim had been dead for six months or less, and noted that the left leg bone showed evidence of having been cut. Marks on the right leg revealed that someone had tried to cut it as well, suggesting that the body had been intentionally dismembered.

Dr. Daily speculated that decapitation might have also occurred, which would explain the absence of the skull as well as four missing cervical vertebrae. Since some of the other bones recovered at the scene showed evidence of animal chewing, he acknowledged the possibility that an animal had dislodged the skull and then dragged it away from the area where the rest of the body had been found. However, Daily concluded that in order for a dog to have been able to carry the skull, it must have already been decapitated with considerable skin and muscle tissue still attached. Otherwise, it would have been impossible for a dog, no matter how large, to grip the skull with its teeth.

Although it was a grisly discovery, at the time the Savery Road skeleton appeared to be the product of an isolated, random crime.

Less than two weeks after the discovery of the skeleton at Savery Road, two more bodies were found. On January 29, eighteen-year-old Derek Fisher and his best friend Steven Harrison were hunting birds near U.S. Highway 1 in an undeveloped part of Malabar, about a mile south of Malabar Road. Derek had spotted wild turkeys in the area the day before, and the boys hoped to bag at least one of them to show off their hunting skills. As they walked along the edge of a wooded area, the boys stumbled across a large bone lying wholly exposed beside the railroad tracks. When they realized what they had found, the two boys quickly ran home to tell their parents. The site of their discovery was less than six miles to the east of where the Savery Road skeleton had been found.

Having been alerted by the boys' parents, deputies from the Brevard County Sheriff's Office responded to the scene and confirmed that the bone was a human thighbone. Over the next week, more than two-dozen Sheriff's office personnel cleared and searched a five-acre square area stretching into the woods next to the train tracks. In the densely vegetated area of pine trees, palmetto bushes, and palm trees, they recovered two nearly complete human skeletons. The remains lay scattered near a transient campsite about 100 yards east of power lines, close to a riding trail known to be used by dirt bikers, and a Harris Corporation office building stood less than a mile away. Like the Savery Road skeleton, the leg bones of both newly discovered skeletons showed evidence of having been cut by a saw, a conclusion readily reached due to the unmistakable tool marks left behind and the unnatural location of the bone separation in the middle of the skeletons' femurs. And like the Savery Road body, both Malabar skeletons were missing their skulls.

Using a lower jaw bone recovered at the scene that still had several teeth attached, a forensic odontologist was able to match one of the bodies to a set of dental x-rays from 1980 belonging to a local missing person: twenty-one-year-old Kimberly Walker, a prostitute from Vero Beach. At the time of her disappearance, the blue-eyed, blonde-haired Walker had been a petite five feet, two inches in height and weighed only about eighty-five pounds.

A nearly full-length leg cast found at the crime scene confirmed the positive identification. At the time of her disappearance, Kim had been wearing the cast due to a broken leg she suffered when a van hit her while hitchhiking. An outgoing, free spirit who did not own a car, Kim's usual means of transportation involved walking or hitchhiking. It also provided an easy way to find new customers for her particular brand of personal service. Kim's red flip-flops and crutch were eventually recovered from the same area where her cast had been found.

The day after the discovery of the Malabar bodies, Sherry Valdez, a close friend of Kim's, told investigators that she had dropped Kim off at the Zippy Mart on U.S. 1 in Micco, Florida, on the afternoon of June 14, 1984.

"When I looked in the rear-view mirror, she already had her thumb out hitchhiking," Valdez told police. "That's how she met her dates— hitchhiking."

Kim had been soliciting Johns on that June afternoon because she wanted to get a birthday present for her four-year-old daughter, and she hoped to earn some quick cash so that she could buy her daughter something nice later that night.

The last reported sighting of Kimberly Walker occurred later that day in a Jiffy Mart parking lot at the intersection of Malabar Road and U.S. 1. A witness reported seeing Kim getting into a "plain-colored," unidentifiable car being driven by a "thin, well-dressed man." The Malabar Jiffy Mart was located barely more than a mile from where Kim's skeletal remains were discovered seven months later.

During Kim's February 7 memorial service, her parents noticed a man who they did not recognize. After the service, Kim's father approached the man to find out who he was and how he had known Kim. Although cordial and polite, the stranger would only identify himself as a friend of Kim's. The man told Mr. Walker that he was sorry for his loss and then quickly walked away without saying another word.

On February 26, Kim Walker's skeletal remains and the unidentified remains that had been found alongside her were both sent to Dr. Dailey at Florida State University's anthropology department so that he could conduct a forensic examination. On March 25, Dr. Dailey released his findings. He concluded that one of the skeletal remains – presumed to be that of Kim Walker – belonged to a petite, Caucasian female of approximately five feet, one inch in height. The other remains came from a more heavily built female of unknown race. Dr. Daily noted that many of the bones showed mild to severe damage as the result of animal chewing, most likely from dogs, rodents, and wild hogs. He estimated that both women had died between three to thirty-six months earlier. Both skeletons also showed signs of having been partially dismembered, most likely by the use of a hacksaw.

Hacksaws had become the tool of choice for dismembering human bodies because their serrated teeth—made for cutting through metal— could quickly and efficiently cut through bone. They were also readily available at any hardware store, easily disposed of, and inexpensive.

Now, barely one month into 1985, the bodies of three women had been found in Brevard County within close proximity to one another. Homicide investigators began to wonder whether the discoveries were connected. They hoped that there would not be more to come.

Gravesite of first Brevard County victim discovered January 1985

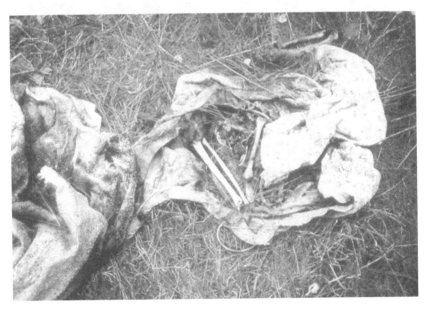

Bones discovered wrapped in blanket on undeveloped property off Savery Road in Palm Bay

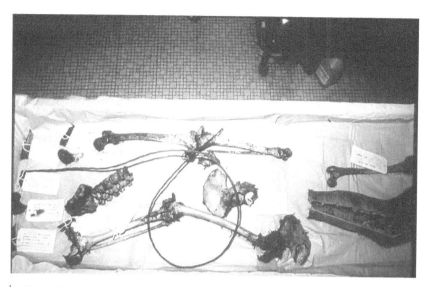

Skeletal remains of Kimberly Walker found in wooded area near Harris Corporation satellite office

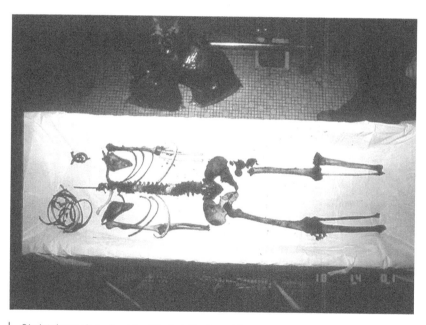

Skeletal remains of unidentified victim found in same area as Kim Walker's body

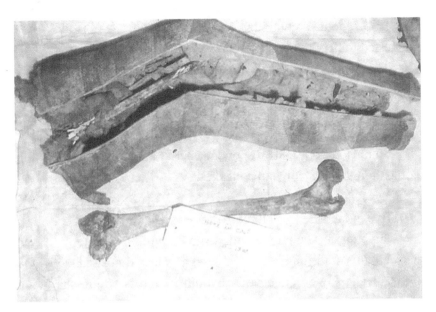

Leg bond and cast that Kim Walker was wearing the last time she was seen alive

By early March, the fleeting Florida winter had once again sounded its quick retreat, fleeing in the face of an overwhelming wave of warmer days. With the new beginning of spring, twenty-nine-year-old Patti Volanski decided to move back to her mother's home in Mims, Florida. She had long since tired of sharing an apartment with her roommate in Scottsmoor, a small town in northern Brevard County, and she decided that it was time for a change.

At approximately 7:30 p.m. on March 15, Patti called her mother, Alta Pratt, to discuss the move. They were both looking forward to spending more time together, and they joked about the sleeping arrangements and what time Patti's curfew would be. Near the end of their discussion, Patti told her mother that nearly all of her things were packed and that she would finish packing in the morning.

"How about I come by and pick you up tomorrow?" Alta suggested to her daughter.

"That would be great, Mom, thanks," Patti replied, "I'll call you in the morning when I'm ready to go."

"Ok, and if you want we can grab some breakfast to celebrate," Alta offered.

"Sounds good," Patti responded, her stomach slightly growling at the thought of bacon and pancakes.

"Bye, Mom!"

"Bye, honey. See you tomorrow."

Alta hung up the phone with a smile on her face, happy to have her daughter returning home. Although Alta did not realize it, that pleasant telephone conversation would be the last time she would ever hear her daughter's voice. Patti would never make the move.

After speaking with her mother, Patti wanted a cigarette. An empty, crunched-up package on the counter reminded her that she had smoked her last one several hours earlier. She was overdue for her next nicotine fix, but there was no store nearby. To make matters worse, Patti did not own a car. She begged her roommate for a ride, but he was too busy to take her. That meant she would have to walk over a mile to the closest convenience store if she wanted to purchase another pack. Prodded on by her nicotine craving, Patti left her apartment sometime between 4:30 and 5:30 p.m. and began walking down U.S. 1. It was the last time anyone reported seeing her alive.

When the next morning came and went without a call from Patti, Alta was not sure whether she should be concerned or annoyed. After all, Patti had gone on last minute trips in the past—sometimes lengthy ones—without letting anyone know ahead of time. Yet, something did not seem quite right this time, and Patti's failure to pick up a veteran's benefits check two weeks later left no doubt in Alta's mind. Something was definitely wrong. The benefits checks, issued on behalf of Patti's deceased husband, arrived like clockwork at Alta's house, which Patti used as her permanent address. Patti always came by to claim the checks soon after they arrived, and her failure to pick up her most recent check raised a red flag that Alta could not ignore. On April 1, she filed a missing persons report with the police.

Carrying 165 pounds on her five-foot-two-inch frame with the image of a skull tattooed prominently on each of her forearms, Patti could come across as a rough character, and she certainly projected a rough appearance to go along with an inner toughness. She had not had an easy life and it had taken its toll on her, but she had endured. Two of her sisters had met premature deaths while she was still a teenager, and at nineteen, she had given birth to a son, only to see her family petition the courts to take him away from her because they felt she lacked the maturity to raise a child. Adding insult to injury, the boy's father later committed suicide.

Her older sister, Bonnie, described Patti as a "lost soul," and once warned her, only half-jokingly, that if she did not stop her habit of hitchhiking, she would end up dead in a ditch. Patti tended to be "drawn to down and out people," and often spent too much time in bars. But she had a soft side as well, and at the time of her disappearance, she had made real strides in trying to get her life together. She loved to cook and talk, and she was always willing to help out her mother, often washing the windows or doing yard work at Alta's house, and assisting with whatever other chores needed to be done.

Her willingness to help extended equally to strangers as well.

"Patti would give anybody the shirt off her back," Alta recalled after it had become obvious that something had happened to her missing daughter.

It would take many months, and a surprising discovery, for the police to piece together what happened to Patti Volanski.

Patti Volanski, who disappeared in early 1985.

Florida is not well known for its woods. Sandy beaches and sunny skies serve as its star attractions. But the abundant sunshine brings stretches of an oppressive heat that is only made worse by the state's extreme humidity. During the summer months, the unrelenting heat and humidity can combine to induce heat stroke in the living. They can also quickly skeletonize the corpses of the dead. A human body left exposed to the Florida elements will rapidly progress through the stages of decomposition, quickly deteriorating from initial rigor mortis to bloating, into the active decay of body fluid loss and maggot infestation, then into a state of advanced decay, before final decomposition into skeletonized remains. The process can take many months in cooler climates, but as little as a week in subtropical Florida, and the abundant scavenging animals of the Sunshine State, the countless vultures, coyotes, and feral pigs, hasten the active decay process even more.

On December 15, 1985, nine months to the day that Patti Volanski vanished while walking to a convenience store, three teenage boys, who were hunting squirrels and target practicing in a wooded area between Dairy Road and Hollywood Boulevard in Palm Bay, came across a decomposed human body partially covered by palmetto leaves and other vegetation. The skeletonized body, lying not far from power lines, wore blue pants with purple buttons and a flowery blouse. Police later found a bra about sixty-five yards away. Unlike the three skeletal remains discovered earlier in the year, this body still had a skull, and the pine needles and algae clinging to it evidenced that the body had been lying there for at least one winter. Due to the location of the skeleton and the woman's clothes that covered it, investigators named the unknown body "Miss Hollywood."

In early January 1986, the Brevard County Sheriff's Office sent Miss Hollywood's skeleton to forensic anthropologists at the Smithsonian Institution in Washington, D.C. After analyzing the remains, forensic experts determined that they belonged to a white woman, thirty to forty years old, approximately five feet, six inches in height, who weighed between 110 and 120 pounds. She had long hair and appeared to have undergone considerable bridgework along her upper and lower jaws. After forensic scientists concluded that she had most likely died between December 1984 and June 1985, Sheriff's investigators theorized that Miss Hollywood had been a transient passing through the area, possibly working as a prostitute in southern Brevard County or northern Indian River County.

Skull of victim referred to as "Miss Hollywood" due to location of skeletal remains

Adding Miss Hollywood to the tally, the skeletal remains of four women had been found in Brevard County in 1985, and police believed that the remains of a fifth, Patti Volanski, lay somewhere in the area awaiting discovery as well.

As the more seasoned homicide investigators realized, finding the skeletal remains of one human body within a thirty-five-mile geographic radius could be considered statistically normal. Such a find might arise from something as mundane as a hunter dying of a heart attack in a lonely stretch of woods. However, discovering multiple skeletal remains within a close radius of one another suggested the strong possibility that a serial killer had been working the area. The skeletal remains of the four Brevard County women were all found within a six-mile radius of each other, and plotting their locations on a map showed their shared proximity to the Town of Malabar.

If these skeletons could talk, they would tell tales of abduction, bondage, rape, and terror. They would tell tales about a pale man in a nondescript car who exuded an almost supernatural attraction. They would tell tales of blood, sex, and death. They would tell tales about a vampire.

Part II

A VAMPIRE AMONG US

FOUR

The walking dead

November 22, 1985 – 10:30 a.m.

Dazed and dizzy from loss of blood, Christina Almah slowly staggered down a lonely dirt road. She could only jut each foot forward an inch or so, one at a time, moving in what was more a clumsy, labored shuffle than a bona-fide step. She wanted to run, but the shackles on her ankles made every shuffling-step a painful struggle. With each movement, the cold metal rubbed deeper into her already raw, chafed legs. Her complexion pasty and unnaturally pale, and clothed only in a bath towel draped loosely around her shoulders, she looked like a zombie, more closely resembling one of the ghoulish walking dead than a flesh and blood human being.

As she continued stumbling forward, she noticed a pickup truck rambling towards her. Christina instantly froze in her tracks, fearful that it was her captor having discovered her absence, coming to reclaim his wandering prisoner. But the truck only slowed as it came closer, and she saw two women sitting in the front, a middle-aged driver and a younger one in the passenger seat. Christina called out to them for help, but they both just glanced at her and drove on, leaving her alone again with her fear.

Growing weaker and more light-headed with each passing moment, she continued her laggard march down the street. It was midmorning and she had only managed to make it a few hundred feet away from the house from which she had fled. Only the fear of that nightmarish house and the macabre man inside of it kept her going. She tried to move more quickly, but the leg restraints were rubbing her ankles so raw that they were beginning to bleed.

After inching forward for what seemed like an eternity, she saw another truck approaching in the distance. At first, she thought that it was the same one she saw before, that her nearly delirious brain was replaying the image like a broken record. Although it had only been a few minutes since the first truck had driven by, she could not think clearly or accurately gauge the passage of time. As the truck neared, she cried out in the loudest voice she could muster despite not being sure whether it was real or a phantom of her mind.

"Please help me," she sobbed, the clear desperation in her eyes reinforcing the urgency of her plea.

Her heart sank as she watched this truck pass by just like the previous one. But as her hope began to give way to despair, the truck's brake lights lit up, and then it stopped. After idling for a few seconds, the truck backed up and drew alongside her. A lone man sat behind the wheel. Seized by a moment of panic, Christina's fight-or-flight response temporarily took control until she caught a clear glimpse of the driver's face and realized that he was not the nameless man come to reclaim her.

Seeing a young girl, naked except for a small towel, her feet shackled, and her wrists bound together by handcuffs, Thomas Harper did not know what to think. He was on his way home from the hardware store, where he had purchased some pipe fitting, and his mind had been preoccupied as he pondered how to finish up a repair project that he had started early that morning at the house. Now, at around 10:30 a.m. and about twenty-five feet from the corner of Hall Road and McCain Drive, he was confronted by something well beyond the ordinary.

At first, he thought that the girl lurching along the street must be involved in a strange practical joke or that she was playing some bizarre game. But then he noticed the genuine terror in her eyes. She stood shivering on the edge of the road, pale as death, shaking and swaying as if the next light breeze might send her tumbling over. Although his windows were up, he could read her lips as she mouthed a muffled plea for help.

After stopping his truck, he opened the driver's door and stepped out to see if she was ok.

"Are those play handcuffs," he asked, "are they toys?" The girl stood there in a daze, as if she did not hear him.

"Do you really need help?"

"Ye . . . yes," she finally stammered. "I was held captive all night.

I got away by climbing through a bathroom window."

"Held captive? And you climbed out a window?" he asked incredulously. "Come on, let's get you out of here and get you some help."

Harper helped her into the passenger seat of his truck and then climbed back into the driver's side. He put the truck in gear, and when they had gone no more than a few feet, she pointed her still-shackled hands at something outside the window.

"Remember that house!" she exclaimed.

Harper glanced in the direction that she was pointing and saw a red-bricked house in the distance facing Hall Road.

"Is that the house you escaped from?" he asked.

"Yes," she whispered softly, as if she feared that the vampire would hear her.

They drove a short distance, a few hundred feet or so, and then turned onto a side street. Christina's complexion suddenly went white as if she had seen a ghost.

"You're not going to hurt me, are you?" she asked in a frightened tone.

"No, I'm not going to hurt you," Harper answered reassuringly, his voice filled with pity.

He pulled into his driveway and stopped the truck.

"You stay here a second. I'm going to get my wife."

He opened the door and disappeared into the house. Christina's heartbeat quickened as she remembered how her assailant had done the same thing before attacking her. But after a minute or so, the man walked back out of the door with a woman close behind him. They came to the truck and the woman opened Christina's door. She gasped when she saw the rope burns on Christina's neck.

"It's okay, dear," Harper's wife said, "you're safe with us. You'll be alright now."

She helped Christina into the house and walked her to the living room where Harper's daughter-in-law waited. Christina was extremely weak and she could barely speak. Her face looked as white as a sheet due to the staggering amount of blood that she had lost. Her dark hair emphasized the unnatural paleness of her skin, and in the low glow of the lamplight, the Harpers thought she looked more dead than alive, like some exiled wraith condemned to walk the eternal night.

They gave her a small cup of orange juice, but she could barely raise it to her mouth and managed to take only a couple of sips. As Christina rested, Harper called the police and paramedics, while his wife and daughter in law did their best to comfort her.

As they waited for the authorities to arrive, Harper asked her what had happened.

Still dazed, Christina began to recount her disturbing story. "I was walking to the store yesterday when a man stopped and asked if I wanted a ride," she said, shifting in her seat as if she was more than just physically uncomfortable. "I know now that I shouldn't have done it, but he looked normal and seemed so nice. So when he offered a ride, I got in his car."

"The man told me that he needed to stop by his house," she continued, "and the next thing I knew, he had a rope around my neck choking me. I passed out, and when I woke up, I was tied down on top of a table. The man raped me throughout the night, and he drained my blood multiple times. Each time he drained my blood, he drank it. And he told me that he's a vampire."

The Harpers were too stunned to reply. The house that Christina had pointed out to Thomas Harper was just down the road. Her nameless vampire was not committing his atrocities in some far away place, somewhere remote and out of mind. This was a monster living in their own neighborhood.

Approximately twenty minutes after Thomas Harper's call for help, an ambulance arrived and hurried Christina to Holmes Regional Medical Center in Melbourne.

As the man in the car drew closer to his house, he grew excited by the thoughts of what he would do next with his prize. He congratulated himself for having kept this one alive for so long so that he could savor the situation. He knew that it was dangerous leaving one alive by itself for such a length of time, but he could not resist the urge for more play time. He was like a child eagerly looking forward to coming home to his favorite toy, but as he made his way down the driveway, he noticed something out of place. The bathroom window was open and he was certain that it had been closed when he left.

Audrey Megregian, an advocate for Citizens Against Sexual Assault, was speaking to a group of high school seniors when her beeper went off that afternoon. She responded to Holmes Regional Hospital and found Christina Almah in a "pretty bad" state. It was obvious that she had been traumatized by something terrible and Megregian could tell that she was still horrified about whatever had happened to her.

At first, Christina's fear of the possibility of having to testify in court in front of her abductor made her reluctant to press charges. However, as they talked, Megregian assured Christina that she would stand with her and support her whether she chose to press charges or not. After taking some time to think about it, and realizing that she could keep the nameless man from doing it again to someone else, Christina told Megregian that she had changed her mind. She would prosecute her assailant after all.

FIVE

A brother to dragons

I am a brother to dragons, and companion to owls.
My skin is black upon me, and my bones are burned
with heat.

- Job 30:29-30

Lieutenant Thomas Fair, head of the homicide division of the Brevard County Sheriff's Office, was in his office that November afternoon doing routine paperwork when his phone rang. He answered to find Lieutenant Leonard Lewis from the south precinct on the line.

"Tom, we've got a signal 31 for you."

"Ok, what do we know, Leo?"

"Victim was abducted yesterday afternoon and the assault continued until early this morning. She claims the assailant drank her blood and told her that he's a vampire."

"No shit. And what's the victim's status?"

"She's at Holmes Regional with two deputies."

"Ok, I'll get someone over there to check it out. Thanks, Leo."

After hearing the details about the strange nature of the sexual assault, Lt. Fair dialed the pager number for the nearest homicide agent to Holmes Regional: Agent Robert Leatherow.

Born and raised in New Jersey, forty-one-year-old Bob Leatherow had a well-deserved reputation in law enforcement circles as a straight shooter with a tendency to tell it like it is. Standing six feet, two inches tall and weighing 210 pounds, Leatherow cut an imposing figure that perfectly complimented his no-nonsense personality and bulldog mentality. His father, a precious metals welder, had hoped that his son would follow in his footsteps, but Leatherow chose a different path, one that would lead him to what would become both his profession and his passion.

Upon graduation from high school in 1960, Leatherow served three years in the United States Navy. After being honorably discharged, he took a job at U.S. Plywood Company in Teterboro, New Jersey. It was there, in 1967, that he noticed an attractive woman dropping off one of his co-workers, her blonde hair blowing in the wind through the open car window as she drove away. After that first glimpse, the same woman kept catching his eye every day, her golden hair always streaming out the window as she went on her way.

Six months passed before Leatherow had the opportunity to meet the woman in the car, but when he did he made sure to get her phone number. When he at last worked up the nerve to ask Peggie Ace out, he called her over and over trying to set up a date, but she always had other plans. Finally, she agreed to go out with him, and they made a date for February 14, Valentine's Day. When Leatherow picked her up that night, it was love at first sight. She was stunning and smart, and he was smitten. After a great time at a nice restaurant, they spoke again by phone the following day. They had the sort of chemistry that blends beautifully from the get-go, the type that usually only exists in romance novels, the type that cannot be explained, only experienced. Leatherow was head-over-heels in love, and he knew that Peggie was the woman for him.

On February 16, they went out again and, despite his tough-guy exterior, Leatherow had to fight through nerves as he mustered the courage to propose to her. He told her that he knew it was a quick proposal, but he had to listen to his heart.

While she took a moment to get over the shock and let the proposal sink in, Peggie said that she had a question for him.

"What's your last name anyway?"

"Leatherow. My last name is Leatherow," he answered anxiously.

She sounded the name several times in her head.

"Ok, Bob Leatherow. Yes, I'll marry you, but under one condition. You better make sure that the additional six letters are worth it!" she said with a sly smile.

On April 8, Peggie Ace became Mrs. Robert Leatherow, and the marriage eventually produced two children: a son, Robert, and a daughter, Jodie.

| Bob Leatherow and family

Leatherow had trained to fight ship fires while in the Navy, and his experiences there inspired him to pursue a career as a fireman. He had enjoyed the excitement and danger of rushing into the fires to battle the blazes. However, as he prepared to take the firefighter exam, a friend suggested that he take the police exam too. He sat for the police test and scored so high that he decided to give law enforcement a try, and he soon found that he had a natural aptitude for police work. Leatherow's police academy training went well and he ended up graduating in the upper half of his class. On October 15, 1969, he was sworn in as a member of the Allendale Police Department in Allendale, New Jersey, a small town near New York City. Fate had decreed that he would forge a career in law enforcement.

As a police officer, Leatherow was tough, and like his family name implied, thick-skinned. He did not suffer fools, or criminals, lightly. In one of his first cases with the police force, he was instrumental in the arrest of a juvenile who had bombed the local high school as well as a main street liquor store, blowing out the windows of many of the downtown stores in the process. Finding himself the first responder at the scene, Leatherow made his way to the second floor of a nearby apartment building so that he could have a bird's-eye view of the damaged liquor store and survey the extent of the damage. As he observed the area from his overhead vantage point, he spotted the suspected bomber standing in the crowd of onlookers that had gathered. Before the bomber could slip away into the night, Leatherow made sure that he was properly fitted with a shiny new pair of handcuffs.

Leatherow was promoted to sergeant in 1978 and subsequently earned a four-year degree in criminal justice. In 1983, he received word that he had been accepted into the FBI Academy's three-monthlong police training program in Quantico, Virginia. During the coveted program, he took classes on firearms, law, and gambling, but the class that he most enjoyed and excelled in was a course on serial killers taught by FBI special agent and famed criminal behavioral scientist Robert Ressler. It was Ressler himself who had coined the term "serial killer," a distinction so well known that, at the close of one of his workshops, his colleagues presented him with a Wheaties cereal box that had been altered so that a rubber dagger protruded from the middle of the cardboard box. In Ressler's class, Leatherow became intrigued by the behavior of serial killers like Ted Bundy and he grew fascinated by how Ressler and his FBI colleagues developed their criminal profiling techniques. After completing the prestigious Quantico program, he returned to his small town police department excited to share what he had learned, yet he could not help feeling some disappointment at the thought that he would probably never have the opportunity to put it into practice.

In 1984, after fifteen years with the Allendale Police Department, Leatherow decided to retire from public service and accept a lucrative offer to work as the chief security officer for a private company. Leaving the police force was a difficult decision for Leatherow, but at the end of the day, he could not pass up the opportunity improve his family's financial situation. Leatherow's dedication to law enforcement and the devout manner in which he performed his duties was so well known that, at his retirement party, one of his fellow officers compared his decision to leave the police department with that of "the pope leaving the Vatican."

As expected, Leatherow made much more money in the private sector, but he was surprised at how dull and unfulfilling he found the work to be. It did not take long for him to realize that he missed real police work. After a few months, he decided that he had endured enough private security work, and he resolved to return to public law enforcement.

In early 1985, a long-time friend informed Leatherow of an opening with the Brevard County Sheriff's Office in Titusville, Florida. After some introductions and interviews, as well as some exploration of the local area with Peggie, he accepted an offer to begin a new phase of his career as a Brevard County Deputy Sheriff. A life-long Yankee, he made the move south in June 1985, unaware that the subject of what would be his greatest case had preceded him in relocating to Florida just two years earlier. Although plucked from his northern roots and transplanted into a Florida landscape that could not have been more culturally and politically different from that of Allendale, Leatherow quickly showed a dedication to his new job, just as he had in New Jersey, displaying an enthusiasm and commitment a notch above the average cop. And his commitment did not go unnoticed. After working six months as a uniformed road deputy, Leatherow received a reassignment to the Sheriff's six-member homicide unit.

Around mid-afternoon on Friday, November 22, Leatherow returned to his Palm Bay home from an autopsy at Holmes Regional Medical Center in Melbourne, where he had been investigating a prison suicide. He was exhausted, having been on the job for the past forty-eight hours. Shuffling into his room, he took off his suit and collapsed onto the bed, looking forward to catching up on some much-needed sleep. That sleep would have to wait. As he started to doze off, his pager began buzzing on top of the nightstand. Groggily, he checked the number and then called in to the office. Lt. Fair came on the line.

"Bob, we have something that's right up your alley. It's a sexual battery case, and get this, during the battery the perpetrator allegedly drained his victim's blood and drank it."

"No kidding," said Leatherow, springing quickly back to life, his interest now piqued. "That sounds like something straight out of Quantico's files."

When Leatherow heard the part about blood being drained and ingested by the assailant, a jolt of adrenaline kicked in. As Lt. Fair had implied, here was a chance to apply his training from the FBI Academy where he had spent three months learning from the best in the business.

"The victim is over at Holmes Regional in the emergency room," continued Fair. "I want you to get over there and check out her story. And let me know what you think once you've talked to her."

Leatherow hurriedly re-dressed, hastened to his car, and made the ten-minute drive back to Holmes Regional in record time. He arrived shortly after 3:30 p.m. and was greeted in the emergency room by a group of nurses anxiously awaiting his arrival. The nurses ushered him to an examination room where he found Christina Almah lying on an adjustable hospital bed. He could see several abrasions on her neck as well as extensive bruising on her wrists and ankles. Her complexion was unnaturally pale, and she literally shook with fright as Leatherow introduced himself. He noticed her hands visibly trembling as she steadied herself to greet him.

Not far away, Christina's nameless assailant cursed himself for having left her alone. When he had seen the bathroom window open, he reassured himself that she could not have had the strength to hoist herself up and through it. But the empty bathtub slammed home the reality of the situation. At first, he had been too angry and agitated to think of what to do, and it took some time for him to think clearly. Once he was able to process the magnitude of what had happened, he knew exactly what he needed to do. Now fully focused, he began his work in earnest, knowing that time had become his enemy. He began gathering what needed to be disposed of.

Back at the hospital, after some peripheral conversation intended to put her at ease, Leatherow asked Christina to tell him what had happened. As the still frightened woman began to recount her ordeal, Leatherow studied her words and body language, trying to gauge the veracity of her story. His first impressions were that she seemed to be very bright and forthright, but deeply shaken from her experience, and her nervousness did not diminish at any point during her recitation of the relevant events.

She described in detail how she had been walking eastbound on Malabar Road at around 1:00 p.m. the day before when a white male wearing a sports coat and tie pulled up beside her in a small, two-door, light-colored car that lacked any identifiable markings. The man looked to be about thirty years old, approximately 5'10" in height, with a thin build and dirty blonde hair. He had offered her a ride, and after deciding that he looked harmless enough, she had accepted, grateful to get out of the rain.

After listening to her for about fifteen minutes, Leatherow felt satisfied that she was telling the truth. He had the nurses move her into a private hospital room to tell the rest of her tale.

When she described the inconspicuous appearance of the man's car, an alarm went off in Leatherow's head. He recalled how, months earlier, the Sheriff's Office had received reports about prostitutes being assaulted by an unknown man in a nondescript car. One of the prostitutes had reported going on a "date" with a thinly-built man in a nondescript car and parking at the Valkaria airport just south of Malabar, where the man had tried to choke her while having sex. Christina Almah's story sounded eerily similar. Something in Leatherow's gut told him that her assailant and the prostitute strangler were one and the same.

SIX

Cheating death

S equestered in a private hospital room, Christina Almah led Leatherow through the details of the rest of her terrifying ordeal. How the pale man who had offered her a ride told her that he needed to stop at his house to pick up a notebook that he had left there. How he had strangled her in his car from the backseat using a nylon rope. How she had lost consciousness and awakened to find herself tied spread eagle on her back on top of an island countertop in a darkened room.

She detailed how the man took her virginity before taking her blood, mounting, and raping her while a video camera on a tripod recorded the terrifying ordeal. Leatherow's interest heightened when she described how the man inserted intravenous needles into her right wrist and along the inside of her left arm. He attached surgical hoses to the needles, and used one of the hoses to suck blood from her arm. He had seemed to enjoy her fear.

When Christina revealed that her assailant had drunk her blood, Leatherow's hair stood up on the back of his neck. He knew that this could be a big case. Her story came across as so bizarre that Leatherow considered the possibility that she might have hallucinated while under the influence of drugs, but the rope burns on her neck and the needle marks on her arms provided convincing corroboration for her story.

She continued her strange narrative by recounting how she had blacked out shortly after the man told her that he was a vampire. She awoke after he had drunk his fill of her blood, when he untied her from the table, handcuffed her around the wrists, and shackled her ankles with a second pair of handcuffs. Then he led her out of the kitchen area and down a hall, but she was too weak to walk and collapsed several times in the hallway, passing out again the last time. When she woke up, she was on the floor, and the man pulled her up onto her feet. He took her into a bathroom and removed her earrings, telling her that they were in the way. She shivered as he began sucking on her neck, and forced her onto her back in a yellow bathtub. Then he warned her to be quiet and stay still.

"You better be quiet or my brother, Paul, will hear you. If he finds out that you're here, he'll kill you."

As he started to leave, he paused in the doorway and turned around, placing his raised finger over his lips with an assertive "shhh!" before pulling the door closed behind him.

Christina stayed motionless in the bathtub, too scared to move. Aside from being dizzy and weak, she felt sick to her stomach. She drifted in and out of consciousness, but eventually gathered her senses together long enough to survey her surroundings. She could see a transparent shower curtain hanging outside of the tub, colorfully adorned with images of red, green, blue, and yellow parrots. Several bath toys were stacked beside the tub, placed next to a towel decorated with red and white clowns. Under the bathroom window, she saw a child's soap dish shaped like a navy sailor sitting next to a polka-dotted clown towel. After what seemed like hours, but may have only been minutes, the bathroom door opened and the nameless man reappeared. He lifted her from the bathtub, slowly led her out of the room, and guided her back into the hallway. They continued further down the hall and into a bedroom.

Once they were in the room, the man handed her a pill and told her to swallow it. She had no idea what the pill was, but she was afraid of angering him so she did not hesitate in swallowing it. After she swallowed the pill, he removed the handcuffs from her arms and ankles and pushed her onto a king-sized bed. She felt as if she were floating in the air and noticed that she was laying on a waterbed covered with brown sheets. While the bed's waves rocked her up and down, she saw a wide tapestry on the wall with the word "Mexico" stitched in large, red letters along the top. The waves intensified as the man crawled onto the bed beside her. She felt the soft, warm wetness of his tongue as it moved along the lips of her pelvic area. She had begun bleeding from below due to her menstrual cycle, and she felt a sucking sensation between her legs as the man tasted that blood too.

Then he climbed on top of her. He grabbed her knees with icy hands and pushed outward, parting her legs. She felt a painful pressure between her thighs as he once again entered her. The pain continued as he moved his hips up and down, sliding in and out of her. She had grown so weak from loss of blood that, despite the intense discomfort, she drifted on the verge of unconsciousness.

Although not wholly coherent, she heard him ask repeatedly if she was enjoying it. She closed her eyes and tried to pretend that it was not really happening, that it was all part of some hideous dream, a nightmare from which she would soon awaken.

As the nameless man continued grinding back and forth, he whispered in her ear between rapidly drawn breaths.

"I'm not supposed to do this . . . I'm getting attached to you."

With those words, he put his hands around her neck and began to strangle her again. She felt the pressure from her neck rise into her head. And then . . . nothing.

When she regained her senses, he was still on top of her.

"Why do you keep choking me?" she murmured. "Do you have a thing for necks or something?"

"Yes, I like necks," he replied. "I like to squeeze them."

Then with a final thrust and orgasmic, animalistic grunt, he finished, and his breathing began to slow.

He rolled off of her and yanked her back to a standing position beside the bed. She noticed a large red stain on the bed sheet where she had been laying.

He gazed at her and grinned. "We need a shower."

She struggled to stay awake as he led her back to the bathroom and started the water. The sensation of the water shocked her. It was icy cold like his hands.

The cold water partially revived her, and then he began rubbing a creamy white lotion on her. The lotion felt warm on her skin and caused a tingling sensation as if her arm had been asleep and the blood was rushing back to where it had been temporarily blocked.

After showering, the man led her back to the waterbed and lay down behind her on his side with his arms locked around her waist. Although she tried to fight it, she could not keep from falling asleep. She was much too tired and weak.

She awakened to a bitter smell. Jolted back from the comforting nothing of unconsciousness, she opened her eyes and saw the man holding something under her nose. It was dark outside and the bright red display of a digital clock showed the time as 4:00 a.m. Seeing that she was awake, the man turned her over and mounted her from behind, raping her for the third time, once again asking her repeatedly if she liked it. Too scared to really speak, she meekly answered "yes" each time so as not to provoke him. While he continued his deep, painful, unrelenting thrusts, he began to choke her some more, and she started feeling disconnected from herself, as if she was simply a spectator watching the events from a distance.

In this dazed state of awareness, she saw the man handcuff her again.

"I'm hungry," he said as his eyes fixed on her with an unnerving stare.

She watched with a detached curiosity as he placed a rubbery hose around her left arm, and inserted an intravenous needle into a vein on the inside bend of the arm. She looked on with a growing awareness of the deadly seriousness of the situation as he licked the blood that slowly oozed out of the spots pierced by the needle. The feeling of fear intensified as he attached a clear length of surgical tubing to the other end of the needle and drained her blood into a beaker-shaped glass jar, at times sucking on the hose like a straw to make the blood flow faster. When it was about halfway full of the crimson liquid, the man lifted the beaker to his lips. Christina heard swallowing sounds as he drank deeply. When he stopped and lowered the container from his mouth, globules of blood dripped from the top of the jar while a small pool of the sanguine fluid settled at the bottom.

"Your blood tastes good, but I didn't drink it fast enough," the man said with wet, red-stained lips. "Some of it coagulated. Next time I'll drink it faster."

Her mind raced as she struggled to comprehend her dire situation, desperately attempting to understand why. Her mind flashed back-andforth between thoughts of confusion. *Why is this happening to me? This can't be real. This can't really be happening. Should I try to resist? Or reason with him? Or should I do whatever he wants? Would he then eventually let me go?*

Why did I get in the car with him? So stupid! I never should have accepted a ride. I never should have left the trailer. I should have just waited for Von to get home.

Fighting the urge to scream, Christina tried to appeal to whatever good lay hidden in her captor's heart.

"Will you please let me go?"

His answer came quickly, without the slightest hesitation, as if it was a dialogue he had participated in countless times before.

"No, I can't. You're not trained yet."

At first it had seemed unreal, but she could tell from the distant look in his eyes that he had no intention of letting her go. She thought of her family back home in California. She would never see her mom again, and never again give her dad a good night hug.

Having drunk his fill of her blood, the man took her back to the bathroom and forced her into the bathtub again, her wrists and ankles once again handcuffed, and this time blindfolding her with thick masking tape. He repeated his previous warning about not attracting the attention of his homicidal brother, 'Paul,' and then he left the room.

Too terrified to move, thinking every moment could be her last, she kept utterly still. She stayed silent, listening, straining to hear any noises that might be coming from the house beyond the bathroom door. She was like a sentinel mutely attentive at her lonely post. At some point, she heard what sounded like a door closing in the distance, but then she could discern nothing more. When the quiet had persisted for what was—as best she could tell—a long period of time, she raised her shackled hands and removed the tape from her eyes.

She thought of trying to open the bathroom door, but the possibility of the man's murderous, unseen brother lurking somewhere in the house beyond it stopped her. Pulling herself up from the bathtub, she slowly looked around the room. She spotted a small, metal-framed window to the right of the bathtub about four-and-a-half-feet above the floor. As she studied the window, she thought that she might be just small enough to squeeze through its narrow opening.

She could see that the window had locks on both sides, but it was the only other way out, so she convinced herself that she had to give it a try. Grabbing a towel from a nearby rack, she pressed one of the locks in with both of her handcuffed hands and pushed up on the window with all the strength she had left. Slowly, stubbornly, the glass enclosure moved.

Although Christina did not realize it at the time, she had been extremely fortunate. One of the bathroom window locks was broken.

Leatherow would later stress how lucky she was that one of the locks had been broken because if both of them had been working properly she almost certainly would have died that day. Located at each end of the approximately thirty-inch-wide window, the two locks were supposed to work together so that both had to be pushed inward simultaneously in order to release the window. With both locks working properly, it would have been impossible for someone restrained by handcuffs to open the window. The locks were simply too far apart for a handcuffed person to reach both of them at the same time. Had both window locks been working, Christina would not have escaped from her deadly prison.

The front portion of the home showing bathroom window through which Christina Almah escaped.

(Left) Close up of bathroom window that Christina squeezed through to escape. (Right) Interior view of bathroom window showing dual locks— one of which was broken, allowing Christina to escape

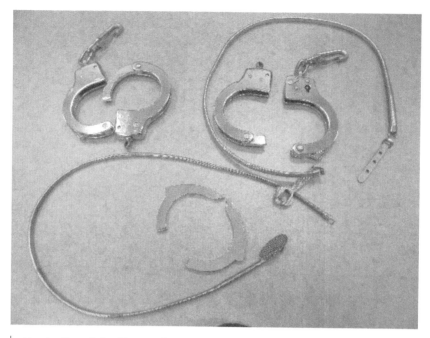

Handcuffs and shackles used to restrain Christina Almah. She was wearing them when rescued by a passing motorist

Having successfully opened the bathroom window, Christina was able to knock out the window screen by repeatedly kicking against it with both feet. Struggling with great effort, and with the towel she had grabbed still in hand, she managed to push through the window's narrow opening. She fell face first onto a grassy area four feet below, her arms and legs severely scratched by jagged bricks lining the outside of the window. After a bruising landing in the grass, she gathered her legs under her and managed to stand.

Disoriented and close to collapsing due to her anemic condition, only the overriding thought of getting away from the house kept her moving forward. She stumbled across the front yard, straining to move her shackled feet in tiny steps that amounted to nothing more than short hops. Shuffling to the edge of the yard, she tripped through some bushes and had a hard fall into a shallow, weed-covered swale. Propping herself up with handcuffed hands, she saw that the swale ran alongside a narrow dirt road. She crawled up the other side of the swale and began hobbling down the street, naked but for the towel draped loosely over her breasts and partially covering her waist.

"And eventually a truck came, but kept going," she recounted to Leatherow. "It had two women in it, but they didn't stop. They just looked at me and kept going. But after a while another truck stopped and a nice man helped me and called the ambulance that brought me here."

Even now, after having received urgently needed medical attention, Christina nearly blacked out several times while conveying her story, and Leatherow could see that she was extremely nervous.

She's probably afraid that she's going to die right here in the hospital, Leatherow thought to himself.

As he listened to her story, Leatherow's training at Quantico kicked in.

Picked up by a seemingly harmless man in a non-descript car.
Choked into a state of unconsciousness.
Confined by handcuffs and leg shackles.
Held prisoner and repeatedly sexually assaulted while restrained.

The essential facts all combined to raise a red flag in Leatherow's mind that he could be dealing with a serial sexual offender. Draining and drinking the victim's blood made the crime even more alarming.

After completing his interview with Christina, Leatherow spoke with Dr. Ronald Stern, the emergency room physician who first attended to her when she arrived at the hospital. Dr. Stern advised that upon examination, Christina displayed extensive visible trauma including puncture marks on her arms and right foot, and scratches on her wrists, ankles, legs, and stomach. She also had vaginal lacerations, consistent with having been raped.

"She was a very lucky young lady," Dr. Stern told Leatherow. "She had lost a significant amount of blood, which left her blood pressure dangerously low."

Leatherow learned that Deputy Roy Osbourne had been the first responder to the hospital after Christina's arrival. Osbourne arrived at 10:35 a.m., finding Christina reclined on an examination table, still handcuffed at the wrists and ankles. Deputy Tony Graziano arrived shortly thereafter and began questioning Christina about what had happened to her. At one point, he asked her if it had been her boyfriend who assaulted her. Emotionally exhausted and physically debilitated, and just wanting to be left alone, Christina indicated to Graziano that she did not want to press any charges in connection with the assault. After Deputy Osbourne managed to remove her handcuffs, Christina signed a Decline to Prosecute affidavit at 11:55 a.m. Shortly afterward, Osbourne and Graziano left the hospital to attend to other matters.

At 1:45 p.m., Audrey Megregian contacted Osbourne and advised him that Christina had changed her mind. She wanted to prosecute after all. Megregian explained that Christina had declined initially because she was too nervous and upset to think coherently, still traumatized from what she had been through. The thought of having to testify with a courtroom full of strangers staring at her and judging her, not to mention with her blood-drinking assailant leering hungrily at her with the same wolfen eyes she had grown to fear, was too much to bear. When she first met with Christina, the frightened girl told Megregian that she just wanted to go home to California, "where people are sane." Megregian assured Christina that whatever decision she made about whether to pursue the case would be fine. Megregian would support her either way. They talked for a while and after thinking it over Christina informed Megregian that she would be willing to prosecute because she did not want any other women to be subjected to the nightmare that she had endured. Although Megregian did her best to comfort Christina, a nurse checking on her several hours later noted in her chart that she was still upset and shaking.

Christina would spend the next two days in the hospital before being deemed healthy enough to be released. She had nearly died from losing over forty percent of her body's blood volume, and the creature who had fed on her blood was still at large, free to hunt new prey.

SEVEN

Hidden in plain sight

It was the height of the materialistic Eighties, an age of excess, an era of intemperance and self-indulgence, and John Crutchley appeared to be living the American Dream. He had an attractive wife, a healthy young son, and an impressive house on a spacious 2.5-acre property complete with a Jacuzzi and a covered pool. A child of his times, he lived an epicurean existence of self-indulgence and self-gratification that extended to sex and other matters of the flesh.

Standing five feet, ten inches tall and weighing about 150 pounds with blue eyes and dirty blonde hair, most women found him to be easy on the eyes. Of course, he thought very highly of himself too, and over the years he had developed a sizeable ego, but he also had the mental awareness and discipline to hide the vain, self-centered side of himself.

Possessing a brilliant mind for mathematics and computers, he developed classified computer language for the United States Navy and earned a substantial salary as a computer engineer at a prestigious communications company specializing in advanced technologies. To all outward appearances, he seemed to be a model citizen, an exemplary family man, and a pillar of the community. But his carefully crafted appearance concealed a secret truth, something sinister lurking just below the polished surface.

***

John Brennan Crutchley, "JB" as he preferred to be called, came from a middle-class family. He was born on October 1, 1946, in Clarksburg, West Virginia, a small town in a scenic region of north-central West Virginia, just off of Interstate 79. Nestled on the Appalachian Plateau that spans the western part of the Appalachian Mountains, Clarksburg's claim to fame was serving as the birthplace of revered Confederate General Thomas J. "Stonewall" Jackson.

JB's father, William Frederic, was born in Woodville, England in 1904, and immigrated to the United States from England in 1914. JB's mother, Mildred Burnside, was a Clarksburg native, born in October 1910. After a normal courtship, the two married in Clarksburg in 1930.

William worked for Consolidated Natural Gas for over forty-four years, the majority of them in Clarksburg, and rose to be a Vice President of the company before retiring in 1969. William and Mildred traveled around the country searching for the perfect place to build their retirement home, but in the end they came back to the Clarksburg area for the simple reason that they could not find any place they liked better.

JB had an older brother twelve years his senior named William II, but called "Sunny" by his parents. He also had an older sister, Donna June, who was born in 1931, but passed away under peculiar circumstances in 1944. At just thirteen years of age, Donna died in an operating room from circulatory collapse as doctors attempted to remove a "foreign body"—a glass tube—from her bladder. The circumstances of how a glass tube ended up in her bladder were long kept secret by JB's parents. Even decades later, when asked by investigators how Donna had died, Mildred Crutchley claimed, "We don't know. She died suddenly." The elder William elaborated that Donna died of "a nervous collapse right when they were just getting ready to give her the anesthetic. She went into convulsions . . . she was frightened to death for some reason or other." JB eventually came to believe that Donna had died as the result of injuries inflicted while masturbating with the glass tube. Whether Donna had been alone at the time, and whether the injuries were self-inflicted, would remain forever unclear.

Another sister, Carolynn Adele, came five years after JB's birth, but that was not soon enough for his mother who never hesitated to say that she had wanted another daughter after Donna died. Indeed, she often told the young JB that she wished he had been a girl. Born several months premature, JB's very existence represented failure to his mother, embodying her disappointment and prolonging her bitterness as a living reminder of her beloved lost daughter. Mildred's desire for another daughter so consumed her that she raised JB as a girl for the first five years of his life, dressing him virtually exclusively in girls' clothes. As JB wrote to Carolynn decades later, "When Donna was killed, Mom desperately tried to replace her lost daughter. The tip of the truth of that event only began to emerge when Mom & Dad last visited me in Fairfax . . . Mom really bared her soul when she told me the details of Donna's demise and she asked that we not talk about it anymore." JB's father did not intervene on his behalf, deferring to Mildred as to how to best raise him during his early adolescence. Even at the tender age of five, the continual humiliation of being made to dress as a girl caused JB to feel angry and exhausted, alienated and alone. Mildred's insistence on treating him like a girl caused JB considerable confusion during the years most influencing the formation of his identity.

Adding to his sense of isolation, growing up JB was not particularly close to either of his siblings. He tended to ignore his younger sister, and the twelve-year age difference between him and his brother kept them from ever bonding. Although they also had poor relationships with their mother, JB's brother and younger sister succeeded both academically and professionally. Sunny graduated from medical school and went on to run a successful thoracic surgery practice in North Carolina. Carolynn also studied medicine and became a forensic psychiatrist in Pennsylvania. Both also married, but eventually divorced their spouses.

On the outside, the Crutchleys seemed to be a close-knit, caring family who enjoyed frequent vacations to popular destinations like San Francisco, New York City, Niagara Falls, Yosemite National Park, Washington D.C., and Disneyland. However, JB remembered his relationship with his parents as being primarily "painful." He yearned for affection from them—his mother in particular—but the affection that he so deeply desired never came. His father never made any attempts to bond with the young JB and avoided any physical signs of affection, leaving JB to feel unimportant and ignored. The comfort he craved did not come from his mother either. Instead, Mildred often acted indifferently toward him, leading JB to develop permanent feelings of inadequacy and unworthiness of love.

While parental affection rarely made an appearance in the Crutchley household, discipline tended to be arbitrary and inconsistent. What would not elicit a reprimand one day might evoke severe punishment the next. Mildred practiced what close observers described as "harsh love," treating JB particularly strictly and sternly. But the harshness of his childhood went beyond that. JB's mother could also be abusive and sometimes beat him for minor misbehaviors. JB claimed that on one occasion, she burned his fingers with a curling iron, and on another, she nearly beat him unconscious with a belt. Throughout his adolescence, although JB desperately wanted parental approval and affection, he knew only coldness and emotional isolation.

JB coped with the conditions of his childhood by erecting emotional barriers, sealing himself in a psychological cocoon that insulated him from the individuals whose approval he so desperately but futilely desired, while also preventing him from forming psychological attachments or establishing emotional connections with others. Considered by neighbors to be a "weird child," JB once went so far as to electrify the doorknob to his bedroom to keep his mother out.

Since JB's father had been raised in the shadow of the Church of England, his parents became active in the Episcopalian Church. They expected JB to follow their faith and regularly made him attend Sunday Mass. However, where they found comfort, he saw only hypocrisy, starting with the piety of his mother whose supposedly saintly ways did not deter her from lashing out at her young son, verbally or physically. As he grew older, JB battled conflicting feelings about his mother, deeply resenting her lack of affection and arbitrary disapproval of him, while simultaneously desiring more than anything to please her.

Although described by those who knew him as "incredibly knowledgeable and incredibly bright," the "hyperactive" JB struggled in school, not due to a lack of intelligence, but because of boredom and an inability to pay attention. While he made straight A's in physics and math, other subjects held no interest for him. He "couldn't care less" about the social sciences and foreign languages, and he had to take Spanish II three times before passing it. His teachers "loved him, but hated him because he had so much intelligence and wouldn't use it." As his father recalled years later, "the major problem we had with John in his younger years was his disinterest in school work—he took five years to get through high school, and five more to get a four-year college degree." Blessed with a genius level I.Q. of 168, which put him in the same intellectual sphere as Einstein, Bill Gates, and Stephen Hawking, JB simply could not stay focused on the subject matter covered in school. It was too basic and boring. To escape the mindnumbing dullness, he passed much of his time in school daydreaming, fantasizing about a reality more stimulating than his mediocre, mundane life.

Despite the poor relationship with his parents and his shoddy performance in school, the young JB managed to stay out of any serious trouble. He never had any run-ins with the police, and according to his mother, he "never drank beer or caroused with girls." But Mildred Crutchley later recalled that her second son "always had to prove things to himself and hated to be told he had to do this or that. If you said that is hot, don't touch, he would touch and get burned."

As a boy, JB read *Treasure Island*, *The Scarlet Pimpernel*, and other adventure tales normally enjoyed by adolescent males. However, he also developed a taste for stories about murder and other violent crimes and amassed a small collection of books focused on that subject matter.

When JB was ten, his father was transferred to another Consolidated Gas location, and the Crutchley family moved from their home at 123 Alexander Avenue in Clarksburg to 2500 Giant Oaks Drive in Upper St. Clair Township, just outside of Pittsburgh. It was there that JB's life-long fascination with electronics began. He started fixing his Upper St. Clair neighbors' television sets after school, and by the time he was in the sixth grade he had earned a reputation as an "electronics wizard."

While in school, JB learned that acting up diverted attention from his social and emotional shortcomings. He began to bully his classmates, even those who were physically stronger than him. He became a "disciplinary problem" and his bullying behavior earned him paddlings and other forms of corporal punishment that were liberally administered by his teachers. Looking back decades later, he observed, "Sometime around elementary school I discovered being obnoxious was an effective way of covering up my lack of 'social skills' which others seem to come by naturally, but are quite difficult for me." This psychological self-defense mechanism enabled him to mask his insecurities, but reinforced his emotional distance from others. Spurred on by the unpredictable mood swings of his mother, JB learned to limit his emotional connections. He knew love only as an abstract concept, something foreign to his own life. Indeed, in an era of promiscuity and free love, JB remained a virgin until he was twenty-one years old because he was "afraid of women."

Prior to starting high school, JB's grades dropped significantly. To get back on track academically, he briefly attended Christ Church Episcopal Boys School, a prep school in Christ Church, Virginia. During the same time period, his parents sent him to a psychiatrist to identify the cause of his plummeting grades, but after several sessions with JB, the perplexed psychiatrist informed his parents: "I don't know who's interviewing who, if he's interviewing me or I'm interviewing him." Despite multiple consultations with the psychiatrist, JB's academic problems continued.

JB's deficiencies in the classroom paralleled poor social ties to his peers. "I always shrank from affection because I didn't know how to deal with it," JB would later recall. "It scared me. I had no social skills and was scared of the opposite sex like crazy." Although brilliant in some ways, he was "stupid in others," especially in social situations. He suffered from a dual condition of emotional deprivation and social isolation, a psychological state stemming from his emotionally sterile childhood—a childhood that had discouraged development of his brain's capacity for feeling empathy or compassion. Due to his extreme emotional insecurity and lack of fundamental social skills, he stayed away from girls, rather than dating like most teenaged boys. Instead of pursuing the romantic attentions of young women, JB's insecurity limited him to fantasizing about sex. But his were not the typical hormone-driven fantasies of a lustful teenaged boy. Instead, his fantasies focused on controlling the girls involved, often through aggressive acts and violent methods.

JB graduated from Upper St. Clair High School in June 1965, ranked 173 out of 193 graduating seniors. The next month, he began taking classes at Defiance College in Defiance, Ohio, the "only college" his parents could get him into because of his poor grades. While attending classes and working part-time at the Zeller Corporation, JB's impressive skills at assembling computers and other electronic devices continued to grow.

His college classmates voted him "Most Likely to Self-Destruct," a title he earned due to an obsessive need to match wits against others and an insatiable desire to play mind games. His strange sense of humor and insistence on seeking revenge for perceived slights, no matter how small, also became well known around the campus. If a classmate ended up on JB's bad side, he might find that sugar had been poured into his gas tank. If a target of his obsessive affections turned him down, she might discover that water had been injected into the lock of her car door on a freezing day so that her keys would break when she tried to unlock the door.

It was at Defiance College that JB had his first bisexual experience. While not unheard of for a student in college exploring his sexual identity, JB's sexual experimentation would not be a transitory event. It would continue and expand throughout the course of his life. The seeds of his bisexuality had been planted in childhood during years of being forced to dress as a girl, all the while subjected to the repeated refrain of how much better everything would be if he had been born a girl instead of a boy. The resulting sexual confusion germinated easily, firmly taking root in the psyche of his self-identity, forever impairing the development of a healthy sexual self-conception.

During his time at Defiance College, Defiance police also

suspected JB of being involved in several thefts at the college, behavior that would be repeated throughout his adult life. While at Defiance, he began even more nefarious activities as well, activities that would not come to light until two decades later.

| Crutchley's ninth birthday party, October 1, 1955

Crutchley with toy train set, January 2, 1956

Crutchley in his Easter outfit, April 1958

Crutchley at twelve-years-old dressed in Boy Scouts uniform (left).
Crutchley riding his bike in 1959 (right)

Crutchley on Christmas Day 1960

Crutchley in front of his family home April 1962 (left). Crutchley standing in front of family home the day he left for Defiance College (right)

After five semesters at Defiance College, JB was put on academic suspension with a 1.4 grade point average, a product of his inability to focus while taking a difficult course load of economics, physics, calculus, electronics, and German.

In September 1967, JB transferred to Point Park College in Pittsburgh in another effort to improve his grades. While at Point Park, he became involved with twenty-one-year-old Maude Moats, a petite, brown-haired, blue-eyed girl whom he met while attending classes. With Maude's encouragement, he was able to make his way back to Defiance College after one academic year.

Beginning in 1968, JB began working part-time as an engineer at WONW Radio while he continued school. The next year, at the age of twenty-two, he married Maude. He did not love her. He had never really loved anyone. But she was always eager to please him and fulfill his sexual needs. After a small church ceremony, the two of them moved into a trailer at a mobile home park in Defiance.

At WONW, JB continued to show an uncanny ability to repair electronic equipment, and he formed a friendship with Ray Malone, who had an IQ comparable to his own. The two had a "love-hate relationship" in that they admired one another's talents and electronic skills, but they often fell into heated disagreements.

Co-workers at WONW remembered JB as a loner with few friends other than Malone. "Not a people oriented person," JB seemed to prefer being alone, a workaholic who kept to himself. When he did try to socialize, he often came across as awkward and uncomfortable. On one such occasion, when introducing his wife to co-workers at the station, he raised eyebrows by stating, "This is Maude. Don't pay any attention to her. She's a sex maniac." At other times, he displayed poor emotional control, such as when he threw a heavy glass bottle at a fellow employee after becoming angry.

JB lost his job in 1970 amidst accusations that he had electronically bugged the station by installing sound surveillance equipment in the attic so that he could eavesdrop on other employees. After leaving WONW, JB held a similar engineering position at Kennedy Television from November 1970 to March 1971. Then he took a job as a project engineer at General Motors' Central Foundry Division in Defiance. In August 1971, he finally graduated from Defiance College, earning a Bachelor's Degree in Physics, and continuing his pattern of academic underachievement by ranking 249 out of 261 graduating students.

After two years with the Central Foundry Division, JB moved to Kokomo, Indiana, to take a position with GM's Delco Electronics Division. However, Maude did not make the move with him. Instead, she filed for a divorce, which became final in July 1973.

*Crutchley and first wife dressed for a ball in December 1968 (left).
Crutchley dressed for a wedding in June 1969 (right)*

Years later, Moats remembered her former husband as a man driven by sexual impulses with an explosive, unpredictable temper, a man she ultimately came to fear. She described him as "crazy and capable of most anything," a man whose appetite for group sex and wife swapping gave way at times to violent behavior. Moats recalled a number of instances in which JB, frustrated with repair projects, threw computers across the room, smashing them to pieces. His impatience, propensity for violent outbursts, and petulant hostility did not limit themselves to inanimate objects. On several occasions, he lashed out at Moats herself.

After they married, JB started shoplifting, not out of necessity, but simply for the thrill of seeing whether he would get caught. When the excitement of shoplifting began to wear off, he switched to stealing from his employers and the schools he attended. JB's habit of stealing from his employers had frequently ignited arguments between him and Moats, arguments that often escalated and turned physical. JB began to beat her, and on one occasion held his hand over her face to prevent her from breathing. The beatings became so common that Maude came to the somber realization that she had to get away from him if she wanted to survive.

"I was afraid of him for four years," she explained. "When I filed for divorce he threw me on the floor, tried to strangle me, and threatened to kill me."

She also described how JB enjoyed strangling her during sex. He had done it on multiple occasions and seemed to enjoy the strangling more than the sexual act itself. He only stopped when, during one of the episodes, she choked him back in self-defense.

Following his divorce from Maude, JB moved in with blonde-haired, green-eyed Lisa Baker, a friendly, petite girl he met in October 1972. The two were introduced at a party being held by a couple of disc jockeys at a local radio station in Fort Wayne, Indiana, north of Kokomo. JB had been invited to the party by a DJ he knew from a short stint of working in college radio. Lisa was immediately attracted to JB's warm smile and she enjoyed how easy it was to talk to him. The night they met, JB invited Lisa to go on a trip with him to Jamaica. She thought he was joking, but six months later they went.

The two quickly started dating, and within ten months, they were living together. Lisa completed her undergraduate studies while JB worked as an engineer. They spent hours playing card games together, UNO being a particular favorite, and Lisa marveled at JB's ability to create computer puzzle games. Both liked to talk about politics and they held similarly liberal political views. They shared a love of The Beatles and The Rolling Stones and Lisa often complimented JB by telling him that he looked like John Lennon, his favorite singer. The two also enjoyed traveling and they took frequent road trips in JB's convertible MG, a tiny, British-made, two-seater sports car. A tour to Morocco and Spain, where they spoke broken Spanish with the locals and enjoyed the beautiful Mediterranean sunsets, ranked as their favorite overseas trip.

They had an open relationship, sometimes swapping sexual partners with other couples, and Lisa gave JB the freedom to indulge his bisexual desires. They occasionally met couples with similar interests through sexually oriented magazines, usually by arranging a weekend rendezvous in Indianapolis. To supplement his sexual diet, JB also developed a habit of picking up women during business trips in New York. Due in large part to the amount of sexual space she gave him, JB became more attached to Lisa than any other woman with whom he had developed a relationship. The closeness of their relationship was revealed years later when JB referred to Lisa as a "member of my family."

While JB's brilliant mind captivated Lisa, his child-like approach to life, a seemingly never-ending curiosity about the world, maintained her attraction to him. She loved his ever-present smile and enjoyed his optimistic nature and positive outlook. Above all, JB's compassion for others and his openness to experiencing new things were her favorite things about him. The only negative trait she ever noticed was a tendency toward stubbornness. The unpredictable monster that Maude Moats had described seemed to have gone away.

From September 1974 to May 1975, JB attended Ball State University in Muncie, Indiana, earning eight hours of graduate credit in Business Administration. He remained with Delco Electronics in Kokomo during that time, working there for five years in total. In May 1977, he quit his job in lieu of being fired for the suspected theft of $4,000 worth of light-emitting diodes, a charge very much in line with his ex-wife's accusations of an addiction to stealing. His supervisor at Delco described him as "immature" and voiced concerns about an inability to exercise good judgment, noting that JB seemed to have an uncontrollable urge to seek revenge if he felt he had been wronged in some manner. Another colleague at Delco recalled that while JB did not get along very well with his male co-workers, he seemed to relate better to women.

In late May, JB and Lisa moved to Fairfax, Virginia, so that JB could take a job with Logicon, Inc. However, three months later, he was terminated for having falsified information on his application about his salary while employed at Delco. An internal correspondence from Logicon dated August 26, 1977 reflected that JB "displayed considerable technical expertise." However, he could not perform his job satisfactorily because it required him to have "considerable interface with technical and non-technical personnel" and his lack of social skills too frequently interfered with his ability to perform that function. Logicon discovered the falsified salary information on JB's application when Logicon management, concerned about his poor people skills, contacted Delco to inquire about his social skills while he had been employed there. Consistent with his past practice, on a subsequent employment application, JB wrote "Poor job fit" as the reason for leaving Logicon.

The same month that JB lost his job with Logicon, Lisa abruptly ended their relationship, and left JB to pursue a job with GTE. Devastated from feelings of abandonment due to the loss of the one person with whom he had experienced an emotional connection, JB retreated behind the same psychological walls he had hidden behind as a child.

A couple of months later, JB found work at Information and Communications Applications (ICR) in Rockville, Maryland, and in January 1978, he enrolled at George Washington University in nearby Washington, D.C. to pursue a master's degree. On January 6, 1978, he met Debbie Fitzjohn, and the two dated for several weeks. Then she disappeared.

In addition to his need for absolute control of romantic partners, JB often obsessed over women to whom he developed any sort of attraction or attachment. Once he fixated on a woman, he could not handle rejection or a lack of reciprocity of his affections. He began keeping an index card file on his sex partners, meticulously recording various personal information about them, including ratings of their sexual performance. The index card file would eventually grow to 72 people, mostly women, before he stopped maintaining the records in 1980.

In March 1978, barely a month after the disappearance of Debbie Fitzjohn, he wrote to the latest of his obsessions, blonde-haired, blue-eyed Patricia Hofer of Reston, Virginia.

> *Greetings!*
>
> *This may appear a bit like a strange letter – in fact, I may keep it a while before giving it to you – but I've been alone, quiet, and thinking a lot all day today! – About you – and me – and things in general – and all sorts of things!!*
>
> *. . . .*
>
> *I am an impatient person sometimes – but – occasionally – maddenly a realist also – even though I often times tend to live in a dream world! Sometimes I'm a bit spacy – so spacy that NASA can't even appreciate where I'm at! But at the same time – I never drag anyone into my world unless they want in!*

A few weeks later, on April 23, he wrote her again, his fear of rejection already readily apparent.

This weekend has been very quiet and I've had a good bit of time for reflecting – on all sorts of things! It seems hard to believe but it has been a month ago that you were off for a week!

Something's bothering me a lot – a month ago I started a letter to you to put my feelings on paper so you'd know where I was coming from – and with one thing or another I didn't give it to you. And that's what has been bothering me – because I'm afraid my holding off might have been the cause of my losing the close affection of the best woman I have ever met! Please read it and talk to me a while – I really want to know – I still want you more than anyone or anything else in the world and my stupid head is driving me nuts!! Please call!

P.S. No matter how you feel, you'll always be a rare first-class person in my mind – so far – the only one that I have ever dreamed of having a child with! I mean that very sincerely – Love,
John
P.P.S. I really want to keep you as a friend!

Following a series of desperate late-night phone calls, realizing that the object of his obsession had slipped out of his grasp, he wrote Hofer a final time on April 28.

Dear Patty,

I'm not sure where to start – Last night was the first time I cried myself to sleep since I was a kid. It's hard for me to admit it, but I wanted you more than anything else in the world. The card that's enclosed, I made for you two weeks ago but didn't send it 'cause I was afraid of scaring you away! – It seems dumb now, but I still want you just as much! And I still want to be your friend! – Arrghhh!!! Because my feelings don't change easily – it might be better if you didn't call next week – I want to talk to you so much right now that I can almost taste it! – But it wouldn't be fair to you.

. . . .

You're so playful and such a free spirit, I find it hard to imagine you're letting someone else control you to the point of who you see – but then I'd probably do the same if you asked me too!

. . . .

I'm returning your picture – you didn't want me taking it! And it's not fair keeping it! Somehow it hurts to remember the hours I've cherished thoughts of you and your picture was always smiling at me when I wasn't with you. Funny – I've never carried a girl's picture in the front window of my wallet before – But I never felt so intense about anyone else before either!

Despite the professed intensity of JB's feelings, or perhaps more accurately, because of them, Patty Hofer cut off further contact with JB to avoid becoming any further entangled with him. Years later, after learning more about him, she called JB a "threat to women both past and present."

JB stayed with ICR until December 1979, when he took a job as manager for the electronic systems section of TRW's Defense and Space Systems Group in McLean, Virginia. The creative environment at TRW was a hothouse in which his individual genius blossomed and flourished as he oversaw the design of new computer systems. During his three-and-a-half year tenure at TRW, JB designed and developed a new computer communications language for the United States Navy. His TRW identification badge included the notification that "the holder of this card is a member of the TRW Defense and Space Systems Group Emergency Response Team and will be permitted access to all areas during an emergency." His judgment and character were held in such high regard that he received a secret security clearance from the federal government in December 1979, followed by a top secret security clearance in December 1980, with open access to much of the Pentagon and other restricted military buildings.

When his work brought him to the Pentagon, JB dealt drugs on the side, amused by the fact that he could sell his illicit product in a place of such intense security, in the heart of the nation's military command. He did not peddle drugs because he needed money. He did it solely for the thrill of getting away with it, the same reason that he had shoplifted and stolen from his employers.

| Crutchley's Pentagon I.D. card

During the same period of time that JB worked for TRW and routinely visited the Pentagon, the body of a missing female employee was found in the Pentagon's vast parking lot. The victim had been strangled in her own car. No one was charged with her murder.

Despite working on high-tech government projects in a cutting edge environment, little in life excited JB, and the few things that did never seemed to do so for long. He lived as if half-asleep, languishing from one moment to the next, suffering a constant feeling of emptiness, as if an unfillable hole had opened up within the center of his soul. His life was monotonous and dull, each day too much like the last, the same surroundings and routine rendering everything meaningless. He lived like Eliot's Prufrock, meekly measuring out his life with coffee spoons.

Unable to find spiritual or emotional fulfillment, JB plunged back into a wild, hedonistic lifestyle that revolved around sex and drugs. In the metropolitan playground of the Washington, D.C. area, he frequented sex clubs and experimented with bondage, group sex, partner swapping, bi-sexuality, and sadistic-masochistic sex. He gravitated toward people who had the financial ability to do whatever turned them on without worrying about the consequences. He sought out women with low self-esteem who were emotionally and sexually submissive, and he did not have any problem finding them.

"My self-image was very, very weak," JB later remembered. "I started running around with a lot of people like myself, really lost souls. Everyone I dated wanted to die."

In time, even life in the fast lane with its attendant excess of parties, drugs, and sex failed to sufficiently stimulate him. He wanted something different, something that would take away the persistent feeling of emptiness that clung like a parasite to his soul.

He began dating several nurses in the D.C. area, including one who introduced him to vampirism, tutoring him in the art of drawing and drinking blood and instructing him in the rites of ritualistic sex. She taught him how to take blood using intravenous needles, syringes, and surgical tubes, and he learned how much blood could be taken before reaching a level that might be life threatening. She also showed him a spiritual side of vampirism, teaching him a darker form of communion, convincing him that drinking human blood could purge his sins.

Having found the sacrament for a new religion, JB developed an insatiable thirst for blood. Beyond the spiritual side, there was something primal and innately sensual about it. From his very first exposure to the practice of bloodletting, he had found it inherently erotic, and fantasizing about it aroused him as well. As an essential element for human life, blood represented power. Taking blood from another person and ingesting it made it his own. Feeding on the essential life fluid fed his need for dominance and control.

After his first intoxicating taste of blood, he craved more and his need grew like a drug addict's need for his next fix. The psychological need grew to such an intensity that when he could not find a partner to satisfy it, he sometimes withdrew a pint or two of his own blood to temporarily satisfy the craving.

And the malevolent darkness inside him continued to grow. It had become his dominant self, his primary sense of identity, but to the outer world he maintained the appearance of a strait-laced, professional computer engineer. He became adept at compartmentalizing his life, concealing his true nature within an external shell of normalcy. To his coworkers at TRW, JB acted friendly and polite, and he seemed to always be happy-go-lucky, perpetually in a positive frame of mind. But behind the mask he viewed people solely as objects to be manipulated, tools he could use to meet his needs. His sole focus in life became self-gratification, and he thought nothing of betraying the deepest trust in order to satisfy his desires.

Accurately described as being "hung like a donkey" by one individual familiar with his anatomy, JB discovered early on that certain women appreciated his unusual physical attribute, and he was not shy in sharing it with them. One of his many affairs involved Judy Carter, a married woman in the Washington, D.C. area with suicidal tendencies. JB enjoyed bondage sessions with Carter in which he would sadistically whip her, one time doing it so severely that the whip eventually broke. After another lengthy session, he took a black and white photograph of her and was excited to see that all of the bruises on her body were clearly visible in the photo.

Another of JB's sexual partners, Kathy Moseley, introduced him to her best friend, Karen White Lulie. Though married at the time, Karen began dating JB in early March of 1980. Tall and thin with long brown hair, many thought that Karen bore more than a passing resemblance to Meryl Streep, and she quickly fell under JB's spell. Though at times afraid of him, Karen nonetheless found herself irresistibly drawn to him. Following a brief courtship, JB and Karen married in November in the small town of Brookettsville, Maryland. As had been the case with his first wife, JB did not love Karen, but he valued her unquestionable loyalty, secure in the knowledge that she would do just about anything that he asked her to do. For JB, it was another marriage of convenience; he viewed it as a logical way to maintain appearances and have a reliable sexual outlet. JB found Karen's reserved, almost mousy, personality particularly attractive since he had an absolute need to dominate any sexual relationship.

Within six months of his wedding, JB completed his graduate work, earning a Master's Degree in Engineering Administration from George Washington University in May 1981. Seven months later, Karen gave birth to a son, Jason, at Fairfax General Hospital in Falls Church, Virginia.

In March 1983, JB interviewed with Harris Corporation at a Washington, D.C job fair. Specializing in communications equipment, Harris Corp primarily built communications systems for the government, including both satellite and terrestrial systems, and Harris's clients included classified and non-classified entities and organizations. On March 22, JB completed Harris's Application for Professional Employment seeking a position in engineering management. On his application, JB highlighted having over fifteen years of management, design, and applications experience in digital and analog control, data acquisition, communications, and systems engineering. He stressed his experience managing the development and production of a safety monitoring system for nuclear facilities, and he emphasized his central role in designing and developing combat communications systems for the U.S. Navy.

Shortly after his interview, JB was offered a position as an engineer at Harris's headquarters in Palm Bay, Florida. Hired to work in Harris's Government Electronic Systems Division as an Associate Principal Engineer, JB would earn an annual salary of $47,000, a hefty sum at a time when the average yearly income stood at just over $22,000. His job duties would be centered on working as a network engineer designing complex computer network systems for various government agencies. An internal Harris document memorializing the decision to extend an offer of employment to JB noted his "very good" potential to advance in engineering management.

After a couple of house-hunting trips to Florida, JB and Karen purchased a four-bedroom home in Malabar, located just east of Palm Bay. They moved into their new Florida home on June 1, 1983, and JB began working at Harris five days later.

On July 6, he typed a letter to some family friends to let them know of the move, obviously excited about the secluded location of his new home.

Well, since you've seen the address, you probably have guessed it, we've MOVED!

. . .

We went and finally did it to Florida!! In the process, we bought a house that came with 2.66 acres, a stable, an enclosed (screened) pool, a Jacuzzi (heated), palm trees, and lots of privacy!!! It's on an unpaved road with few neighbors, so there's very little traffic, and it would be very hard to have a party that would bother anyone!

. . . .

I started work at Harris Corporation, in Melbourne, about 5 minutes away, on the 6th. I'm managing a design engineering group that puts computer and communications systems together. The work is similar to what I was doing at TRW, but the climate here is much more to our liking!!!

. . . .

If you're going to be in Florida sometime in the future . . . we'll send you a map on how to find us. Without directions it is unlikely that anyone will accidentally drop in 'cause the roads around our house aren't on any of the maps we have seen!

At Harris, JB came across as a goofy, apparently harmless computer geek. He had a distinctive way of carrying himself, often walking in a loping, bouncy way that seemed intended to attract attention, and he never wore socks, even when dressed up in a suit and tie. JB's Harris colleagues found him to be a little eccentric, but most overlooked his odd mannerisms since he always seemed to be smiling and in good spirits. If someone asked him how he was doing, they were likely to receive an enthusiastic "Peachy!" in response.

JB was well versed in computer technology and well connected in the aerospace industry. Performance evaluations described him as "very enthusiastic in performing his work and in his interface with others in the workplace." Although his Harris evaluations noted that he sometimes expressed his opinions "too firmly, putting others in a defensive position," he received generally good performance appraisals and annual merit-based salary increases. He was a good company man, religiously attending office parties and other "official" work gettogethers. Though typically friendly toward his co-workers, few of them knew him very well. To most, he was the computer geek with the goofy personality who enjoyed flirting with the women around the office. Even those who worked closely with him rarely caught a glimpse of the manipulative, controlling side of his personality.

No one could see that behind his carefully adorned mask of a hardworking family man, JB suffered from a deep-seated insecurity, an insecurity that had plagued him since childhood. The seeds of this affliction had first taken root when he became aware of his mother's disappointment and resentment toward his very existence. The feelings of inadequacy that sprouted while he was a young boy grew exponentially over the years, infecting his very soul, blending with his essential sense of self. They spawned a psychological need for power and control that spread through his wounded psyche like a cancer, growing stronger and more dangerous over time.

And yet, despite his insecurity, JB wanted to be liked by others. He had a psychological need for a certain degree of popularity and peer approval. Although he generally avoided socializing at public places, JB and his wife hosted several lavish parties at their Malabar home, as well as smaller get-togethers with other couples. One Christmas party at their house drew over 150 guests, and at least seventy people attended their Halloween party. The Crutchleys also hosted a shishkabob dinner for the ten colleagues in JB's engineering group. As Karen recalled, "we entertained a lot."

A November 1984 letter to a friend provided a glimpse into what seemed from the outside to be a normal, middle-class American life.

It's suddenly getting colder, and doing it earlier this year!! Last night, the temperature actually dropped below 60! (Since it was election night, and so many of the candidates were giving each other the cold shoulder). Actually, we have had company this past week – Karen's folks are visiting from Maryland, and we've decided they were responsible for bringing all of the cold with them!

They were hoping to see a Space Shuttle launch this morning, but, as things go, they postponed the launch 'till tomorrow. They also missed their opportunity to vote, but Florida voters are much more patriotic than Marylanders, and now, I think they wish they'd gotten absentee ballots! Around here, we had about a 90% turnout at the polls, which says something good!! Since there is so much government defense related business here, you can guess which (Reagan) presidential candidate took the place by a landslide! It was strange that Mondale took D.C.!

In other happenings, around here things have been awfully quiet this year! But, that's why we moved to the place we did!! Shux, when you live in Paradise, you really shouldn't complain about the quietness!!

So far, we haven't gotten horses to fill the stables, yet, but I've finally gotten around to mending most of the fences in the pastures, so now when we find some animals at a good price we'll be ready!!

The big news of the summer is the underwater UNO marathon I participated in a couple of weeks ago! A bunch of local divers got together and carried on a continuous game of UNO – UNDERWATER – for almost 58 hours! We did it all at the Palm Bay Ramada Inn's swimming pool. The press was here, people from the makers of the UNO game, and lots of others . . . When the final news photo was taken, I was already in the water, winding up a three hour session!! Hopefully, the event will make it into the Guinness' Book of World Records! Whether it does or not, it was a lot of fun!

Cheers!

The following year, on April 18, an excited JB sent out a family news update entitled "Ye New Malabar Meanderings," which continued to foster the appearance of a normal, middle-class family man.

Greetings!

The big news around here is the acquisition of a "real" computer for the house. It's an IBM XT, with 640k of memory, 10 Meg of hard disk, double density floppy, a Hayes 1200 baud SmartModem, and an Epson FT-Plus printer.

. . . .

Otherwise, in the newsy realm, let's begin in December. Jason's third birthday party started off the festivities on the 8th with 5 other kids, and some of their parents. He was the "sweetest, cutest, handsomest, smartest boy in the world! Everybody says that!" (Karen's words, quoted directly!).

. . . .

We threw a Christmas party on the 15th of December for two sections of people from work. The turnout was somewhere around 150 people (or more), kids included! The party began in the middle of the afternoon, with beer, swimming, and volleyball, and continued 'till whenever.

. . . .

Karen and Jason went to Washington, DC for a week in March.

. . . .

Party, again! We had John's section over for an all day Saturday cookout, volleyball, swim, and beer party . . . It started about 1 and leisurely meandered through to somewhere around 1 AM when the last of the partiers left!

. . . .

We still haven't gotten any horses, but we've mended he fences

in the pastures, and this year new gates go in, so, as soon as we
find a good

> *vet, and then the right animals*

> . . . .

Enjoy!

On September 24, 1985, an apparently civic-minded JB attended a Town of Malabar City Council meeting, where he voiced concerns about a lack of protection for the town's areas designated as rural residential. He feared that the encroachment of commercial developers would change the peaceful, quiet character of the town. Just two months later, that cherished small-town innocence would be irreversibly altered, banished by his own actions to the shadowy realm of memory.

EIGHT

Capturing the Vampire

Shortly after Christina Almah finished telling Leatherow about her nightmarish ordeal, Brevard County Sheriff's deputies learned that the Malabar house in which she had been raped and held prisoner belonged to a young married couple, John and Karen Crutchley. In anticipation of obtaining a search warrant for the house at 2180 Hall Road, Lt. Fair instructed Corporal Barry Liford, a member of the Sheriff's Office SWAT team, to position himself nearby the residence without being observed so that he could obtain a physical description of the dwelling sufficient to support a warrant. Having been advised by Agent Al Fuller that the Crutchley residence was located in the northeast quadrant of the intersection of Hall Road and McClain Road, Fair planned on driving Liford to a position northwest of the intersection, where Liford could exit the vehicle with minimal chance of being observed.

Fair drove Corporal Liford to the northwest quadrant of the intersection, unaware that Agent Fuller had erroneously identified the location of Crutchley's house, which was in fact located on the northwest quadrant of Hall and McClain Road, as opposed to the northeast corner as Fuller had advised. As Liford exited Fair's vehicle, a car turned onto the road and proceeded towards them, threatening to illuminate Liford with its headlights. To avoid being seen by any occupants of the Crutchley residence, Liford quickly jumped into a ditch beside the road and ended up crouched in the bushes that bordered the edge of the property. There he found an unexpected surprise.

To his astonishment, Liford found himself face to face with John Crutchley, who was armed with a pistol in his hand, and who had been hiding in the bushes watching the police as they staked out his house. Startled, but even more exasperated, Crutchley demanded to know what Liford was doing on his property. The plain clothed deputy pretended that he had just been out for a late night stroll, but Crutchley was not fooled by Liford's story. He stated in no uncertain terms that Liford could be shot for trespassing. To avoid escalating the situation, Liford identified himself as a Deputy Sheriff and retreated from the property.

When informed of what had happened, Lt. Fair became concerned that Crutchley—now keenly aware that the police were closing in on him—might flee from the area or dispose of vital incriminating evidence. With time clearly working against them, Fair hurried to Crutchley's front door, knocked loudly, and announced himself as a police officer investigating a report of a prowler in the area. He asked Crutchley if he could come inside the house to ensure that it was secure, but Crutchley did not fall for the ruse and did not respond.

Recognizing the urgency of the situation, Fair established two surveillance points for the house and then sent Leatherow and Beau Russell to the Sheriff's south precinct at Sarno Road to prepare a search warrant. Leatherow and Russell met Assistant State Attorney Michael Hunt at the precinct and assisted with preparing the warrant. At 1:30 in the morning on Saturday, November 23, Brevard County Judge Lawrence Johnston signed the search warrant. Leatherow and Russell raced back to Crutchley's house fearing the worst, but hoping that they were not too late.

At approximately 2:37 a.m., Fair and Leatherow knocked on the back door of Crutchley's home and announced that they had a warrant to search the house. A ghostly face briefly appeared in an unlit window on the north side of the house, peered out from the shadows, and then melted back into the darkness. For several tense minutes, silence prevailed as the police began planning their next move. Knowing that time was of the essence, Lt. Fair cut the screen on the door that connected the carport to the house, but as he reached in to unlock the door, it slowly creaked open. The assembled officers watched anxiously as a man's head peeked out languidly through the partially open door. It was the opportunity that Fair was waiting for. He grabbed the man roughly by his nose and yanked him outside. In the illuminating yellow glow of several well-focused flashlights, they discerned that the man matched the description of Christina Almah's abductor. Uniformed deputies quickly placed him under arrest and read him his Miranda rights. As the other deputies secured the house and made sure no one else was lurking inside, they walked the man back into the house and sat him down in the dining room area in handcuffs.

The immediate interior of the house seemed unremarkable. The living room, kitchen, and dining areas looked entirely normal in appearance. It looked like the type of house where the deputies' sons and daughters might attend a friend's birthday party, eating ice cream and playing pin the tail on the donkey. Upon a casual glance, nothing suggested that it served as the lair of a vampire.

Restrained at a round breakfast table, Crutchley listened as Bob Leatherow carefully and methodically read the six-page search warrant and supporting affidavit. As Leatherow continued to read, Crutchley interrupted him several times, asking if he could tell his side of the story.

"I know why you're here," he said resolutely. "I screwed up. I messed up. You don't have to read the warrant to me."

"It's procedure," Leatherow replied coolly. "It has to be done. We have to read the warrant to you."

Leatherow resumed his recitation of the terms of the warrant.

"That Manson girl wanted it. She begged me to do it!" Crutchley suddenly blurted out.

Leatherow ignored him and continued reading, and when he finished, Agent Bo Russell re-advised Crutchley of his Miranda rights.

As the other deputies on the scene began going room-to-room searching the house, Crutchley began to cry.

"I screwed up. You've got me now," he dramatically declared, like some stereotypical villain caught red-handed by the good guys in an old Hollywood movie.

Then he fell silent for a time, as if reflecting on his own words and regretting what he had said.

"I think I should talk to an attorney," he announced abruptly.

"Hey, no problem. If you don't want to talk to us, we're happy to stop right now," Leatherow responded. "Do you have an attorney?"

"No," Crutchley replied blankly, his face betraying no hint about what he was thinking.

Lieutenant Fair, who had been listening to the conversation, motioned to Leatherow.

"Bob, make some calls and find us a public defender."

Leatherow glanced at his watch, not particularly surprised to see that it read 2:53 a.m. Even with all of the excitement of the arrest, he was tired. Long overdue for some real sleep, the adrenalin could only do so much at such an hour in the dead of night. Even in his exhausted state, he knew that getting a public defender on the phone at that hour of the night would be challenging, if not outright impossible.

After Leatherow left the room to make his phone calls, Crutchley turned to Fair.

"Do I need a lawyer?"

"John, you're a smart guy," Fair replied. "What do you think? Only you know if you need a lawyer."

"Well, if I invoke my rights, who do I call?" Crutchley asked.

"I can't recommend a lawyer to you," Fair answered, "but we're trying to track down a public defender for you."

"If you were in my shoes, who would you use?" Crutchley asked.

"If I was in your situation, there are three lawyers who I'd consider, and I'd probably call Joe Mitchell, but you can't afford him."

"You don't know what I can afford," Crutchley replied curtly.

As Fair and Crutchley talked, Leatherow called back to his office and told the operator that he needed to reach an attorney from the Public Defender's Office. He waited patiently as the operator put him on hold. Five, ten, fifteen minutes went by without an attorney coming on the line. Then Leatherow heard Fair's voice hollering at him from the living room.

"Forget about the public defender, Bob!" he heard Fair shout. "Mr. Crutchley has decided that he wants to talk with us now."

Leatherow sighed, hung up the phone, and walked back into the dining room. Crutchley still sat handcuffed at the table.

"Mr. Crutchley just called Joe Mitchell and Joe has agreed to represent him," Fair explained to bring Leatherow up to speed.

Unbeknownst to Fair or Leatherow, Mitchell had told Crutchley that he could answer Fair's questions if he chose to do so, but that he should not trust anyone else associated with the Sheriff's Office.

Agent Russell spoke next.

"Mr. Crutchley, did you understand your rights as they were read to you?"

"Yes."

"And is it your desire to talk to us at this time?"

"Yes, I want to tell you my side of the story," Crutchley answered calmly. Since speaking with Mitchell, he had become "very friendly," almost warm, toward Fair and Russell.

Fair and Russell sat down across from Crutchley at the table and gestured for him to begin while Leatherow stood beside them.

"Yesterday began like any other day," Crutchley told them. "I spent the morning working at my office, and then went home for lunch because I'd left a notebook at the house that I needed for work that afternoon. My wife had taken our son to visit her parents in Maryland for the Thanksgiving holiday, so I had the house to myself. And I was enjoying the time alone. My wife and I had been experiencing some problems for a while and we thought it would be good to spend a little time apart."

He paused and asked for a glass of water before resuming his story.

"I was on my way home from the office, and I spotted a girl hitchhiking on Malabar Road."

"What time was that, John?" Fair asked.

"It was about 1:00 in the afternoon as best I can recall," Crutchley answered before continuing. "As I slowed down to get a better look at her, she waved me over and called out to me. I could read her lips as she shouted to me: 'please, please!' She looked as if she had never been out in the sun. Her skin was chalky and quite pale, and she looked kind of spooky, like a ghost or something, but I felt sorry for her, so I agreed to give her a ride to Melbourne after I picked up the notebook that I needed for work."

He glanced at Leatherow who was busy jotting down notes in a small flip pad.

"When we got to my house, I parked in the carport and started to get out of the car to go inside and get my notebook when the girl suddenly told me that one of her fantasies was to struggle. She said she wanted to be roughed up and my mind just kind of got away from me. I had some rope in the car so I grabbed it and said ok."

Crutchley grew visibly excited as he recounted how he choked the girl and forced her into the house.

"I had the rope in the car for my canoe. I grabbed the rope and wrapped it around her neck, and said 'Is this how you want it?' I pulled until I choked her out. She had struggled for a little while, about fifteen seconds or so, before she passed out. Then I dragged her into the house."

After she went limp, he had continued pulling on the rope a bit longer to make sure that she did not regain consciousness too quickly, but he thought it better not to mention that to the police. Only when he was satisfied that she would stay out did he relax his grip on the rope and remove it from her neck. Grabbing her under her shoulders, he pulled her out of the backseat of the car, dragged her across the carport, and hauled her into the house. From there, it had not been difficult to lift her onto the island countertop and bind her by tying her wrists and ankles.

"When she woke up she said she wanted to do something 'freaky.' So I grabbed my IV needles and surgical tubing and drained some of her blood."

"Did you perform oral sex on her on the table?" Russell asked.

"No, but I put my face between her legs to smell her," Crutchley replied, now even more animated.

"She was cleaner than I thought she would be."

Crutchley boasted to Russell and Leatherow that the girl had virtually begged to sleep with him.

"She said that normally she's the very shy type, but I had excited her. She told me that it was her dream to go to bed with Charles Manson."

They eventually made their way to the bedroom and had sex.

"I think she was a virgin," Crutchley added casually.

"Why do you think that?" Russell asked.

"She was very, very tight when I entered her," Crutchley bragged. "She said it hurt. She even moaned and cried a little when I stuck it in."

Later, they had oral sex in a sixty-nine position on the bed. Crutchley chuckled as he described to Leatherow and Russell how Christina had not been very good at fellatio.

"I could tell that she didn't have much experience sexually speaking."

As the night progressed into the early morning hours, they had sex several more times, some of which Crutchley videotaped.

The next morning, Crutchley had to get to work for an 8:00 a.m.

meeting, so he put the girl in the bathtub in a bathroom. When he came home for lunch around noon to check on her, she was gone.

"After I came home and discovered that she wasn't there, I freaked out. I grabbed the videotape of us having sex and erased it. I took her clothes, the IV needles, and the jar that I drained her blood into and tossed them all into her handbag and threw it in my car to get rid of it. I ended up on I-95 and drove north until I came to the Sarno Road exit. That's where I dumped the handbag, on the side of the exit ramp at Sarno Road."

Front view of Crutchley's home in Malabar

Aerial view of Crutchley's home showing large property with barn and pond on adjacent property

Although Leatherow and Russell subsequently accompanied Crutchley to the Sarno Road site after his arrest, no trace of the handbag or other items could be found. The three walked the area around the ramp without finding anything. As Leatherow recalled, Crutchley became "very, very hysterical that we couldn't find anything." He started ranting, insisting that he had thrown the handbag there. They walked the area one more time and then returned to Crutchley's house empty handed.

Leatherow later learned that Crutchley had actually discarded the handbag by throwing it into a dumpster next to a Winn Dixie on Malabar Road. He had lied to the police to keep them from finding the items. His dramatic ranting had been part of the deceit, a purposeful performance to throw them off the trail.

As Crutchley continued his account of the events, he alternated between an enthusiastic narrative and something closer to a sob story, sometimes eagerly telling what happened, other times recounting events with a tone of regret as the reality of the situation dawned on him. Perhaps intending to offer an excuse for his actions, he revealed that he had recently been having problems with his wife and that the two of them had not had sex in at least six months. However, when Leatherow asked him about the accusation that he had taken Christina's blood, Crutchley grew visibly excited, clearly ardent in wanting to talk about it, blithely telling Leatherow, "I drank of the blood," his eyes fixed in a trance as if reliving a spiritual experience. "I'll show you the beaker," he added after appearing to refocus his attention.

Crutchley sat forward, literally "on the edge of his seat" as he described draining and drinking Christina's blood. He had wielded so much power over her, he had exercised such complete control, that if he had wanted to he could have drained her very life force away. He exultantly told the deputies that he had withdrawn blood from his wife in a similar fashion and drank it "hundreds of times" since having been introduced to the practice by a nurse in the Washington, D.C. area years earlier. He had been taking blood from his wife and previous girlfriends ritualistically, almost religiously, ever since. Not even the specter of AIDS had stopped him.

Thought to have originally entered the United States in 1969, Acquired Immune Deficiency Syndrome had rapidly spread throughout the country, and had quickly reached epidemic proportions during the first half of the decade with the number of reported cases rising to over 13,000 by 1985. By the end of the summer of 1985, a majority of Americans ranked AIDS as the second most serious medical condition affecting the country, trailing only behind cancer, and well ahead of heart disease, the country's leading cause of death. On October 2, 1985, amidst extensive media attention, widely beloved actor Rock Hudson died from AIDS-related complications, further demonizing a disease that had already frightened a majority of the country. Yet, despite the growing danger, Crutchley's thirst for blood did not diminish.

Pursuant to the warrant from Judge Johnston, Sheriff's personnel went room to room searching Crutchley's house. The kitchen area, bedroom, and bathroom precisely matched the descriptions that Christina Almah had given them. Investigators found numerous items of interest during their search of the premises, including Christina's driver's license, which they found hidden in the back pocket of a soaking wet, white and blue-striped men's bathing suit hanging on a backyard clothes line. Although the time that elapsed between Christina's escape at approximately 10:30 a.m. and the execution of the search warrant over sixteen hours later had given Crutchley plenty of time to get rid of incriminating evidence, he may have forgotten about the driver's license or concluded that the police would overlook it hidden in plain sight in a pair of wet swimming trunks.

Leatherow offered his own explanation.

"John felt he'd beaten us. He'd gotten rid of all the victim's stuff, but he had to keep her California driver's license. He couldn't let it go. He figured no one would pick up a wet bathing suit."

Investigators had done some quick research on Crutchley as they waited for the judge to sign the search warrant. Based on the value of Crutchley's home and his employment with Harris Corporation, they knew that he was well educated and worked a white-collar job. Deputies realized that "he was not your average run-of-the-mill rapist that we encounter," but they were still surprised by some of the things they found in his house.

Over forty items were seized during the search, including videotapes, nylon rope, a video camera, surgical tubing, a glass beaker, and intravenous needles and syringes. In the master bedroom closet, they found a large assortment of leather dog collars, even though Crutchley did not own any dogs. They also found chains, several plastic bags containing hair clippings, a plastic baggie of marijuana, and identification cards belonging to Maude Moats and Lisa Baker. They came across a copy of the biographical book, *Killer Clown*, among Crutchley's belongings as well, which detailed the killing career of notorious serial killer John Wayne Gacy.

Other items discovered in Crutchley's home included about twenty women's medallions and necklaces hanging beside the clothes in his closet, well away from where his wife kept her jewelry. There was also a personal computer set up on a desk in Crutchley's study. Although personal computers were not common at the time, deputies left the computer undisturbed, at Lt. Fair's direction, because it had not been included in the search warrant. For his part, Leatherow regretted not seizing the computer that night because he knew that failing to do so had given Crutchley the opportunity to erase evidence of other crimes from the computer's memory.

A gold Honda motorcycle and blue dirt bike were parked in the carport, as was a light beige-colored, two-door 1982 Nissan Stanza with a hatchback. Strangely, all identifying emblems on the vehicle, including the "Stanza" emblems on the back, sides, and wheels, had been completely removed or covered over with black electrical tape. The Nissan was seized and taken to the Sheriff's criminalistics lab in Titusville for closer inspection. There investigators discovered that the car had also been rigged by Crutchley so that he could pull a knob next to the radio and lock the passenger side door via a wire that ran behind the dash board to the passenger door. It was obvious that the car had been rigged to prevent unwilling passengers from escaping.

As the search of his home continued, Crutchley called his wife in Maryland shortly after 4:00 a.m. Deputies overheard him telling his wife, "I picked up this chick . . . brought her home and things got out of hand . . . Yeah, I got the camera out for her."

At approximately 9:00 a.m., Leatherow and Russell transported Crutchley to the Brevard County Jail in Titusville. They charged him with sexual battery, aggravated battery, kidnapping, possession of marijuana over twenty grams, and possession of drug paraphernalia. The Arrest Form completed by Leatherow reflected that the "Victim almost died from the severity of the crimes."

So began the strangest, most intensive investigative effort of Leatherow's career.

JOHN B. CRUTCHLEY

Booking photo of John Brennan Crutchley

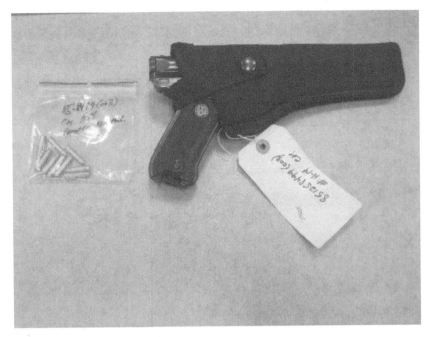

Crutchley's handgun found in his home

Women's necklaces and pendants hanging in Crutchley's closet far away from his wife's jewelry

Crutchley's nondescript car used to abduct his victims. All identifying decals and labels on exterior and interior of the car were removed or covered by Crutchley to make the car more difficult to identify.

Interior photo of Crutchley's car showing black knob that he installed near the steering wheel that allowed Crutchley to lock the passenger side door, preventing any passenger from escaping.

NINE

What may man within him hide

O, what may man within him hide, though angel on the outward side!

— Shakespeare

In a decade where appearance was everything, Crutchley did not appear to be anything more than a clean-cut, white-collar professional, a hard-working and devoted family man. In all respects, he seemed to be the happy, successful guy next door, but there was more than meets the eye with the erudite, unimposing computer genius. When performing his public persona, he presented himself as a talented, well-educated professional working for a prestigious high-tech communications company. He had learned enough about emotions to be able to pretend to experience them himself so that he could appear normal. If a coworker tearfully told him that her mother had just died, he knew how to look and sound sympathetic despite the fact that he lacked the ability to experience any empathy. In truth, such news actually impacted him less than the thought of what wine he would be having with dinner that night. If he heard that a friend's newborn daughter had been diagnosed with a life-threatening case of bacterial meningitis, he knew how to come across as caring and concerned when it actually meant no more to him than discovering a broken zipper on his jacket or a button missing from one of his shirts. Behind closed doors or concealed by the shroud of night, his darker, depraved side emerged with a ghoulish addiction to blood and driven by a demanding hunger appeased only by sexual dominance and death. In an age of appearance, Crutchley became a master of wearing masks to disguise his true nature.

Katherine Ramsland, a noted author and Professor of Forensic Psychiatry, underscored one of the most troubling things about the man who had held a helpless nineteen-year-old girl prisoner, draining and drinking her blood while repeatedly sexually assaulting her.

"The most frightening thing about John Crutchley is that he gives off no signals that would alarm you," Ramsland said. "You would never see him coming. He could pass as anybody. He seems normal. There's nothing about him that would lead you to believe that he's anything other than an engineer."

Indeed, neighbors in his Malabar neighborhood described Crutchley as a nice person and quiet neighbor, an altogether unassuming man.

And yet, despite his seemingly harmless appearance, a creature of darkness had made the Sunshine State his home. For more than two years, unbeknownst to his Malabar neighbors, a vampire had been living among them, concealed as one of them, hidden in plain sight in an unobtrusive house next door.

When the citizens of Brevard County, the greater Orlando metropolitan area, and surrounding parts of central Florida unfolded the morning edition of their November 24 *Sun Sentinel* newspaper, they were greeted by a strange headline: "Rape Victim Tells Police Attacker Drank Her Blood." It heralded the beginning of what would become extensive media coverage of the case. Meanwhile, Crutchley's neighbors continued to express astonishment at the arrest of the reclusive engineer and apparent family man. He had always seemed so normal to them, a quiet guy who worked hard, enjoyed riding motorcycles, and even occasionally attended Malabar town meetings as a concerned member of the citizenry.

Thomas Harper, who had rescued Christina Almah as she stumbled dazedly along Hall Road, voiced a common theme among the local Malabar residents.

"It all took me by such surprise," Harper explained. "It's always been so quiet here—no break ins. We've always been so happy here." Another neighbor, Vincent Glatter, expressed a similar reaction.

"I thought he was quite a decent, respectable fella," Glatter said. "He drove on his motorcycle a good deal of the time, and I was always out in the garden and he would wave. We would talk sometimes when he stopped by on his motorcycle."

According to Glatter, Crutchley had always come across as a "warm person," never hesitating to strike up a pleasant conversation.

Another resident, Ivy Harper, added: "Most people in this area are nice folks and you wouldn't have known any different. It's just beyond the scope of imagination."

They never suspected that the face Crutchley had worn was not his own, that something sinister lurked beneath the surface, sequestered behind superficial charm.

Crutchley's mother professed the same level of astonishment about her son's alleged acts, speculating that his bizarre behavior was so unlike him that it must have been caused by a brain tumor.

"Something snapped. It just had to," she insisted. "I just can't believe it of John. He's never been in any trouble. The only problem we ever had was getting him to eat when he was a baby and getting him to study when he was in school."

Sounding a similar note, his former live-in girlfriend, Lisa Baker, was "shocked" to hear of his arrest. She could not imagine him capable of committing the criminal acts for which he stood accused.

"When I knew him, he would never intentionally hurt anyone," she asserted.

On Monday, November 25, Leatherow met Christina Almah at Von Bane's trailer in Enchanted Lakes Estates, and then drove her to the Sheriff's precinct for a polygraph examination. Though just released from the hospital and still shaken from her horrific experience, Christina easily passed the lie detector test, which showed no deception in her assertions about the abduction and nearly twenty-two hours of sexual assaults and captivity. In reviewing her account of the relevant events, Christina remembered an additional detail that had previously eluded her.

"The man told me he was going to kill me several times – it was pretty clear what he was intending to do."

Later that day, Leatherow met with Bobbie Imhuff, a home-maker whose husband worked at Harris Corporation. Mrs. Imhuff informed Leatherow that she and her husband had attended a party at 312 Avenue B in Melbourne Beach on November 9. The party, which had been a going away celebration for another Harris employee, took place less than two weeks before Crutchley's arrest. Crutchley also attended the party, and Imhuff recalled that he had been acting very strangely. He showed up at the party without any shoes and wearing a shirt with some sort of sexual expression on it, the exact words of which she could not recall. He had a camera with him and Mrs. Imhuff noticed that he took photographs of all of the women at the party, while also grabbing or fondling most of them. His behavior towards the women became so obnoxious that the party's hosts eventually asked Crutchley to leave, and he stalked out of their house shortly after midnight. The next day, Mrs. Imhuff read in the newspaper that a rape had occurred in Melbourne Beach on the same night as the party, just one street over on Avenue A. She wondered whether Crutchley might have been involved in the rape so she contacted the Sheriff's Office to share her information. Leatherow assured her that he would look into it.

After having time to analyze the items taken from Crutchley's residence and to review photographs of various items in his house that had not been seized during the November 23 search, Leatherow felt strongly that they should go back and get Crutchley's personal computer, an IBM PCXT model with an Epsom FX-80 printer. His gut and Quantico training told him that the computer could be the key to connecting Crutchley to other crimes. Leatherow pitched the idea of retrieving Crutchley's computer to his superiors at the Sheriff's Office, but they did not share his urgency in doing so. They felt that they could wait and take possession of the computer later if need be.

While at home watching the evening news, Kimberly Walker's father saw a story about Crutchley's arrest. During the news clip, Crutchley's face flashed across the TV screen. Strangely, unexplainably, Crutchley looked somehow familiar to him. All during dinner, and for hours afterward, the feeling that he had seen Crutchley before kept gnawing at his brain. Then, when he was brushing his teeth, it finally hit him: although his hair had been a little darker at the time, John Crutchley was the unknown man who had attended Kim's memorial service years before.

On December 2, Crutchley strolled out of the Brevard County Jail after posting bond. Since he was a first-time offender with a family and white-collar job he had been deemed a low flight risk, and his bond had been set at $50,000, a relatively small amount considering the seriousness of his alleged crimes. He was free to do as he pleased pending trial on his criminal charges.

The next day, Leatherow met with Robert Collins, an attorney for Harris Corporation, to request access to Crutchley's office at trailer 823 of Harris's Palm Bay facility. Collins advised that he would need some time to arrange it, but assured Leatherow that the office would not be disturbed in the meantime since, as of the day before, Crutchley had been prohibited from using Harris facilities or equipment, including his office at the Commercial SATCOM Division of the company's main facility.

A few days later, Leatherow received a phone call from Special Agent Robert Ressler of the FBI Academy's Behavioral Science Unit in Quantico, Virginia. Leatherow was happy to hear that Ressler remembered him from the three-month training program that he had attended several years before. Ressler had heard about the Crutchley case and wanted to know more about it. He asked to review the case reports and Leatherow agreed to send him a copy of them. The two talked about the case for nearly half an hour, and before hanging up, Ressler suggested that Leatherow check Crutchley's car to see if it had a cut-off switch for the license plate light or any similar devices for concealing the driver's identity or making it difficult to describe the car.

Back at his Malabar home on bond, Crutchley sent a package of unknown items to Lisa Baker, asking her to hold on to the contents for him until the heat from the Christina Almah case died down. Baker would later deny that she ever received the package.

On December 9, Crutchley wrote a letter to his mother.

Dear Mom,

I have received both of your letters, and I am finally getting a few words on paper in reply. In your first letter, you said that it is a shame that I was sitting on the top of the world and lost it all with doing drugs. That is not the case. I was in a position in life where I felt no real return coming to me from life. Thus, there was not much to lose. The reasons are rather complex, and most painful and difficult for me to simply write down in a letter. I would like to put all of the details in this letter, but I don't fully understand them all myself, at the moment.

. . . .

What is happening to me may be the best thing that has happened to me in a long time, in spite of how it looks at the moment. The root of my problem has a lot to do with religion. My impression of church related things has been colored heavily by my observations of all of the hypocritical things happening in what I saw of the church as a child. As a result, I developed my own religion, which I am quite sure you would never approve of. It seemed to fit better than any other alternatives I saw, and I got through a surprising lot by following it. However, as I have finally come to realize, it was a false friend.

Crutchley did not specify which "hypocritical things" he witnessed in church and did not elaborate why his "own religion" turned out to be a "false friend."

The day after he wrote that letter, investigators returned to Crutchley's house with another search warrant. The stack of at least twentyfive credit cards, clearly visible in a photograph taken during the original search that showed the contents of Crutchley's safe, was nowhere to be found. And that was not the only item of interest that had disappeared. Crutchley's personal computer was missing as well. Later, while having a blood sample taken, Crutchley told a jail guard that the police had missed their opportunity. They should have taken his computer the night of his arrest. Now two potentially incriminating pieces of evidence had vanished without a trace. Leatherow eventually learned that when Karen returned from Maryland following her husband's arrest, she removed his computer from the home and delivered it to his colleague, George Hurley, for "safe keeping."

On December 11, Audrey Megregian called Leatherow to let him know that she had recently received a phone call from Von Bane's mother, Suzanne, who, coincidentally, worked at Harris Corporation. During their conversation, Bane mentioned something to Megregian that she thought might be of interest to Leatherow: Crutchley's password on his office computer at Harris. According to Bane, the password began with one word: "Vampire."

A photograph taken of the contents of Crutchley's safe, showing a stack of approximately twenty credit cards. The credit cards later vanished after Crutchley was released on bail.

Later that day, in Sacramento, California, Hugh Scrutton bent over to pick up a package that was sitting outside by the entrance to his computer store. As he lifted the package off the ground, it exploded with ear-shattering force. The thirty-eight year old Scrutton died instantly. He became the first fatality in the bloody bombing campaign of Ted Kaczynski, the infamous "Unabomber."

TEN

Gathering evidence

Crutchley's arraignment went forward on December 17 at the Brevard County Courthouse in Titusville. Three days later, Harris Corporation formally cut ties with him, terminating his employment on grounds that the "circumstances surrounding his legal situation rendered him ineffective." The same day, Leatherow and Lieutenant Joe Crosby arrived at Harris's Palm Bay location on Palm Bay Road. They met with Human Resources officer, Glen Nichols, and Crutchley's former supervisor, George Webber, to conduct a search of Crutchley's office in room 112 of trailer 8-23.

After entering the trailer, the four men walked down a dimly lit hallway lined with faded brown carpet. At the end of the hall, they reached a corner office. Leatherow and Crosby followed Nichols and Webber into the office and found themselves in a ten-by-ten-foot windowless room with a plain grey desk positioned a few feet to the right of the door. A PC computer and dot matrix printer sat perched on top of the desk. Two chairs were situated in front of the desk and two matching metal bookcases stretched across the opposite side of the room, with an assortment of binders and computer manuals haphazardly stacked on their shelves. A heavy metal filing cabinet stood against the wall opposite the door.

Over the next few hours, Leatherow and Crosby observed as Nichols and Webber searched throughout the room. They found several items of interest among Crutchley's personal belongings. In the top right drawer of his locked desk, pushed to the very back of the drawer, they discovered a plastic sandwich bag containing Patti Volanski's Florida identification card, Social Security card, library card, and voter registration card, along with two photographs of Patti's son.

In Crutchley's filing cabinet, they found a yellow five-by-seveninch box filled with over seventy photographs of bound and gagged women who had been posed in various graphic sexual positions. In some of the photos, a man's hands could be seen wrapped around a woman's neck, apparently choking her.

In the same filing cabinet, the investigators discovered a card file box containing seventy-two three-by-five-inch index cards. Each card had a woman's name typed or written at the top along with her address and phone number, astrological sign, and how Crutchley had met her. Most of the cards also contained miscellaneous other personal information about each woman, such as her sexual preferences or what her hobbies included. One index card included the note "very interesting – rather do someone's mind than their body." Another stated, "wants to do dirty pix!" while a different girl's card identified her as a "cockteaser – very self-centered." Many included what appeared to be coded ratings delineated as "b" and "f." The card for one of the women, Elizabeth Camelo, read:

100# 5'. Student, Met @ Dateline party 21 Feb 78.
28 Feb – VIRGIN!
19 May 78 – Non Virgin!
B 14 Feb 54. b = 8.

To begin pill Tues 23 May 78.
1ˢᵗ real orgasm 29 May 78.

The top of another card contained the name Debbie Fitzjohn. It included extensive notes about her:

Office administrator, met at work, lunch 19 Jan 78.
Strong on women's position in work force, art major,
working for associate in Business Administration, wants
teaching certificate.
Does not smoke cigarettes.
Very creative, likes antique jewelry.
Married in 72, divorced in 73.

Debbie's card ended with an ominous hand written notation:

"Disappeared 27 Jan 78."

The four men found a business card lying next to the card file box. The front of the business card read:

Diversified Detection Services, Inc. Oakton, VA
James Wilt – President
21 Mar – 569-1176

They also found a box of slides and reams of computer paper that appeared to contain classified information about U.S. Navy operations, including submarine deployment data and satellite images of ships in the Middle East. Leatherow turned over the Navy information to federal agents who determined it to be of "significant national security interest." Although Leatherow anticipated that federal espionage charges would follow, none were ever filed against Crutchley. Federal authorities may have ultimately concluded that Crutchley stole the information for his own use, or perhaps they did not want to draw attention to the fact that he had been granted a top-secret security clearance. In speaking with Crutchley's coworkers at Harris Corporation, Leatherow learned that Crutchley at times acted a little eccentric, but he fit reasonably well into the engineering group. Depending on the project involved, he oversaw four to six engineers, but he never became close to any of them because he moved around a lot due to the nature of the projects that he worked on. Crutchley had what some called a "California personality" in that he would not hesitate to invade a colleague's personal space when discussing a particular topic, and he seemed to lack the social skills to recognize when he had offended someone. He was notorious for flirting with most of the women at work, and it was a poorly kept secret that he had slept with at least one of the married secretaries, but aside from his overactive libido, he came across as harmless. His coworkers were all shocked to hear of his arrest because they never would have suspected him of being capable of committing such a crime.

George Hurley, who shared Crutchley's interest in motorcycles and computers, had formed the closest bond to Crutchley than anyone else at Harris, and the two often ate lunch together. Hurley remembered Crutchley as being very bright and having an animated, friendly personality, someone who never seemed to get angry and was always smiling and upbeat. However, Hurley also noticed that Crutchley was a "fast talker" who enjoyed manipulating others. He could also be a bit vain, and he sometimes gave off an air of superiority. Hurley made it a point to tell Leatherow how Crutchley also had an odd way of walking at work, which he did with a certain panache, taking exaggerated strides and bouncing on the balls of his feet, a walk that seemed intended to draw attention, a walk that Hurley described as being almost feminine.

For the majority of Crutchley's coworkers, the only quirky or outof-the-ordinary things they could remember about him were that he never wore socks and he once pinned a nude photo of his wife to his office wall. They never would have guessed that he had a hidden dark side.

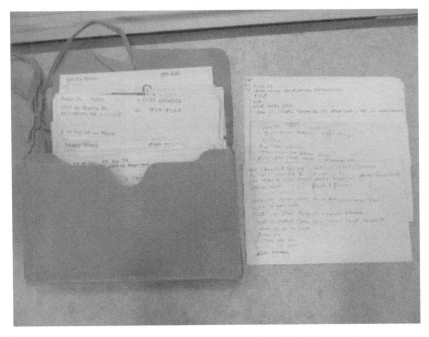

Index card file found among Crutchley's belongings. The index cards contained detailed information about women who Crutchley had dated or was interested in dating.

likes travel, astrology, art, camping
plays piano, guitar
b-6.5   5'1" 110#
Office administrator, met @work, lunch 19Jan78
strong on women's position in work force
art major, working for assoc. in B.Admin.
wants teaching certificate
does not smoke cigarettes
very creative,

Back of index card for Debbie Fitzjohn with Crutchley's handwritten notation at end: "disappeared 27 Jan 78."

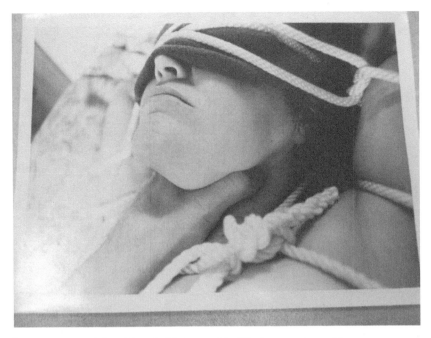

Photograph of Crutchley choking an unidentified woman bound by ropes.

Another photograph of a bound woman being choked.

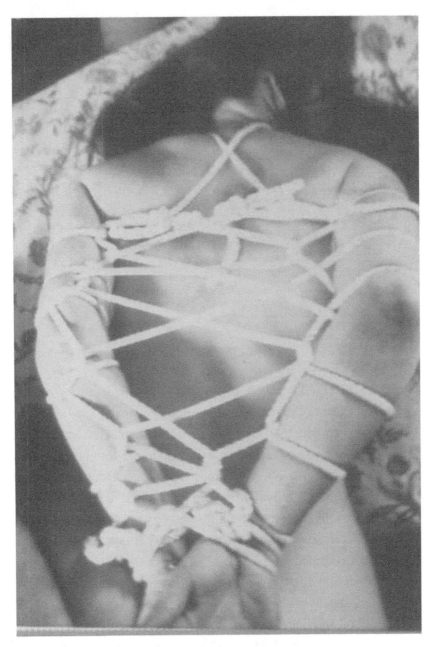

Photograph found among Crutchley's belongings depicting a woman bound by extensive roping.

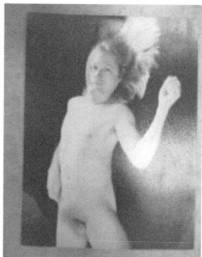

Undated photographs of Crutchley found in his belongings suggesting a narcissistic side to his personality.

After the successful search of Crutchley's office at Harris, Joe Crosby returned to the precinct and, after a few calls, tracked down Maude Moats, Crutchley's first wife, by telephone. Moats told Crosby that her ex-husband had a bad temper and could turn violent without warning. He often became extremely jealous and would frequently manipulate her, trying to make her feel guilty about things that he did. She left him after he began beating her, and she still feared him. He told her on multiple occasions that he did not get mad when someone wronged him, "he got even."

When they had sex, he enjoyed choking her until she passed out, and the sex steadily became more and more violent.

"He liked to choke me when we had sex," Moats told Crosby, "and he said it excited him to hear me gasping for air when he strangled me. I finally had enough and the next time he started choking me, I put my hands around his neck and squeezed as hard as I could.

He screamed, 'Stop, it hurts!' and then knocked my hands away. But he never tried to strangle me again after that."

Moats said that while they were married Crutchley became fascinated by group sex and partner swapping. After persuading her to give it a try, Crutchley arranged for them to swap partners with Walter and Beverly Dickman, a couple who lived in Defiance, Ohio. When they arrived at the Dickmans' house, they found Beverly fully nude and tied to a chair in the living room. Too disturbed by the situation, Maude refused to go through with it.

Moats also shared some things with Crosby that Crutchley had told her about his childhood, including that his mother had abused him mentally and physically. According to Crutchley, Mildred had burned his fingers with a curling iron when he was a child, and he showed Moats the scars to prove it. With venom in her voice, Crutchley's mother also repeatedly told him, while he was a toddler and young boy, that she had wanted a girl instead of him, and that she did not like boys.

"I wasn't all that surprised to hear those things about his mother," Moats advised Crosby. "John was always obsessed with trying to please his mother, and he often imitated her voice when he wanted to make a point. I think his mom's constantly negative comments about wishing that he was a girl really messed with his head. He told me many times that he would have liked to have been a woman and that he often imagined himself as a woman."

Moats also recalled that Crutchley had told her that he had been in a sexual relationship with his sister, Carolynn, for a period of time. According to Crutchley, the two had sex on the sofa in their parents' home on the night that he graduated from Defiance College, and the incestuous relationship had apparently lasted for several years.

After speaking with Moats, Crosby tried to contact the other women in Crutchley's index card collection, ultimately reaching about a third of them. Most of them were surprised to hear about

Crutchley's arrest, and told Crosby that he had always seemed like a "nice guy." Some mentioned that he had dated "a lot of girls," but otherwise "noticed nothing unusual" about him. However, one of the women, Sue Goldman, told Crosby that she had met Crutchley at a bar, but refused to go out with him because he kept asking her "weird questions about her sex life."

On December 21, Leatherow met with a team of investigators, including Commander "Speedy" Dewitt, Lt. Crosby, and State Attorney Norm Wolfinger, at the State Attorney's Office in Titusville to discuss the new evidence that he and Crosby seized from Crutchley's office. Speedy Dewitt was a pioneer at the Brevard County Sheriff's Office, having formed its homicide unit with great success, achieving one of the highest clearance rates for murder cases in the state as well as the country. Dewitt implemented a "96-hour rule" which mandated that no homicide investigators could return home while working a new homicide case until at least ninety-six hours had passed from the time that the murder was first reported. Dewitt's "old school" approach was tough on the homicide detectives, but it had produced exemplary results, as ninety percent of the Sheriff's Office's murder cases were solved within the first ninety-six hours of having been received. A "no nonsense" commander, Dewitt looked and acted like J. Edgar Hoover. He kept meticulous records of meetings and conversations and he "had the dirt on everybody." Yet, he zealously kept his real name a secret, going so far as to have his driver's license and high school records purged. Though he grew up in Erie County, New York, Dewitt relocated to Florida and most people assumed him to be southern by birth as he was frequently fond of pronouncing that he "never met a Yankee cop who was worth a damn."

After the group meeting, it was Leatherow's turn to work the phones. First on his list was Detective Fred Pfeiff of the Fairfax County Police Department, whose business card had been found among the items in Crutchley's desk at Harris Corporation. To Leatherow's surprise, the call went straight to Pfeiff, who was working at his desk when the phone rang. After a brief introduction, Pfeiff informed his Brevard County counterpart that he was intimately familiar with Crutchley because Crutchley had been investigated by the Fairfax County Police Department in connection with a homicide that had occurred in Fairfax County, Virginia a few years prior. Like Leatherow in the Florida case, Pfeiff had been the lead investigator in Virginia, and he agreed to send Leatherow copies of the case reports. It was the first time that Leatherow learned of the disappearance and murder of Debbie Fitzjohn.

ELEVEN

Early prey

In his cover letter accompanying copies of the Fairfax County Police Department's case file on Debbie Fitzjohn, Detective Fred Pfeiff asked his Florida counterparts to keep him posted about their investigation of Crutchley "because I sure would like to make him on my case or yours." When Leatherow finished reviewing the Debbie Fitzjohn case file, he knew that Fitzjohn must have been one of Crutchley's first victims. The facts of the Fitzjohn case made it crystal clear in his mind.

Seven years earlier, on October 15, 1978, three relic hunters searching an area of woods in Fairfax County had stumbled upon a human skull. A subsequent search of the area revealed a badly decomposed human body about one hundred yards north of a row of power lines. The nearly skeletonized remains were unclothed, lying in a shallow grave in the rural area of Chantilly, Virginia, about twenty yards away from Pleasant Valley Road. The "grave" really amounted to nothing more than a depression in the ground, only a foot or two deep, but the body had been well concealed because it was partially covered by tree branches that had been stacked end-to-end on opposite sides of it. Some strands of light brown hair were found in the dirt at the end of the grave where the body's head should have been. Most of the body's dirty-white and greyish-yellow ribs and leg bones bore bite marks, which had most likely been caused by dogs or other large animals chewing on the corpse.

Due to the advanced state of decomposition of the body, Fairfax County homicide investigators sent it to the Smithsonian Institution in Washington, D.C. for identification. A forensics expert at the Smithsonian ultimately identified the skeletal remains as those of Deborah Rita Fitzjohn, a 25-year-old woman from Centreville, Virginia. Affectionately known to her friends and family as "Dee," Fitzjohn had disappeared about ten months earlier on January 27, and her grandmother reported her missing the next day. The forensic report noted that examination of the body's jaw showed a faint degree of "pink teeth," suggesting that the cause of death had been asphyxiation by strangulation.

Debbie was born in Alexandria, Virginia, and grew up in the Fairfax County suburbs of Washington, D.C. When her parents separated and moved out of the area in 1964, she was adopted by her paternal grandparents, Herman and Milda, who raised her from childhood. At the time of her disappearance, she was a petite, attractive girl with hazel eyes and honey blonde hair, standing about five feet, two inches tall and weighing approximately 105 pounds. A shy, creative person, Debbie played both the guitar and piano, and she had also recently begun writing a short story about a lonesome woman who picks up a hitchhiker. She enjoyed travel, art, and camping, and she maintained such a positive outlook on life that her grandmother called Debbie her "shining star."

Debbie worked as an office assistant in the consumer relations department of Texaco Oil Company's office in Rockville, Maryland. She was thankful to have her job with Texaco, but deep down she wanted to do something more with her life. At night, she took classes in math and public speaking at George Washington University in pursuit of a degree in business administration. Having divorced five years earlier, she lived alone in a two-bedroom condominium not far from her grandparents' house in Centreville. As her stepmother, Edna Fitzjohn, recalled, "She was a super kid who worked for everything she had. Everybody I know dearly loved her. But she was such a trusting kid, I guess it would have been easy to pull the wool over her eyes."

At the time of her disappearance, Debbie had been dating John Crutchley for about two weeks. The two met in the cafeteria of the office building where they both worked, and shortly thereafter they went on their first date. Debbie was quickly captivated by the articulate, well dressed Crutchley's intelligence and wit.

Like Debbie, Crutchley had recently started taking classes at George Washington University, and like Debbie, he had been divorced and single since 1973. The two also shared some interest in the occult, but while Crutchley was interested in hard-core astrology and had become fascinated by Satanism, Debbie had only a fledgling curiosity about horoscopes and tarot cards.

Like her granddaughter, Milda Fitzjohn could not help being impressed by Crutchley, at least initially. Employing all of his charm, he easily made a positive first impression on both of the Fitzjohn women, but as she spent more time with him, Debbie began to see another side of Crutchley. Mildred had been a bit surprised when, after returning from one of her dates with him, Debbie spontaneously remarked to her grandmother, "Granny, he's a nutball." And as it turned out, that "nutball" ended up being the last person to see Debbie alive.

On Friday night, January 27, 1978, Debbie had dinner with her grandmother as she frequently enjoyed doing. Though naturally goodnatured, on this particular evening Debbie was in an especially talkative, upbeat mood because she had recently learned that Texaco would pay the majority of her tuition to take courses in public speaking and math at George Washington University.

"She was as happy as a lark," her grandmother recalled.

After dinner, Debbie drove home, departing her grandparents' house at about 6:30 p.m. Shortly after getting back to her residence in Newgate Condominiums, Debbie treated herself to a hot bath. The tub was draining and she was still drying off when the phone rang. It was Crutchley calling. He invited her over to his trailer at Waples Mobile Home Estates in Fairfax, just a ten-minute drive down Lee Highway.

"Hello?"

"Hey, Dee, it's JB. Do you have any plans tonight?"

"Hi, JB. Not really. I thought I might have a quiet night at home, maybe watch a movie or something."

"I've got a better idea. Why don't you come over to my place and we can have a quiet night together."

"Well . . ."

"Come on. I really want to see you. I've been thinking about you all day. And I promise I'll be good."

"Alright, but only for a little while. Let me get dressed and I'll be over there around 7:30 or so."

At approximately 7:25 p.m., Milda Fitzjohn was washing dishes when she saw her granddaughter driving past her open kitchen window.

"Granny, I'm going to Fairfax," Dee yelled with a wave. "I'll be back."

Milda nodded and smiled. She watched Debbie's blue 1976 Subaru station wagon pull away and grow smaller and smaller until it disappeared down the road.

It was the last time Milda ever saw her granddaughter alive.

Early the next morning, Crutchley stepped out of his trailer, got into his car, and left town.

When Debbie failed to return home on Saturday, January 28, Milda immediately became worried. She had never fully recovered from the loss of Debbie's younger sister, fifteen-year-old Barbara, in a car accident seven years earlier, and she could not bear to think of something happening to Debbie.

Too worried about Debbie to just sit around waiting for her to show up, Milda decided to go out looking for her. Later that afternoon, Milda spotted Debbie's station wagon sitting in the parking lot of Hunter's Lodge, a country music nightclub located about a mile from Crutchley's trailer. There were not any footprints or tire tracks visible in the snow-covered ground around the car, and no one at the club knew how the car had ended up there.

When Milda called Crutchley to see if he had any idea where Debbie might be, he told her that Debbie had left his trailer around 11:00 p.m. on Friday, January 27, and that he had not heard from her since.

Her concern quickly escalating to fear, Milda contacted the Fairfax County Police Department to report her granddaughter's disappearance. Although the police prepared a missing person's report, they told her that since Debbie was an adult and there was no obvious sign of foul play, they would not be able to do much to help her. Young adults sometimes run off, they told her, and Debbie had a right to privacy with regard to her whereabouts. Even so, Detective Fred Pfeiff agreed that Debbie's disappearance raised some red flags.

"Her disappearance was an abrupt change in her personal habits," he acknowledged, "but there's no indication of foul play. We don't know what the heck has happened to her. We just know she's gone."

While there was nothing concrete suggesting foul play, nothing suggested that Debbie had voluntarily left on a prearranged trip either. For starters, she had not packed. None of her clothes were missing from her Centreville condominium. In addition, although she generally never carried more than $10 cash with her, she had not used her credit cards in the days leading up to her disappearance or afterward. The last activity on her bank account was a check payable to People's Drug Store dated January 27. Another red flag was that Debbie had not called her mother on the morning of January 28 to wish her a happy birthday, something she never failed to do.

On January 30, Detective Pfeiff drove to the Hunter's Lodge parking lot to inspect Debbie's 1977 blue Subaru. The car was locked and Pfeiff noted in his report that "there were no signs of any foul play or any indications of any type of struggle occurring in or around the vehicle." The owner of the Hunter's Lodge told him that the car had been parked there since the night of Friday, January 27, yet the bartender, manager, check-in girl, and five waitresses all said that they had not seen Debbie at any time that day.

The next day, Pfeiff spoke with Crutchley, who told him that Debbie had come over to his trailer the night of January 27, but that he had fallen asleep shortly after she arrived. Debbie left while he was sleeping and he did not know where she went. Crutchley said that he left the next morning for North Carolina to visit an ex-room-mate, and he did not return home until Sunday night on January 29. Pfeiff thanked him for his time and asked Crutchley to contact him if he remembered anything else about where Debbie might have gone.

Debbie Fitzjohn, who disappeared about ten days after she started dating Crutchley.

Frustrated by a lack of progress in the case and what they considered to be lackadaisical police work, Debbie's grandparents decided to seek assistance elsewhere. A mutual friend suggested that they contact private detective James Wilt.

Sharp-eyed with a narrow, chiseled face and a stocky build, Wilt had twenty-eight years of law enforcement experience, including a stint with the Fairfax County Police Department, before starting a private detective agency with his wife in 1975. After speaking briefly with Milda and Herman Fitzjohn over the telephone, Wilt drove to their home to meet them. The Fitzjohns hired him on the spot, and it did not escape their notice that after they hired Wilt, the police became much more active in investigating Debbie's disappearance.

Shortly after being hired, Wilt prepared a missing person poster using a blow-up of a recent photograph of Debbie. He distributed and displayed hundreds of copies of the poster around the Centreville area, starting with the Hunter's Lodge. He also questioned additional Hunter's Lodge employees, but none of them remembered seeing Debbie the night she disappeared. He interviewed Debbie's friends, who all said that she was not the type of person to just take off without telling anyone what she was doing or where she was going.

Meanwhile, the missing person posters were generating a lot of calls, and Wilt followed every lead that came in. One tipster reported seeing footprints in the snow around a lake and spotting something white underneath the ice. The tipster thought that the white thing might be Debbie. Wilt hired divers to search the lake, but they found no trace of Debbie. Another caller remembered seeing Debbie at a 7-11 the night she disappeared. Wilt interviewed the 7-11 employees, but none recalled seeing her. Another tip came in that Debbie had been seen walking near the Centreville railroad tracks. Wilt and Debbie's father walked miles of the tracks looking for some sign of her, but found nothing.

Private Investigator James Wilt (left) and the missing poster he made for Debbie Fitzjohn (right).

On February 4, Fred Pfeiff interviewed Crutchley at his trailer in Fairfax. Crutchley repeated essentially the same story about the events of January 27 that he had previously told Pfeiff on the telephone, but this time he remembered that Debbie had mentioned something about having plans on January 28 for her mother's birthday. He also told Pfeiff that Debbie had seemed depressed or despondent before she left. In response to Pfeiff's questioning, Crutchley confided that he did not have an intimate relationship with Debbie and the two of them had not engaged in sexual intercourse.

Almost a week later, a letter from Crutchley arrived at Debbie's condominium. When Milda Fitzjohn noticed the name "J.B. Crutchley" on the return address, her brow furrowed. She squinted to make sure that she had read it correctly. She wondered why Crutchley would have sent a letter to Debbie when he knew that she was missing. The letter was dated February 4, the same date that Crutchley had been interviewed by Pfeiff at his trailer, but it had not been postmarked until February 8. She opened the envelope and took out the letter to read it.

Dear Dee,

I'm sorry that I fell asleep on you again – but please don't hold it against me! When you get back, please call me! I don't know you very well, but in spite of your want for a new job & all, I know it's not like you to stay away for long – Your grandmother and I talked about you the other day & she sounds as super as you said she is!

I know you're probably upset with my falling asleep every time you come over, but I'm not always tired!! – work & all has been heavy this month, especially with the cold weather!

From what you've told me, I know you're awfully lonesome! – I, too am lonely many times, in spite of dating! – Sometimes dates seem to be all empty meetings with people who are in some other space & as you say – most imperfect!

I like you a lot – I know that my Libra possessiveness is an affront to your Gemini want for freedom, but I really want to be your friend!!

I could hardly blame you for not calling me back – I've been quite a bit less than stimulating – but I'd really like to talk to you again!!

Please call me & talk – or at least leave a message on the tape – it'll record up to 3 minutes when it answers! – At least answer my call! – Or drop me a card! – I promise not to bother you with calls at weird times like you get from that other guy! – Please call!

Love,

John

After reading the letter, Milda called Detective Pfeiff to let him know about it, and then she gave the letter to Wilt for safekeeping. Wilt found the letter, which Crutchley wrote nearly two weeks after Debbie's disappearance, to be extremely suspicious. To his trained investigator's mind, the letter smelled of an attempt at creating an alibi, a scheme by Crutchley to try to convince the police that he really had no idea about what had happened to Debbie. His vague reference to the "other guy" near the end of the letter stood out as an especially clever touch. Wilt asked Milda about Crutchley, but she did not know much about him, only that Debbie had not been dating him for very long when she disappeared.

After getting Crutchley's phone number, Wilt tried calling him several times, but could not seem to catch him at home. The first time Wilt tried the number, an answering machine greeted him with the theme music from the television show, *The Twilight Zone*, followed by Crutchley's voice mimicking the show's well-known introduction. "You are now entering . . . the Twilight Zone."

That's strange, thought Wilt, *this guy is thirty-one years old, but he sounds like he's a sixteen-year-old kid.*

Although Wilt left several messages on the answering machine, Crutchley never returned his calls. Finally, on the fifth try, Crutchley answered the phone.

"Hello, is this Mr. Crutchley?"

"Yes, who's this?"

"Mr. Crutchley, my name is James Wilt. I'm a private investigator and I've been hired by Deborah Fitzjohn's grandparents to look into her disappearance."

"I see. How can I help you, Mr. Wilt?"

"I'd like to ask you some questions about Deborah's disappearance if you don't mind."

"Sure, I'll do whatever I can to help. I've been worried sick about

Dee, wondering what happened to her."

"Ok, I appreciate that."

"Sorry I didn't call you back before. It's been really busy at work lately. I feel like I've barely had time to breathe."

"No problem, I understand. Can you confirm for me that you saw

Debbie on the night of January 27?"

"Yeah, she stopped by my place for a while that night. I'm not really sure how long she was here though. I dozed off shortly after she arrived and when I woke up she was gone."

"Could we set up a time to talk about it in person? I'd like to meet you and see if we can come up with any leads. Could I come by your place some time to talk some more about her?"

"Sure, that'd be fine. Just give me a call first to let me know that you're on your way."

"Ok, great. I'll be sure to do that," Wilt replied.

Now nearly three weeks had passed since Debbie vanished.

On February 20, Wilt drove to Crutchley's trailer at unit 221 of Waples Mobile Home Estates. Though initially a bit standoffish and evasive, Crutchley warmed up to Wilt when he found out that the two had something in common: they had both grown up in West Virginia. After swapping stories about their West Virginia upbringings, Crutchley invited Wilt inside and offered him a cup of coffee. During the nearly forty-minute interview that followed, Crutchley told Wilt that Debbie had been to his trailer on three or four occasions before her final visit on January 27. According to Crutchley, on the night Debbie disappeared, he called her to invite her over, and then stretched out on the couch to watch television while waiting for her to get there. Debbie arrived around 7:35 p.m., shortly after the show, "CPO Sharkey," had started. Crutchley said that he fell asleep as Debbie was taking off her coat and boots, and then he woke up sometime later as she was leaving.

Crutchley did not act nervous or seem uncomfortable as he answered Wilt's questions. To the contrary, he came across as quite calm, but Wilt still found some of Crutchley's story fishy. For starters, he thought it odd that Crutchley would invite a woman as attractive as Debbie over to his home only to fall asleep right after she arrived. It just did not make sense.

What idiot would fall asleep with a pretty girl in his trailer? Wilt kept thinking to himself.

When Wilt asked Crutchley to describe what Debbie was wearing that night, Crutchley was able to do so off the top of his head with an astonishing amount of detail. He told Wilt that Debbie had been wearing a red full-length coat with a hood, white knit gloves, a brown scarf, a multicolored print blouse, blue jeans, and brown knee-high boots, along with a purse, a watch, a silver necklace, and several rings. Wilt thought the extensiveness and specificity of Crutchley's recollection particularly odd since he claimed to have been so exhausted that he fell asleep as soon as Debbie arrived.

If he was so tired that he fell asleep right after she arrived, it doesn't make sense that he would notice so much detail about what she was wearing, Wilt thought.

"He remembered all of that, and it was almost a month later," Wilt said afterward, "I've been an investigator all of my life, and I couldn't tell you what I wore to work a week ago."

No matter how many times he kicked it around in his mind, Crutchley's story did not seem right to Wilt.

The next time Wilt telephoned Crutchley, he seemed to be a different person than the polite man he had shared coffee with a few days earlier during a pleasant interview. This time, Crutchley lashed out at Wilt because the police had been following him and asking him questions ever since Wilt dropped by his trailer to interview him. Crutchley was so incensed that Wilt could almost feel his hostility though the phone line. It did not take long for Crutchley to accuse Wilt of working with the police.

"Ever since you showed up, those goddamn police have been on my ass," Crutchley shouted angrily, "Every time you show up, the police are ten minutes behind you!"

Wilt assured the livid man on the other end of the line that he was not working with the police. To try to calm Crutchley down, Wilt suggested that he take a polygraph test to clear himself of any wrongdoing in connection with Debbie's disappearance.

"If you have nothing to hide, that's the sure-fire way to get the police off of your back," Wilt said, trying to persuade him.

"The police want me to do a polygraph too," Crutchley replied testily, "but I'm not going to do it."

"Let *me* give you the polygraph," Wilt continued, "that way the results can be kept confidential. If you pass the test, I'll go to bat for you. I'll let the police know that you had nothing to do with Debbie's disappearance."

Crutchley thought about it for a few moments and then reluctantly agreed. Having a former member of the Fairfax County Police Department vouch for him would go a long way in clearing him of a crime. They set up a date for Crutchley to come to Wilt's office to take the polygraph exam, but when the agreed upon time came, Crutchley never showed up. When Wilt called him to find out what happened, Crutchley lashed out at him again. He was furious that the police were still following him.

"Those sons of bitches follow me everywhere I go now," Crutchley growled indignantly. "I'm not taking a fucking polygraph!"

Wilt heard an abrupt click and the phone line went dead. He never spoke with Crutchley again.

A few days later, Detective Pfeiff showed up at Wilt's office. Robert Horan, the Commonwealth Attorney, had sent him to retrieve the letter that Crutchley mailed to Debbie at her condominium. Though more than a little annoyed that the police would suddenly appear and demand the letter after what he perceived to be considerable footdragging in the case, Wilt reluctantly handed the letter over, careful to make a copy of it first for his own file.

A few weeks later, Fairfax County police finally persuaded Crutchley to take a polygraph test. Detective Pfeiff contacted Crutchley on March 6 and the two agreed that he would appear for the test two days later. Even though Crutchley would have preferred to avoid taking a polygraph, the temptation to beat the police at their own game became too much for him to pass up. On March 8, Crutchley showed up at Fairfax County Police Headquarters for the exam.

In anticipation of the polygraph, Crutchley had prepared a timeline of events about the night that Debbie disappeared. After arriving at the police station, Crutchley handed Pfeiff the timeline, which presented the events of January 27 as follows:

Evening of 27 Jan 78: (Times approximate, +/- 15 minutes or so)

6:45: Dee called, she had been busy and had to wash (dry) her hair etc. and might be a few minutes late. She was originally planning to arrive around 7:00.

7:15: Dee arrived, parking across the end of the driveway, driving blue/green Subaru. Inside, she removed her coat, scarf, gloves, and boots (shoes).

7:20: She showed me her new contacts, replaced after the previous ones had been damaged. She had a problem telling which side should be out (soft lenses can get reversed). We went to the bathroom where the light is brightest and I taught her how to do the "taco test" which is a process of folding the lens and observing the manner that it deflects, indicating the lens's position.

7:25: She asked to play my TV games after learning the taco test. She enjoys the pinball and breakout games quite a bit. We began playing pinball, with each of us operating one flipper, trying to keep the ball on the other's side. After a few games of pinball, she asked to play breakout, as I was losing the ball too much. As she began playing breakout, I leaned back and began to doze off.

8:00: Evidently noticing me asleep or tired of playing breakout alone, she shook me and asked if it would be OK to watch TV. I said it'd be OK, and noticed that the program which was starting was "CPO Sharkey" with Don Rickels, a comedian I enjoy. I resumed my reclining position and dozed off after a few minutes of minimal program activity.

8:30: (?) Dee woke me to ask if I wanted the TV off & I said OK. She turned it off and kissed me good night. She left the room & went to the bathroom or down the hall.

8:40: Dee was seen by her grandmother (per account of J. Wilt).

10-12: (?) I woke up and called her name. On no answer I looked out a window and saw that her car was gone, so I turned the light off and went to bed for the night.

Dee was wearing:

Red/maroon coat with white knit gloves, brown scarf, and boot shoes (dark colored). Multicolored print top, blue jeans, several rings, watch, and silvery necklace.

Dates we met:

18 Jan 78 – Met at lunch in building cafeteria – ½ hour.
20 Jan 78 – Dinner at my place – 2 hours.
24 Jan 78 – Visited her place – 1 hour.

27 Jan 78 – Above.

Plus 2 or 3 evening phone conversations of about 1 hour each.

The polygraph itself lasted barely more than a half-hour because a clearly agitated Crutchley kept pressing the examiner to finish his questions. Since the exam had been terminated before he could complete it, the examiner found it difficult to gauge Crutchley's veracity and he recommended that Crutchley sit for another examination. Pfeiff re-established contact with Crutchley and set up the second polygraph for March 17. As the date of the second polygraph approached, Crutchley informed Pfeiff that they should postpone it because, due to severe anxiety that he had been suffering during the past week, his doctor advised him to take a couple of weeks of vacation. Pfeiff assured Crutchley that the examiner would account for his nervousness, and convinced him that it would be better to get the test over with rather than continuing to drag it out. On March 17, Crutchley appeared for the second polygraph test as had been agreed.

As part of the second polygraph, Crutchley filled out a Polygraph Personal History form, listing his height as five feet, nine inches and his weight as 135 pounds. His only entry under the section for "Arrest Record" listed a speeding offense in Ohio for which he had paid the customary fine. The section for "Physical Condition" noted that "Today had EKG. Having funny feelings."

While watching the exam from a two-way mirror in the observation room, Pfeiff noticed that Crutchley was having difficulty answering some of the questions and he appeared to be extraordinarily nervous. As the session continued, Crutchley became obsessed with the thought that someone might be watching him in the observation room. But throughout the examination, Crutchley remained resolute in his denial of any knowledge about, or involvement in, Debbie's disappearance. After nearly three-and-a-half hours of questioning, the examiner concluded the polygraph test and Crutchley hastily exited the building.

Afterward, the examiner informed Pfeiff that the results of the second polygraph test indicated that Crutchley had been deliberately deceptive during parts of the exam. Moreover, he had not been cooperative at times, refusing to answer any questions about the extent of his sexual activity with Debbie Fitzjohn. The test results suggested that Crutchley had some "deep seated psychological problems," and the examiner concluded that he had almost certainly been deceptive in response to several questions in particular, including:

- Have you told me the complete truth?
- Did you intentionally lie to any question?
- Did Deborah Fitzjohn walk out of your house?
- Did you drive her car on the night of January 27?
- Do you know where she is now?
- Did you physically hurt her?

Following the examiner's interpretation of the polygraph results, they were shared with another polygraph expert who concurred with the original examiner's assessment. Both experts concluded that Crutchley "definitely possessed knowledge as to the whereabouts of Deborah Fitzjohn" and both determined that the test results indicated that Crutchley was directly involved in her disappearance.

On March 28, Pfeiff contacted the Clarksburg Police Department in Crutchley's hometown in West Virginia to check further into his background. The Clarksburg police advised Pfeiff that Crutchley had no criminal record and that they had never had any reason to investigate him. However, they did reveal something that Pfeiff found noteworthy: when Crutchley was born, he had a stillborn twin.

Not long after the second polygraph, Detective Pfeiff and his partner stopped by Crutchley's trailer to ask him some follow-up questions. This time, Crutchley reacted with such outright hostility that at one point Pfeiff's partner came close to drawing his gun and shooting him.

On June 21, Pfeiff received a teletype from the Robinson County Sheriff's Office located nearby in North Carolina. The report concerned a badly decomposed body that had been found, estimated to be that of a white female, fifteen to eighteen years of age, 110 pounds, with medium-length brown hair. Pfeiff thought it possible that Crutchley had a connection to the body since he was known to have traveled to North Carolina several months earlier to visit Lisa Baker, who lived not far from where the body was found. However, his inquiries into the matter with the Robinson County Sheriff's Office did not result in any leads, and his full caseload would not allow him to pursue it any further.

Milda Fitzjohn knew that Debbie would never have just run off without letting her know what she was doing or where she was going.

"From the very beginning, I felt it was foul play with Deborah," she said.

Debbie's father, Herman, felt the same way.

"I know she was murdered. We knew that she was dead when she didn't come home that night. And I know who did it."

After spending hundreds of hours working on Debbie's case,

James Wilt shared her father's belief. He too was convinced that Crutchley had killed her. It may have been that Crutchley grew tired of Debbie rejecting his sexual advances. Perhaps he came to resent the power she wielded in the sexual arena, and unable to cope with further frustration, he decided to take that power for himself, raping her while his hands constricted her neck, his fingers eventually collapsing her fragile throat.

On October 26, Pfeiff interviewed Lisa Baker in North Carolina. Baker shared details about her sex life with Crutchley, including that he enjoyed risky sexual experimentation and bondage, and kept four ropes on the corners of his bed to tie up his male and female sexual partners. Baker also revealed that during one sexual bondage session, Crutchley had put his hands around her neck and started squeezing, choking her hard enough to cut off her air supply. However, he had stopped after a few seconds when she began to struggle. According to Baker, Crutchley had recently begun seeing a psychological counselor, but she did not know the counselor's name. Baker thought that his seeking psychological help had something to do with the fact that, as a child, Crutchley's mother had "totally rejected him." She knew that Crutchley continued to struggle with that childhood experience as well as "many other hurts in his life." Aside from any psychological disturbances that he might be suffering, Baker emphasized that Crutchley was extremely intelligent and enjoyed trying to manipulate and outwit people, even to the point of lying. Indeed, from what she had seen, he could be extraordinarily deceptive at times. But more than anything else, the attribute that particularly stuck out to Pfeiff from his interview with Baker was Crutchley's obsession with enacting various "kinky" sexual fantasies.

Some of the same traits showed up when Pfeiff interviewed Patricia Hofer, whom Crutchley had met at a bar in February. As he had with Baker, Crutchley tied Hofer up numerous times during sex and choked her, though he had never squeezed with more than a moderate amount of pressure. She also mentioned that Crutchley sometimes wore a mask during sex, and since he was so "physically well endowed in his sexual organs," he "hurt her" sometimes. Hofer described Crutchley as being "somewhat weird" overall, and told Pfeiff that Crutchley went through severe mood swings, acting "hyper" one moment, while other times seeming to be depressed.

Over the weeks that followed, Fairfax County police received complaints from several women who reported that Crutchley had brought them to his trailer, bound them with rope, and choked them. Shortly thereafter, the badly decomposed body of a fourteen-year-old girl was found in another wooded area of the county, concealed in much the same way that Debbie Fitzjohn's body had been hidden. But Pfeiff could not connect the girl to Crutchley. If their paths had crossed, Crutchley had covered his tracks well.

On November 28, Pfeiff interviewed Kathy Moseley, who had been dating Crutchley since July 13. In September, she moved into his trailer. Like his other sexual partners, Moseley engaged in bondage sessions with him, but she reported that although Crutchley sometimes put his hands around her neck during sex, he had never choked her hard enough to prevent her from breathing.

At this point in the investigation, based on what he had learned about Crutchley's sexual appetites and what he knew about Debbie Fitzjohn's last known whereabouts, Pfeiff declared Crutchley the "most positive suspect" in Debbie's disappearance.

On December 7, an anonymous caller to the Fairfax County Emergency Operations Center conveyed a warning to the police investigating Debbie's murder. The caller claimed to know Crutchley and warned investigators that they were "dealing with an unstable person." The caller also advised that Kathy Moseley was "bananas" and "had become more and more unstable" since moving in with Crutchley.

Sensing the increased focus on himself as a suspect in Debbie's murder, Crutchley decided to go on the offensive. He filed a formal harassment complaint against Fred Pfeiff and his investigative partner, Officer J.P. Riddel. On December 12, he appeared at the Fairfax County police station to give a statement in connection with his complaint. Crutchley claimed that Pfeiff and Riddel had slandered him and were harassing both him and his fiancée, Kathy Moseley, by telling Moseley that he "murdered somebody" and that she "was living with a murderer."

In the process of recounting the events leading to his complaint, Crutchley provided some insights about his personality and the women he sought as sexual partners.

> I'm not just an ordinary, average type of person . . . I'm just very difficult – you know – to associate with, and there's very few women that I can get on the same wave length with.
>
> . . . . .
>
> I'm a very quiet type of person, and I just don't share my feelings well, and I've been hurt – I've been hurt many times, and I just don't let my feelings out where people can hurt me. And I need another somebody that – you can sense – you kind of get a feeling that they have been hurt also. That's the kind of person that I want.

Crutchley claimed that Kathy was one of the only women that he had ever felt connected to and that they had "every intention of getting married." However, due to the incessant hounding by Pfeiff and Riddel, Moseley's nerves were "just shot." Crutchley sarcastically lauded the two investigators for succeeding in their attempts to "scare the living daylights out of her." He claimed that they had been so effective in their efforts to upset Moseley that she had needed to take considerable time off work.

Crutchley detailed how Pfeiff and Riddel had dug into his past and tried to use what they discovered against him. They had learned about a situation he had experienced a couple of years earlier in Kokomo, Indiana, "involving a young lady and her ex-husband who literally beat me to an inch of my life . . . and broke ribs, and a jaw and a finger in the process." It had taken him two months to recover from the attack. After finding out about it, the two investigators had been trying to scare Crutchley by telling him that Debbie Fitzjohn's father was a "very mean S.O.B., and that he was out to kill me." They tried to intimidate Crutchley by telling him that they could only keep Mr. Fitzjohn away from him if he agreed to answer additional questions about the case.

Crutchley also alleged that they had "terrorized" Patty Hofer, who he had dated prior to Moseley. According to Crutchley, he and Hofer had been "very, very close." Then one day Pfeiff and his partner paid her a visit.

"Suddenly she wouldn't talk to me any more. All of sudden it was like night and day, and she wouldn't say another word to me."

They had similarly harassed Lisa Baker, and tried to scare her by telling her that Crutchley had killed someone.

Crutchley warned the police who were taking his complaint that he had already consulted with an attorney about filing a lawsuit against Pfeiff, Riddel, and the entire Fairfax County Police Department. Although he claimed to have a "very high respect for the police" and emphasized that he had been a member of the Fraternal Order of Police for several years when he lived in Ohio and Indiana, Crutchley insisted that he had been "terrorized" for two months by Pfeiff and Riddel. Their overzealous investigative efforts had caused "irreparable damage" to his relationship with Moseley and had made him "feel like a criminal." He primarily blamed Pfeiff for the harassment and did not try to disguise his disgust for the detective.

"If I saw Pfeiff out there on the street, and somebody was holding a gun on him, I would just close the door," he said angrily.

Crutchley concluded the interview by insisting that he had told the police everything he knew about Debbie Fitzjohn's disappearance and that from now on he would refuse to discuss the case any further.

> I have no other pertinent information in the Fitzjohn case. I refuse to even recall anything about it. I have just wiped it out of my mind. And that's my – if I even see somebody out there committing a crime, it's out of my mind from now on. I've learned my lesson. I'll give no more information.

An internal affairs investigation ultimately deemed Crutchley's harassment allegations to be unfounded, but the complaint had its intended effect by derailing the Fairfax County Police Department's investigation of him. Understandably, Herman Fitzjohn felt betrayed when he found out that the police had ceased their investigation due to Crutchley's threats of legal action.

"The police didn't even completely investigate Debbie's murder," he said bitterly. "They just stuck it in the dead file. They just backed off."

After reviewing Pfeiff's case file on the Debbie Fitzjohn murder, Leatherow pronounced Crutchley's filing of the harassment complaint to be a "brilliant" move, a strategic maneuver that "showed Crutchley to be very, very shrewd."

On December 18, the skull that had been found two months earlier was positively identified as Debbie's by comparing her dental records to evidence of amalgam and plastic fillings still attached to the skull's jawbone. Three days later, the Centreville United Methodist Church held a memorial service for Debbie in her hometown of Centreville, Virginia. It was the type of day that reminded those attending of the beauty in life, as well as its fragility. The clear skies and sunshine perfectly complemented the crisp chill of winter, invigorating the body and soul with an abundance of brisk December air.

Stationed inconspicuously in the background, a police surveillance team carefully monitored the funeral attendees, hoping that Debbie's killer could not resist making an appearance to see the effects of his handiwork first hand. James Wilt and his wife attended the modest service, and from their seats in one of the front pews of the church, listened to a reading from Psalm 90.

We are like weeds that sprout in the morning
That grow and burst into bloom
Then dry up and die in the evening.

Wilt had put much of himself into Debbie's case. In some irretrievable ways, too much of himself, certainly more than what the Fitzjohns had paid for. The case had become personal, and he felt terrible about what he knew in his heart had happened to Debbie.

"She was such a pretty little girl," he said to no one in particular, shaking his head at the thought of the promising young woman's life being so suddenly and tragically snuffed out. "It's such a shame. She had her whole life ahead of her."

Shallow gravesite where Debbie Fitzjohn's skeletal remains were discovered

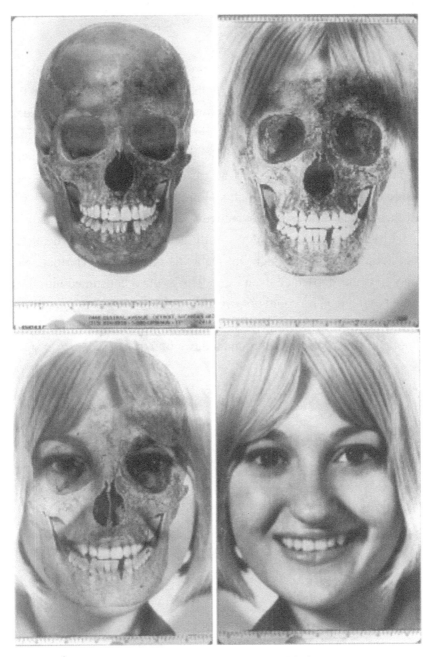

Reconstruction photographs of Debbie Fitzjohn's skull

As the days drifted by, Fairfax County prosecutors sifted through all of the evidence the police had gathered against Crutchley. In the end, without explanation, prosecutors deemed it insufficient to seek a criminal indictment from a grand jury. There would be no criminal prosecution of Crutchley for Debbie Fitzjohn's murder. There would not even be an arrest. The case subsequently went cold, set aside by Fairfax County police and prosecutors, pushed to the back of the storage shelves, and eventually forgotten.

Milda Fitzjohn could never fully accept the untimely death of her adopted granddaughter, but Debbie's grandfather, Herman, Sr., may have been affected even more. His grief so consumed him that, to his dying day, he could not even bear to talk about her.

"She was his pride and joy," Milda explained, wiping away another tear. "Dee was her granddaddy's breath."

TWELVE

Every wickedness

The belief in a supernatural source of evil is not necessary; men alone are quite capable of every wickedness.

- Joseph Conrad

The facts of the Debbie Fitzjohn case cemented Leatherow's belief that he had a serial killer on his hands. The more he learned about Crutchley, the more concrete that belief became. As he dug deeper into Crutchley's past, Leatherow noticed a recurring pattern: young women went missing in areas where Crutchley lived, and the disappearances drastically decreased or stopped after he moved away. He and other Brevard County investigators began to suspect that unsolved homicides in Florida, Virginia, Maryland, and Pennsylvania could have a connection to the Vampire Rapist.

While researching the out of state cases, Leatherow learned that the Naval Criminal Investigative Service had begun a preliminary investigation into the possibility of Crutchley's involvement in the murders of two women at the Naval Air Station in Norfolk, Virginia. Both murders had occurred in the early 1980's when

Crutchley had been working for defense contractor TRW with job ties to the Naval station. In one, Navy messenger Pamela Kimbrue, aged twenty-three, disappeared shortly after 3:00 a.m. on March 25, 1982. Her body was found the next day, tied up in the back seat of her car. She had been raped and strangled, but she was still alive when her attacker sent her car down a ramp into ten feet of water. Ten months later, twenty-one-yearold Navy courier Carol Ann Molnar disappeared from a Norfolk nightclub. Her body was found on May 2, 1983, wedged under the rocks of a sea wall at the Naval Air Station. Although the Navy would neither confirm nor deny it, at the time of their deaths, Kimbrue or Molnar may have been carrying the microfilm containing classified images of the Navy's Sixth Fleet, images that were later discovered in Crutchley's home. In one of the murder cases, a car was seen leaving the area where the body was found, and investigators later found the car owner's name in Crutchley's personal address book. However, despite their suspicions, NCIS agents could not link Crutchley to either of the murders with sufficient evidence to support charging him.

To test a theory about how Crutchley could have disposed of his victims, Leatherow drove his squad car from the back of Crutchley's Hall Road property through the woods to the Kimberly Walker crime scene, located near a Harris Corporation building in which Crutchley had maintained a satellite office. The short, relatively easy drive confirmed Leatherow's belief that Crutchley could have transported a body in the dead of night without encountering any witnesses. In addition, at the time of his arrest, Crutchley owned a dirt bike and neighbors reported that he had ridden it frequently since moving to Brevard County. The dirt bike connection intrigued Leatherow because most of the bodies found in Brevard County in 1985 had been discarded near power lines. Since he knew that dirt bikers frequently used the cleared areas along power line routes as riding trails, it stood to reason that the Walker crime scene was a familiar area to Crutchley. Putting two and two together, Leatherow pronounced it quite probable that Crutchley transported Kim Walker's body from his house to the wooded field where it was eventually discovered.

While most were well into the holly-jolly holiday spirit, Christina Almah was having a hard time getting into a festive mood. On December 23, she received a disturbing letter at her home in Westminster, California. Dated December 19, the unwelcome correspondence had been sent by Mildred Crutchley in Bridgeport, West Virginia. Mildred had written the letter at her son's request in an attempt to get Christina to change her mind about prosecuting the case.

> *Dear Christina,*
>
> *First I want to say how sorry we are to learn of your experience with our son John. I still can't believe such a thing of him. I know he would do anything to make it up to you, he must have gone out of his mind.*
>
> *I wish you and John could settle your affairs just between you. As it stands now, they are trying to raise his bail so he can't make it and throw him in jail. John is not a harden[ed] criminal, he has never been in jail and I am worried what it will do to him . . . John is a very intelligent person and is well considered in the computer world as having great potential.*
>
> *Just to give you some idea of his background may I say a few words. John had one of the highest I.Q.'s in school. When we moved in Pittsburgh he delivered papers. His customers all thought the world of him as he was always doing little extra jobs*

for them fixing their T.V.s . . . One day he came home on his bike holding his chest and I ran out thinking he had been hurt. He had stopped at Mrs. Chippa's and she was so upset as the duck had hatched her eggs all but one and deserted it. He brought it home and we fixed up lights and at 2:00 in the morning I talked him into trying to crack the egg a bit and see if it would come out. It did and we kept it a few days then took it back to the others. It was funny to see the duckling leave the rest when John started to leave. Finally by inching away he finally was able to leave it.

We never had trouble with John in school except getting him to study. He was bored and only liked the sciences . . . He attended Defiance College and never gave us trouble. He didn't even drink beer.

. . . .

John and Karen have been going to Church and are going tonight, for which I am thankful as I have been praying all these years that they would as John always attended the Episcopal Church when he was home.

. . . .

Love & Prayers,
Mildred Crutchley

The letter did not have its intended effect. It traumatized Christina by dredging up dreadful memories, and it frightened her further to realize that her tormentor knew where she lived, but she did not waiver in her decision to prosecute him.

On the same day that Mildred Crutchley's letter reopened Christina Almah's psychological wounds, Lt. Joe Crosby was listening to an audiotape that had been seized from Crutchley's office. The strange tape contained a recording of three separate voices, two belonging to men and one to a woman. They spoke off and on about seemingly unrelated subject matter, their voices frequently unintelligible and difficult to follow. As he continued listening, Crosby heard heavy breathing and undecipherable moaning sounds, followed by muffled murmurs and what could only be the sound of someone choking and coughing. At one point, the distinct tone and tenor of Crutchley's voice could be heard shouting: "Give me more gauze! More gauze!" The meaning of his cryptic request would baffle Leatherow and Crosby for the remainder of their investigation.

The day before Christmas, Leatherow and Crosby interviewed Karen Crutchley at the south precinct of the Brevard County Sheriff's Office, with Crutchley himself also in attendance. The interview failed to yield any new information, as Karen completely clammed up. She responded to virtually every question with "I don't remember" or "I don't recall," often glancing at her husband before parroting her answer. Leatherow likened it to trying to interview a potato.

On Christmas day, Leatherow took a break from the Crutchley investigation, spending a peaceful holiday with his family in Palm Bay.

The day after Christmas, Leatherow was back at work, viewing a videotape that had been seized from the closet of Crutchley's study area during the initial search of his house back on November 23. The videotape contained a recording of a television program called "Painting with Ilona." A few phone calls later, Leatherow learned that the show aired on November 22 at 2:30

p.m., which coincided with the time period in which Crutchley discovered that Christina Almah had escaped from his house. Leatherow surmised that Crutchley must have recorded the television show to tape over incriminating evidence, most likely the video footage of his vampiric assault and rape of Christina Almah.

Later that day, Leatherow and Crosby viewed another videotape found during the search of Crutchley's house. The tape, which was self-dated March 13, 1985, looked like an amateur porn film. It depicted a fully nude Crutchley binding his equally unclothed wife with ropes, posing her in various positions, and then engaging in sex acts with her. At one point, he attached nylon ropes to metal hooks that were secured to the ceiling of the kitchen area of their home, the same area where Christina Almah had been tied up. Using the ropes, Crutchley manipulated his wife up off of the floor and then lowered her so that he could enter her from behind, then he continued lifting and lowering her in a steady rhythm as he moved in and out of her. Peculiar music played in the background, and at times, Crutchley could be seen snorting powdery white lines off the countertop.

On December 27, Joe Crosby interviewed Kathy Moseley by telephone. She had dated Crutchley from 1977 to 1980, and began living with him in September 1978, not long after Debbie Fitzjohn had disappeared. She said she became scared of Crutchley when he started showing violent tendencies, including in the bedroom, where he enjoyed strangling her during sex. Moseley told Crosby that she moved out in May 1979 after Crutchley began beating her.

Moseley also revealed that Crutchley always kept personal items of the women he slept with because he liked to save them as souvenirs to better remember the experiences. Moseley told Crosby that she believed Crutchley so valued the souvenirs that he would never discard or destroy them, even to avoid facing a murder charge. She felt sure that he would not talk to the police about his victims and would never confess to any murders, even if confronted with direct evidence of his guilt.

According to Moseley, Crutchley confided to her that when he was born he had a twin sibling who died at birth, but his parents had hid that fact from him. He only found out about the dead twin when informed by detectives during the Debbie Fitzjohn investigation.

During their time together, Moseley had noticed a particularly peculiar element of Crutchley's personality in that he seemed to be afraid of women, but also liked to control them. As their relationship wore on, other negative aspects of Crutchley's character surfaced, including his extreme vanity, which had been endearing—almost cute—at first, and his vengeful nature, which manifested in many ways, including in his frequent announcements that he did not get mad at people who wronged him, instead he got even.

Moseley also saw how emotionally empty he seemed to be. "John has no sense of conscience," she said. "He never feels bad about anything he does."

Perhaps most interesting of all, Moseley informed Crosby that she had been warned by an Episcopalian priest in Fairfax County that Crutchley had five personalities. Ominously, as if he had stepped out of some B-grade horror movie, the priest urged her to be careful because Crutchley's fifth personality could be extremely dangerous.

As 1985 came to a close, Michael J. Fox's *Back to the Future* beat out Sylvester Stallone's dual contenders of *Rambo: First Blood Part I* and *Rocky IV* as box office champ in what turned out to be a big year for Hollywood. It had been a big year for Bob Leatherow as well. He ended 1985 determined to follow Crutchley's trail back to Debbie Fitzjohn, and if necessary, beyond, but he could not have guessed what the future would hold.

THIRTEEN

The way of the wicked

The way of the wicked is like darkness
They know not on what they stumble

– Proverbs 4:19

Unemployed and hoping for adventure, Jackie Lee Horton left his hometown of Lexington, Tennessee, in September 1985, traveling with a carnival that had been in town for the county fair. A small man standing five feet, eight inches tall and weighing only about 125 pounds, the thirty-one-year-old Horton joined the carnival along with his eighteen-year-old nephew, Keith Keller. In early November, the carnival arrived in Brevard County, Florida, stopping at the Holy Name of Jesus Catholic Church in the Town of Indiatlantic.

On November 6, Horton and Keller were accused of hitting a man with a wooden board, strip-searching him, and robbing him of twentyfive cents behind a restaurant on State Road A1A in Indiatlantic. Arrested and charged with armed robbery and false imprisonment, Horton had been housed in the Brevard County Jail for several weeks by the time of Crutchley's November 23 arrest.

The two men met when Crutchley was placed in a four-man cell that functioned as a holding area for inmates receiving outside visitors. While reading his Bible in the corner of the cell, Horton cautiously eyed the new arrival. Crutchley was obviously upset, so Horton approached him, "shared his faith in Jesus," and "explained what salvation was all about." Crutchley later claimed that, at that moment, he was so inspired by Horton's religious faith that he decided to invite Christ into his own heart.

"During that period, Jackie answered the key questions I had which resulted in leading me to the Lord," Crutchley explained. "During the process, I genuinely received the 'born again' experience. A new creature emerged from within me."

Horton and Crutchley spent the next nine days together in the jail. The two bonded to such an extent that when Crutchley posted his $50,000 bond on December 22, he gave Horton an early Christmas present by posting his $1,500 bond and inviting him to stay at Crutchley's Malabar home until he could get back on his feet.

Karen was home for the first few days that Horton stayed at Crutchley's house. Although she was not crazy about having Horton in her home, she tolerated it because that is what her husband wanted, and on December 26, Crutchley drove her to the airport so that she could visit her parents in Maryland.

Alone at the Malabar house, Horton and Crutchley had the opportunity to get to know each other better. Over the next few days they spent hours talking, and at one point, Crutchley explained that people have five levels of personal space, with level one being the most intimate. Crutchley said that he had let Horton into his third or fourth level, while Lisa Baker had made it to level one.

In the early morning hours of December 30, Crutchley appeared beside Horton's bed with a strange, almost blank, look in his eyes.

Without saying a word, Crutchley began removing his startled guest's clothes. When Crutchley initiated oral sex, Horton felt unable to resist. He was frightened by the look in Crutchley's eyes, but at the same time, they contained what he could only explain as a hypnotic allure. He did what Crutchley wanted, and then submitted to anal sex as well, as Crutchley turned him onto his side and eased into him from behind.

Crutchley came to his bed again the next night. Whether due to fear, a sense of indebtedness, or an unexplained power of attraction, Horton could not refuse Crutchley's advances. They rang in the New Year by sharing the same bed, two hard, tangled bodies blindly groping in the dark.

As one of his first acts of the New Year, Leatherow interviewed Caroline Greathouse, a resident of Valkaria, a small community located immediately to the south of Malabar. Greathouse told Leatherow that her seventeen-year-old daughter, Angela, had babysat for Crutchley on two occasions in January 1985. Crutchley had driven her home on both occasions, and during the second trip he had rubbed his hands on Angela's leg, telling her that he liked her tight jeans. When Greathouse called Crutchley to confront him, he denied doing anything inappropriate. He told her that her daughter was lying to get attention.

On January 4, Leatherow and Crosby departed from Titusville to drive to Quantico, Virginia, for a meeting with Robert Ressler at the FBI's Behavioral Science Unit. The meeting had been arranged by Leatherow, who requested Ressler's assistance with the investigation. On January 6, the two were joined in Quantico by Norm Wolfinger and the trio drove to the FBI building, where they were ushered into a conference room with a large, round table. Around the table sat Detective Fred Pfeiff, Detective Eric

Witzig of the Metropolitan Police Department, and a host of seven FBI agents, including Ressler and John Douglas. Leatherow presented a briefing about the Crutchley case using a Kodak slide carousel that he had put together for the occasion. Detective Witzig talked about several murders that occurred in the D.C. area during the time period that Crutchley had lived in Northern Virginia and worked at Delco. He hoped that someone in the room could spot a connection to Crutchley that he had missed. Pfeiff discussed the Fitzjohn case for the same reason, hoping that someone would point out a piece of evidence that he had over-looked, some missed clue that might decisively tie Crutchley to Debbie's murder.

The group discussed the Crutchley case for most of the day. Ressler and Douglas gave the Florida investigators suggestions on the best way to handle Crutchley to maximize their chances of getting him to confess or inadvertently divulge details about any murders he had committed. Leatherow compiled a step-by-step list of their recommendations.

Ways to Interview John:

1. *Soft interview related to his buying sex objects.*
2. *Soft interview on ESP and dreams.*
3. *Give him something to write on describing his dreams.*
4. *Have quiet room & low light.*
5. *Have file cabinet with his name on drawers, maps of locations, picture of him.*
6. *Start with his book collection, which is non-criminal.*
7. *Be inquisitive but don't act interested in perverted sex.*
8. *Move to partners who he does sex acts with.*
9. *Lead into video about he and his wife, talk about what she didn't like him doing during the movie.*
10. *Talk about what came from his interview with*

psychiatrist, let him know you understand he may have mental motivation to doing things.

11. *Who are the girls in the pictures, where was this done, ask about ropes.*
12. *Let him see as much as possible about what we have been doing.*
13. *Have room with boxes of evidence marked, identified by FBI, maps, pictures, fliers of missing people, possible use of bones or clothing.*
14. *He must sincerely believe you are interested in him & his problem.*
15. *Leave childhood bad things until last, give him a reason for doing bad things.*
16. *Stay away from polygraph as an inducement, save it in the background.*
17. *If John arrested his wife may turn to us for help & guidance.*
18. *Let him see evidence relating to him but not have time to examine it.*
19. *Be nice, give drink, coffee.*

Ressler thought that when confronted with the names and apparent remains of his victims, Crutchley might break down and confess. The FBI had used similar rooms with much success in getting serial child molesters to confess, but Crutchley was another breed of monster.

The following morning, Leatherow, Crosby, and Wolfinger returned for another meeting with Ressler and Douglas, and then departed early in the afternoon for Washington, D.C., where they turned over physical evidence that had been seized from Crutchley's office and residence to the FBI laboratory.

The next day, January 8, Leatherow and Crosby drove to the Fairfax County Police Department to meet with Detective Pfeiff.

When the three visited Crutchley's former residence in the Waples Trailer Park in Fairfax, the new owner of the trailer informed them that Crutchley had dropped by about a year earlier and showed her where a key was hidden in a nearby shed.

The two Brevard investigators accompanied Pfeiff to the wooded area on Pleasant Valley Road where Debbie Fitzjohn's body had been found. Almost immediately after arriving at the Fitzjohn crime scene, Leatherow noticed a number of similarities to the locations where the Brevard County bodies were found. Most prominent among them was that, just as at most of the Florida sites, power lines were not far from where Fitzjohn's body had been found, and the body had been left in a very shallow grave partly concealed by vegetation and debris. All signs pointed to a connection between the Fitzjohn murder and the unsolved Florida homicides.

On the same day that Leatherow and Crosby were learning more about Crutchley's past, Crutchley typed a letter to his mother, looking toward the future and careful to emphasize his professed newfound faith in God.

> *Dear Mom,*
>
> *It was spiritually uplifting to read your words of encouragement. I realize you are worrying heavily about Karen, Jason, and myself in this hour of great change.*
>
> *Karen's new faith in God is helping her a lot. However, last night she read an article which convinced her that she has clinical depression. . . I think her family's telling her to choose between them and me was most unfair to her. True, their only knowledge of me has been during the time in my life when Satan had a strong*

hold on me. So, they think I am a less than desirable son-in-law, and they would like to see her free of me as soon as possible.

. . . .

As to myself, as I told you on the phone, my discovering that Jesus could, in his mind, forgive me of all of my sins, and that I had one chance to be born into the world of the spirit of God has had a profound effect on my life. This is a victory over Satan! . . . In church the other evening, I had a feeling that I was being called to the Outreach Ministry for young couples. I will have to explore this more and tell you about it as it develops.

Crutchley's purported religious faith would soon be tested. The new evidence and information gleaned about Crutchley energized investigators and prosecutors, and painted a portrait of someone who should not be roaming free while awaiting trial. At a hastily scheduled telephone hearing at 2:00 in the afternoon on January 9, State Attorney Wolfinger requested that the court revoke Crutchley's $50,000 bond and replace it with a bond of $500,000. In requesting the imposition of a half-million dollar bond, Wolfinger stressed the seriousness of Crutchley's crime and asserted that Crutchley "poses a substantial danger to the community." After hearing from both sides, the court granted the motion without delay. State Attorney Wolfinger lauded the measure as necessary to get Crutchley "off the streets." He proclaimed that if Crutchley were somehow able to post the new bond, "other action would be taken" to ensure that he remained behind bars until his trial.

As Judge Charles Harris entered his order increasing Crutchley's bond, Leatherow and Crosby made the return trip to Titusville, driving all day and arriving late that night. The next morning, as Leatherow walked into his office, Crosby told him to pack a bag. He was to leave that very day for Clarksburg, West Virginia, to intercept another letter that Crutchley had sent to his mother.

FOURTEEN

A substantial danger to the community

On January 9, Crutchley received an unexpected phone call from his attorney, Joe Mitchell. It was not good news. Crutchley's $50,000 bond had been revoked and increased to $500,000. After an extended discussion, Crutchley agreed to Mitchell's suggestion that he turn himself in to the police. Jackie Horton, who was still staying at Crutchley's house, asked him if there was any way that he could afford to post the bond.

"Murder one has no bond," Crutchley cryptically replied.

Later that day, Crutchley sat in front of his computer and prepared a letter to his mother in Bridgeport, West Virginia. As he typed, MTV blared from the living room television and reverberated down the hall, filling Crutchley's study with the sounds of Animotion's song, "Obsession."

Crutchley liked this song. Its lyrics resonated with him. He identified with the speaker's all-consuming fantasy, a fantasy dependent on achieving absolute control over the objects of his sexual obsession. Crutchley thought about the mementos he had collected over the years from all of the Christina Almahs that he had come across, but as he replayed some of those encounters in his mind, his brow began to furrow. He realized that his fun—his obsession—might be coming to an end now because of a ridiculous error in judgment.

After several minutes, Crutchley finished typing and folded the letter, sealing it along with several other items in a regular, white business-size envelope. He put a twenty-two-cent first-class stamp on the envelope and asked Horton to mail the letter for him. Before sealing the envelope and handing it to Horton, Crutchley placed a couple of other papers inside of it.

Horton watched as Crutchley hurried over to the safe in his large walk-in closet, removed some things that Horton could not see, and put them in a plastic garbage bag. He closed the safe and strode into the computer room, plastic bag still in hand. Horton heard him moving things around in the room and it sounded like he was putting other items into the bag. After a few minutes, Crutchley emerged from the room still carrying the garbage bag. By now, the bag looked to be about half full.

Crutchley abruptly paused and glanced at Horton.

"It would be best if you didn't know what I'm doing. The police might try to interrogate you."

He took the bag into another room, but then returned less than a minute later.

"I just need to run an errand to get rid of some things, some old paraphernalia. Stay in the house until I get back."

Horton watched as Crutchley walked out the side door of the house and made his way across the property to the barn. He ducked into the barn and remained out of sight for several minutes, then emerged from the barn, and wandered back to the carport where he climbed onto one of his motorcycles. As Horton continued to watch, Crutchley drove down the driveway with the garbage bag strapped securely to the back of the bike. He turned onto Hall Road and sped away.

About twenty minutes later, Horton heard the low rumbling of a motorcycle approaching. Crutchley pulled back into the carport and parked. The garbage bag was gone.

Shortly after coming inside, Crutchley picked up the phone and called his former office at Harris Corporation. He told the company operator that he needed to speak to the Human Resources Department because he had personal items in his office that could cause great embarrassment to himself—and to Harris—if he was not allowed to retrieve them. A few minutes later, a visibly angry Crutchley slammed the phone back onto its receiver. Pacing back and forth in the room like a panther in a locked cage, Crutchley caught Horton watching him again. He growled to Horton that the incident with Christina Almah was "nothing" compared to the "damaging evidence" that could be found in his office at Harris.

———

Later that afternoon, Horton rode with Crutchley, Karen, and Jason to Joe Mitchell's office in Melbourne to make arrangements for Crutchley to turn himself in. Jason sat in his father's lap, while Horton read passages from the Bible in the back seat.

At around 3:30 p.m., accompanied by his attorney, Crutchley turned himself in to Deputy Sheriffs at the precinct in Melbourne. From there, he was transported to the jail in Titusville. Jail officials booked him at about 6:30 p.m. and placed him in a closed-security single cell. Shortly after being booked back into jail, Crutchley asked to speak to the news media, but later changed his mind upon the advice of his attorney. Concerned that he might harm himself "because he was very upset," corrections officers checked on Crutchley every fifteen minutes.

That evening, investigators picked up Jackie Horton for additional questioning. During the interrogation, Horton informed Sheriff's deputies about the letter that Crutchley had written to his mother, as well as Crutchley's errand to dispose of the plastic garbage bag containing items from the house and barn. Horton also told them that he had developed a fear of Crutchley while staying at his house.

"I felt the man had the potential of being dangerous," Horton explained. "It was just a feeling I was gettin'. And I actually felt like a prisoner for about a week."

An obviously embarrassed Horton also disclosed that he and Crutchley had twice engaged in sex while alone at Crutchley's house. While being questioned, Horton also revealed that while they were having anal sex, Crutchley had wrapped his fingers around Horton's throat and began choking him. Horton had to strain with all of his might to pry Crutchley's hands away from his neck. At the time, it seemed to Horton that Crutchley had possessed supernatural strength. Horton insisted that he was not a homosexual, but that he had gone along with the sex acts strictly out of fear.

"I had fear for my own life, my own safety," Horton maintained. "I saw something in him that I hadn't seen previously, as if he was really two people."

What Horton saw would stay with him for the rest of his life, haunting him in nightmares until the day he died.

Neighbors subsequently reported having seen Crutchley carrying several large trash bags out of his home while he was out on bail. Although taking out the garbage was not peculiar in and of itself, the neighbors thought it odd that Crutchley had stood at the end of his driveway for several minutes and waited for the garbage truck to arrive, and then placed the bags into the back of the truck himself. Stranger still, before heading back into his house, he stood there and watched the truck drive away, as if wanting to be absolutely certain that whatever was in the garbage bags was gone for good.

After quickly packing and driving to the Melbourne airport to catch a flight, Leatherow arrived in Pittsburgh on the afternoon of January 10. He picked up a rental car at the airport, braved the winding, icy, sloping mountain roads to Clarksburg, West Virginia, and then checked into a Sheraton Hotel.

Meanwhile, back in Titusville, Sheriff's investigators reinterviewed Jackie Horton. During this round of questioning, Horton revealed some new information, including that Crutchley had told him about a girl he dated whose "ultimate dream" was to be choked to death while having sex. He said that Crutchley often spoke to him in what seemed like riddles, but one time Crutchley mentioned having hurt many people in his "past life," a time when "Satan was such a great part of his life."

Doing his best to minimize the damage, Joe Mitchell suggested that Horton had been planted in Crutchley's cell by Sheriff's officials, but Horton's mother denied such a scheme, maintaining that he was a "real friend" to Crutchley. Horton's attorney, Assistant Public Defender Rick Singer, likewise insisted that no deals had been made with the State Attorney's Office.

Later that night, amidst Jason Crutchley's frightened cries, Department of Health and Rehabilitative Services caseworkers and Sheriff's deputies removed him from the Crutchley home, leaving behind his hysterical mother. Citing a dangerous and unstable home environment, Juvenile Court Judge Fran Jamieson had signed a twenty-oneday retention order giving custody of Crutchley's four-year-old son to his maternal grandparents in Pennsylvania.

On January 11, Leatherow met with West Virginia Assistant State Attorney Steve Dolly and H.R. Procter of the West Virginia State Police. The three discussed their strategy for intercepting Crutchley's letter to his mother, and worked on preparing a search warrant for the letter until nearly 3:00 p.m.

The same day, Crutchley wrote a letter from jail to his young son.

Dearest Jason,

I just found out last night the Sheriff's Department had you taken from us. Let this be a lesson to you that you will remember the rest of your life. . . A mistake your daddy made was being with somebody he shouldn't have. The policemen are punishing your daddy right now, as these words are being written. But, the policemen made a mistake and they took you, too! You must forgive them. This is a learning time. Remember it, so you will NEVER want to hurt anybody.

Although he was back in custody, Crutchley considered himself much too smart to be convicted for any crimes, including those arising from his abduction of Christina Almah. He was confident that his superior intelligence would prevent detectives from ever being able to link him to any murders.

Shortly after 2:00 on the morning of January 12, the shrill ringing of the hotel room telephone jolted Leatherow awake. Half asleep, Leatherow fumbled to lift the phone handle from its cradle. In the quiet of the night, the local postal inspector's voice seemed to shout at him through the receiver as he advised that the post office had received a letter originating from Malabar, Florida that was addressed to Mildred Crutchley. Leatherow rolled out of bed, threw on some clothes, and staggered bleary-eyed out of his room to make his way to the post office, where he would view and photograph the letter, being careful not to tamper with it to avoid running afoul of federal postal regulations. Later that afternoon, Leatherow met with the mail carrier who would be delivering the letter in order to brief him on the police stake out procedures. He told the carrier to act normal and deliver the mail the same way he always did so as not to alarm Mildred Crutchley or alert her to the officers' presence.

Late in the morning of January 13, Leatherow, four West Virginia State Police officers, two postal inspectors, and Assistant State Attorney Dolly staked out Mildred Crutchley's home at 231 Ridgeway Drive in Bridgeport, just minutes away from Clarksburg. They parked several hundred yards down the street in unmarked cars to avoid drawing attention to themselves. There had been a snowstorm the night before and a deep blanket of white still covered much of the hilly countryside. Flurries continued to fall as the mail carrier made his way up the steep incline of the icy street. Approaching the house on schedule for his usual delivery time, he deposited the letter in Mildred Crutchley's mailbox.

Within a few minutes of the mail being delivered, Mildred opened the front door and stepped briskly toward her mailbox down a footpath frosted powdery white with snow. As she pulled the mailbox lid down and took out its contents, Leatherow and the other officers sprang into action. Amidst a dazzling array of flashing lights and sirens, their unmarked cars screeched to a stop in front of the Crutchley residence. When she realized why they were there, Mildred sprinted back towards the house, an envelope clutched tightly in her hands. Leatherow jumped out of his car and gave chase, following close behind her as he sloshed and stumbled through the melting snow. Mildred did not slow down as she ran into the house and Leatherow followed closely on her heels. As Leatherow ran through the living room, he spotted Mildred's husband sitting in a leather chair in front of the fireplace. William Crutchley glanced up and gave Leatherow a startled look as he darted by. Mildred started to escape out the back door, but two of the West Virginia State Police, who were entering the house through the rear, grabbed her as she attempted to flee. They took her back into the house, kicking and screaming.

Leatherow took the envelope from her and opened it. Inside, he found a photocopy of Christina Almah's California driver's license. The accompanying correspondence from Crutchley urged his mother to contact Christina to persuade her to drop the case against him. However, there were no incriminating statements in the letter. What had initially seemed to be a promising lead turned out to be empty.

Though disappointed in the outcome of the trip, Leatherow remained resolute in his determination to find evidence to convict Crutchley. He caught a flight home the next day, arriving in Titusville at about 7:00 p.m.

While Leatherow was in West Virginia chasing down Crutchley's letter to his mother, the Brevard County Sheriff's Office staged a "Bones Room" to try to coax a confession out of her son. As Robert Ressler and his fellow FBI agents had suggested, investigators filled the room with boxes bearing Crutchley's name with the names of his suspected victims prominently labeled in large letters. They even lowered the lights in the room to try to produce the desired effect. Now they were ready for Crutchley himself.

The night after his re-arrest, several officers appeared at Crutchley's jail cell door and told him to come with them.

"Where are we going?" he asked, looking up from his cot with surprise.

The officers remained stone-faced, not uttering a word in reply. They led him through a door to a waiting car and opened the rear passenger door. Crutchley stooped to get in and sat down on the back seat, then the car pulled out and headed down the road. After a short period of time, they arrived at their destination: the Parkway Center in Titusville.

Sheriff's personnel escorted Crutchley to a waiting area where they were soon joined by Earle Petty, Commander of the Brevard County Jail. Petty led Crutchley down a narrow hall to a plain, metal door. He opened the door and motioned for Crutchley to go inside. Crutchley stepped through the doorway into a small interrogation room with metal shelves aligned along the walls. The shelves were stacked high with large numbers of cardboard boxes bearing such labels as "Crutchley – Patti Volanski," "Crutchley – Kimberly Walker," and "Crutchley – Unidentified Victim." Most of the boxes were closed, but the tops of two of them were propped open. Parts of what looked to be human bones protruded from the openings.

For a few moments, Crutchley's eyes widened. His skin tone dropped a shade paler as he stared at the boxes. It looked for a moment as if the police ploy had worked and that Crutchley had been scared into confessing. But then the moment passed. He regained his composure and looked Petty in the eye. When he spoke, his words did not come anywhere close to the hoped for confession.

"This is an evil room," he murmured angrily. "Take me back to jail."

Then he sat down on a straight-backed chair and refused to say anything further.

After trying unsuccessfully to get Crutchley to talk, Petty took him back to the county jail. Although the officers' efforts had not elicited a confession, Crutchley's experience in the bones room deeply affected him in a way that would only be fully revealed later.

FIFTEEN

An evil mind

On January 13, anthropology professor R.C. Dailey released the findings from his forensic examination of the skeletal remains found at Savery Road in Palm Bay, as well as his findings regarding the remains of the two bodies found just west of U.S. 1 in Malabar. His overall conclusion supported Leatherow's suspicion that the murders had been committed by the same killer.

"It looks as if there is a connection because they all involved some form of dismemberment," Dailey announced.

Meanwhile, in Virginia, Fairfax County police reopened their cold case file on the Debbie Fitzjohn murder "in light of information" provided by Leatherow and other Brevard County investigators, including that Debbie's white Bible had been found among the items in Crutchley's safe at his Malabar home. In announcing the reopening of their investigation, a Fairfax County police spokesman asserted that "[i]f we find evidence, then Crutchley will be charged" in connection with Fitzjohn's "suspicious death."

After learning that jewelry Debbie wore virtually every day had not been found with her body, Brevard County detectives suspected that it could be among the necklaces and other women's jewelry found in Crutchley's bedroom closet on the day of his arrest. On January 21, they sent several pieces of the jewelry to Fairfax County detectives to see if Debbie's grandmother could identify any of them; however, seventy-year-old Milda Fitzjohn, suffering from the early stages of Alzheimer's disease, could not remember what Debbie's jewelry looked like with any certainty.

As the investigation and pretrial proceedings in Crutchley's case continued, so did the intense media coverage. By now, the macabre acts of the Vampire Rapist had gained notoriety far beyond the borders of Brevard County. Newspapers across the country routinely followed the case, and stories about the Vampire were carried worldwide. The hedonistic creature's appetite for blood captivated the media.

Yet, in a letter to the *Florida Today* newspaper dated January 21, 1986, Crutchley denied engaging in any acts of vampirism.

I do not drink blood, am not, and never have been a vampire, he asserted.

As for why he had picked up Christina Almah and taken her to his home, Crutchley claimed that she asked him to do it.

She stated that it was her desire to have sex. She said her boyfriend had stood her up.

He denied having held her captive in any way and likewise denied having taken blood from her using intravenous needles. Instead, she had been a "willing participant" in an adulterous encounter that was a "one-time thing."

Crutchley explained that much of his life had been spent experimenting with sex in an unsuccessful attempt to find meaning and contentment. His encounter with Christina constituted just the latest in a line of such experimentation.

I had no enjoyment out of life. I was looking for something intimately satisfying, he wrote.

As for the crimes he was charged with committing, Crutchley insisted that he had not really done anything wrong. Christina Almah, a "second generation Charles Manson follower," had wanted what Crutchley offered. He had simply given her what she consciously, or unconsciously, desired.

Everybody I've ever dated had a death wish in one way or another, he contended.

Rather than vilifying him as some abhorrent monster, the media needed to recognize that he was only one of many. Countless others were living similarly hollow lives.

There's a lot of people like [me] who are looking for something to give them meaning to their life, he maintained. *I've met hundreds of people just wandering around waiting for something to do.*

This lack of meaning—this essential emptiness—dictated his actions, not the deranged desires of a demonic sexual predator.

We were looking for the ultimate orgasm, the ultimate turn on, the ultimate satisfaction, he explained.

The roots of his crimes could be traced there, not in any diabolic inclinations or malevolent intentions. He stressed that he had been born again in prison and steadfastly denied having any violent tendencies.

I never physically abused anyone, he wrote. *I'm not a violent type of person. When it comes to inflicting pain, I draw the line.*

A consistent narrative emerged as a comforting response to his new reality, structured around the theme of denial and blaming others. He did not have an evil mind, but he had become an avid reader of alternative, hard-core pornographic magazines such a *Penthouse's* Variations, and it was pornographic magazines and videos that should be deemed responsible for his criminal behavior, not Crutchley himself.

They caused me to do it because they gave me a hope that I'd find something that would be fulfilling.

Despite the considerable evidence arrayed against him, Karen remained steadfastly loyal to her husband, asserting that the Sheriff's Office and State Attorney's Office "just want to persecute him." Much to the amazement of reporters, she characterized Crutchley's terrifying abduction and assault of Christina Almah as a "gentle rape." Attempting to rationalize Crutchley's bizarre behavior, she brushed it off as a symptom of her workaholic husband having suffered a breakdown while she was out of town.

On January 28, Leatherow and Sheriff's Agent Scott Russell met with Harris Corporation security personnel in Palm Bay for another search of Crutchley's office in room 112 of trailer 8-23. This time, the investigators focused on various computer software, seizing forty five-inch floppy disks, twenty eight-inch floppy disks, several computer tapes, and two disk packs.

As Leatherow and Russell searched Crutchley's office in Palm Bay, the Space Shuttle *Challenger* blasted off from its launch pad at nearby Cape Canaveral, rising into the sky at 2,257 feet per second. The large crowd that had gathered to witness the launch stood bundled in sweaters and coats to keep out the unseasonably cold air. The temperature had dropped to a frigid 28 degrees Fahrenheit as the shuttle rocketed skyward with a deafening roar. As the shuttle shot away, the bonejarring sound of its booster rockets steadily diminished, slowly fading to silence as it passed into the upper atmosphere. At regular intervals, as the shuttle's image on the video projection screen grew smaller and smaller, the crowd heard the

Capsule Communicator's radio exchanges with the shuttle's commander.

At 11:37 a.m., CapCom issued a final instruction.

"Challenger, go at throttle up."

"Roger. Go at throttle up," came the shuttle commander's reply.

Within moments, only seventy-three seconds into its inspiring flight, the space shuttle exploded in an orange-red fireball sprouting vast plumes of smoke. Just before the catastrophic explosion, the crew's cabin recorder captured the final words of anyone on board the doomed ship. Pilot Michael J. Smith, recognizing that something had gone terribly wrong, fatefully echoed the last words uttered by many a lost soul, words coming so natural in a situation as hopeless as that, words so quintessentially human.

"Uh, oh," Smith had suddenly said in a tragic, all-too-brief, final moment of awareness.

After the explosion, the booster rockets, no longer attached to the sides of the shuttle, continued to shoot out of control through the clear afternoon sky. As pieces of the shuttle began falling into the Atlantic Ocean off the Florida coast, the NASA public affairs officer announced what was so readily apparent.

"Flight controllers here looking carefully at the situation," he said solemnly. And after a slight pause, he added, "Obviously, a major malfunction."

In the days that followed, the post-crash investigation revealed that air temperatures had dropped so much the night before the launch that it caused the O-ring seal in the shuttle's right rocket booster to fail, resulting in a structural failure of the fuel tank, and causing a catastrophic explosion. Further investigation revealed that NASA managers had known about the potentially fatal flaw in the design of the Oring seals since 1977.

SIXTEEN

Fruitless pursuits

T he same day as the *Challenger* tragedy, Judge Antoon held a hearing on a motion filed by Crutchley's attorney seeking to impose a gag order to prevent the Sheriff's Office and State Attorney's Office from speaking to the media about Crutchley's case. During the hearing, a highly animated Crutchley took the witness stand holding a copy of a recent newspaper article about the case.

Glaring directly at Sheriff Jake Miller and brandishing the front page of the paper, Crutchley accused the Sheriff of deliberately misleading the media about the evidence that had been gathered against him.

"This entire lead story is a 100 percent lie! I challenge you to show the court or the press a single thing in the story that is true. I will plead guilty to anything that you can think of if you can show where I've been asked a single question about the unsolved murders."

Not long into the hearing, Judge Antoon banged his gavel heavily and announced that the court would take a short recess, but not before informing the Sheriff and Norm Wolfinger that he wanted to see both of them in his chambers. A few hours later, the still perturbed judge resumed the hearing and granted Crutchley's motion, imposing the gag order as requested.

After returning to jail following the conclusion of the hearing, Crutchley was promptly shuttled into solitary confinement. Soon after being introduced to his new surroundings, an enraged Jake Miller paid him a visit, his eyes dilating violently and his nostrils flaring open "like a horse running at full gallop."

"You embarrassed the Brevard County Sheriff's Department, and I promise that you'll never live to forget it!" Miller vowed before stalking away still fuming.

Upon reviewing the computer disks that they had seized from Crutchley's office on January 28, Leatherow and Russell found that some files on the discs had been erased by Crutchley and other files were encrypted or encoded. Unable to access the files themselves, they contacted NASA security specialists Andy Casey and Charlie O'Neal to see if they could crack the codes. For seven days, Casey and O'Neil worked nearly nonstop decoding the files. In the end, they were able to decode various text files and games, but nothing that seemed relevant to the investigation.

FBI cryptologists subsequently took at a stab at deciphering the files, but came up similarly empty-handed. Investigators learned of the possible existence of a file named "Casket," but found no trace of the file or its contents. Leatherow suspected that Crutchley kept records about his victims on his computer, using it as an electronic diary of sorts; however, the FBI's computer experts were unable to retrieve any such memoirs. Whatever files had been erased from the discs were gone forever.

As Leatherow continued his investigation of Crutchley's background, he gathered more and more details about Crutchley's bizarre sexual practices and tastes. In April, he interviewed Janice Carter, who had met Crutchley in October 1978, while working as a waitress at a restaurant. Crutchley's good looks and odd charm had immediately attracted her and the two soon began dating. Carter moved in with Crutchley the next year and traveled with him to visit his parents at their house in Bridgeport, West Virginia. During the trip, Crutchley encouraged her to call him by the nickname "Spooky" and mentioned in passing that he did not like his father, although he never elaborated why. The trip had otherwise been uneventful, with Crutchley and his father spending much of the visit alone in the basement watching television.

As they spent more time together, Carter grew tired of Crutchley's sexual eccentricities and demands. She fell into a depression and began entertaining thoughts of suicide. Instead of trying to talk her out it, Crutchley offered to help her kill herself, assuring her that he could do it painlessly by bleeding her to death. He stuck a needle in her arm to drain her blood, but the prick of the needle shocked her to her senses and she changed her mind. Instead of ending her life, she ended their relationship.

In early February, Crutchley called the *Florida Today* to discuss his case. He admitted that he had picked up Christina Almah, but denied raping her or drinking her blood, again insisting that what had taken place was simply an adulterous affair.

"She was just like me," he claimed. "We were looking for the ultimate orgasm, the ultimate turn on, the ultimate satisfaction."

He compared her to many others he had come across over the years, young women who were in their physical prime, but who plodded and staggered through life with a distant, zombie-like detachment. Crutchley explained that his association with such insensate souls had begun in 1977 when he moved to the Washington, D.C. area, where he had turned to sex clubs, partner swapping, group sex, and drugs.

Crutchley painted a bleak picture of life in prison.

"Going to jail is like dying and going to hell, but worse. You're like an animal in a cage. Cockroaches crawl all over your body."

He reiterated his newfound religious faith, admitting that he had done things in the past that he was ashamed of, but that Jesus had forgiven him.

"If it wasn't for the word of God," Crutchley petulantly proclaimed, "I don't know what I'd do."

He also reasserted that law enforcement was out to get him.

"They have a lot of unsolved crimes on their hands and no leads on any of them," he pointed out in an insinuating voice. "Here's a chance for them to make a name for themselves."

Crutchley told the paper that the unrelenting wrongful prosecution had taken its toll on him and his family, both psychologically and financially. The mounting legal bills had even forced his wife to resort to selling their wedding gifts.

"We're beyond broke," he explained.

Soon after his phone interview, Crutchley met with *Florida Today* reporters in a jailhouse conference room. After being led to the interview room from his tiny, one-man cell on the third floor of the Brevard County Jail, Crutchley sat with reporters for an additional seven hours of interviews, during which he projected the blame for his criminal behavior primarily on his parents.

"My parents never helped me to sit down and do any life plans, so I just lived one day to the next," he said as if trying to justify his actions.

Although he had grown up in an upper-middle class family that looked happy and healthy on the outside, Crutchley claimed that he did not have any pleasant memories of his childhood.

"My childhood was not family oriented," he said sullenly, his voice cracking. "I never felt like I belonged anywhere."

The many family vacations and his father's extensive involvement in his Boy Scouts functions were only window dressings presenting the illusion of normality. As a result of an emotionally sterile home environment, he became a loner, spending most of his time holed up in the basement working on electronic equipment, taking apart televisions and radios and putting them back together in different ways to see what would happen. Socially and emotionally isolated, he became incapable of developing real feelings about anything or anyone.

Around the time that Crutchley was trying to deflect the blame for his behavior by clothing his story in a cloak of sympathy, a low-budget production company announced its intention to portray its own version of the Vampire Rapist's story. The company planned to film a horror movie in Brevard County based on a script about a modern-day vampire who captured his prey by picking up girls in bars or along the roadways near his home. Though clearly an instance of reality influencing art, the film's director denied that he had based its plot on the real-life events of Crutchley's case. In an ambiguous statement that seemed to evoke Crutchley himself, the director vaguely described what motivated the behavior of his film's vampire.

"This particular character has certain problems with women because of an incident that happened during his childhood," the director explained.

Over a three-day period spanning February 11 through 13, Leatherow, Croft, and other Sheriff's deputies conducted an additional search of Crutchley's residence and the surrounding properties, including the pond of a neighbor at 2020 McCain Drive. The search team hoped to find evidence of missing women or traces of other bodies, but their efforts ended empty-handed.

Unbeknownst to the investigators who originally searched his house, Crutchley had a hiding place inside his waterbed behind the stacked drawers that were built into the bed's frame. If they had found the secret compartment the night of Crutchley's arrest, they may have recovered evidence sufficient to charge him with murder. But the hiding place went undiscovered until well after Crutchley had bailed out of jail.

On Valentine's Day, Leatherow met with Harris Corporation security personnel about a report of harassment that had been filed by former Harris employee Judy Bowman back in 1984. Leatherow suspected that the incident might be connected to Crutchley, so he interviewed Ms. Bowman after reviewing the report. She told him that in September 1984, while she was still employed at Harris, a picture of her had been stolen from her office. Later that same day, while getting into her car to drive home, Bowman found a sexually graphic photograph that had been placed on the front seat of her car. The photo showed a white male's exposed pelvic area and semi-erect penis. Not long after that, Bowman began receiving obscene phone calls at her house, and twice spotted a prowler outside of her window. The obscene calls stopped in November 1985, just as suddenly as they had started.

Leatherow wondered whether Bowman's obscene caller was Crutchley. After all, he had been arrested on November 23, 1985. The timing of his arrest and the last of the obscene phone calls seemed to be more than a coincidence. Seeking to confirm his suspicions, Leatherow sent the photograph from Bowman's car to the FBI, along with several known photos of Crutchley, to see if a positive identification could be made. The FBI analyzed the photos, but due to the lack of any significant identifying characteristics visible in Bowman's photo, FBI analysts could not determine whether Crutchley was the individual in the photograph.

On the same day, at the request of attorneys for the *Florida Today*, Judge Antoon held a hearing to determine whether to revoke his January 28 gag order that prohibited attorneys, court workers, and Sheriffs' deputies from discussing Crutchley's case with members of the media.

Clutching a Bible, Crutchley took the stand and testified about the notoriety and stigma he had been subjected to as a result of the biased media coverage being orchestrated by prosecutors and the police. He said that it became so bad that he had considered hanging himself while in jail. Only a religious experience in December 1985 saved him.

"I was at the bottom of an emotional pit. I had no meaning in my life," he meekly told the judge, explaining the reason for his suicidal thoughts and fishing for some sympathy.

He accused the Sheriff's Office and State Attorney's Office of manipulating the media to "try to run me out of town," and also asserted that the resulting press coverage was "ruining my chance for a fair trial in this county." After hearing arguments from both parties, Judge Antoon denied the motion, keeping the gag order in place.

On February 17, Leatherow interviewed Harris employee Mary Walker, a married mother of two young children. Mrs. Walker confided to Leatherow that she and Crutchley had engaged in extra-marital sex on two separate occasions in 1985, once at her house and once at his house on Hall Road. Unlike the majority of Crutchley's other sexual partners, Walker had not been choked by him, or if she had, she refused to admit it.

On February 26, Leatherow, Fair, and other investigators undertook another search of the Crutchley property. Leatherow could not shake the feeling that Crutchley still had mementos from his victims, or parts of the victims themselves, hidden on the property. However, once again, their search efforts yielded nothing remarkable or relevant to the case.

The same day, Crutchley wrote a friend from church about his time in the Brevard County Jail, mentioning how he had spent weeks in solitary confinement.

"I liked the safety and the solitude gave me lots of time for Bible study," Crutchley wrote, but then he added that ultimately "loneliness and an oversized dose of self-pity set in."

Still fearful that the extensive media coverage of the case would taint the minds of potential jurors, Joe Mitchell filed a motion for change of venue, requesting that Crutchley's trial be moved out of Brevard County. As grounds for the motion, Mitchell emphasized that the intense news coverage had "poisoned the local prospective jurors" to such an extent that they "couldn't put all the stuff out of their minds and base their verdict purely and simply on what's presented in the courtroom." Mitchell asserted that the "day-after-day-after-day" exposure to slanted media coverage had irreparably damaged his ability to select an impartial jury for the trial. The judge ultimately agreed, ordering that the April 14 trial be moved to Gainesville in Alachua County. However, in granting the change of venue to Alachua County, the judge simultaneously lifted his gag order since its restrictions would no longer be needed to ensure a fair trial in Brevard County.

Mitchell told reporters that his client's spirits were good despite the circumstances in which he found himself. In describing his most recent visit with Crutchley, Mitchell stated that he "seemed to be handling the stress of incarceration very well."

Meanwhile, Leatherow continued to review the facts of the case over and over in his mind. Reflecting on the strange circumstances of Christina Almah's escape from the vampire's lair, Leatherow arrived at what he believed to be the most plausible explanation. Based on the volume of blood that Crutchley took from Christina Almah, Leatherow concluded that Crutchley must have assumed that she would be too weak from blood loss to get out of the bathtub, much less escape by lifting herself up and squeezing through the bathroom window. Having taken the same amount of blood from his past victims, who had all been rendered unconscious or otherwise incapacitated from that amount of blood loss, Crutchley must have believed that Christina would be similarly disabled. For some reason, most likely her younger age, Christina had been stronger than the others. Leatherow believed that Christina's youthful vitality and stamina enabled her to escape the fate of Crutchley's other victims, who, lying naked in a cold porcelain bathtub behind a parrot-decorated shower curtain, had eventually fallen unconscious and died, their bodies gruesomely dismembered by Crutchley with a hacksaw, their blood drizzling and dripping from the saw's serrated teeth before disappearing down the drain.

SEVENTEEN

All of the sinners

O
n April 1, 1986, Lt. Fair interviewed Greg Raub, one of
Crutchley's former cellmates in Cell 210 of the Brevard
County Jail. The jail administrators generally used Cell 210 to
house prisoners who were under medical care, but they had put
Crutchley there to keep him close to the jail officer's desk.
Although designed to be a four-person cell with two bunk beds, Cell
210 did not occupy much space, extending only about 20 feet wide
and around 25 feet in length. It contained a small black and white
television, one toilet, and a single shower. The cell's large, solid
steel door had a narrow food flap below a muffled hole, which the
inmates used to talk to visitors or jail officials. The claustrophobic
compactness of Cell 210 became even more pronounced on March
10 when the addition of Crutchley had increased the number of
inmates sharing the cramped cell from four persons to five.

Crutchley did not make much of an initial impression on Raub.
He had never heard of the Vampire Rapist due to his having had an
extended stay in an isolation cell at Sumter Correctional Institute
before being transferred to the Brevard County Jail to serve out the
final few months of his sentence. Indeed, the isolation at Sumter

Correctional had been so extreme that Raub had not even heard of the *Challenger* explosion until after his transfer to Brevard County.

When he first saw Crutchley, Raub thought him to be no more than twenty or twenty-one years old, and he assumed that a drug or burglary charge had punched his ticket to the jail. With his pale complexion and bowl-type haircut, Crutchley came across as "nerdy," but unexplainably "creepy" as well, and it did not take Raub long to notice that Crutchley possessed considerably more intelligence than the inmates he typically came across. He spoke eloquently, acted politely, and conveyed a calm, distinct confidence.

Raub kept to himself during Crutchley's first day in the cell. However, as typically happens to strangers who find themselves in close quarters for extended periods of time, as the hours and days passed by the two of them began to talk. When Crutchley learned that Raub had come to the jail from a state prison, his curiosity was piqued. He wanted to know what prison was like and peppered Raub with questions about it.

At some point, Raub asked Crutchley why he was in jail. Crutchley expressed amazement at Raub's question.

"Don't you know who I am?" Crutchley inquired, clearly astonished.

"No, why, should I?" Raub asked in reply.

"You're in a cell with the Vampire Rapist," Crutchley announced in a tone conveying an obvious sense of self-importance.

"Vampire Rapist? What the hell is that?" Raub responded, the tenor of his voice in no way disguising his annoyance.

"You mean you haven't read or heard about me?" Crutchley asked incredulously.

"No, man, but I haven't exactly been keeping up with the daily news."

When Raub explained how he had been isolated in solitary confinement and had not even heard that the space shuttle had exploded, Crutchley brandished some newspaper articles about himself and, after a deliberate dramatic pause, handed the clippings to Raub. Raub could tell from Crutchley's attitude and mannerisms that he obviously thought of himself as some sort of celebrity.

Over time, Raub gained a better understanding of his infamous cellmate.

"He didn't seem like a violent person or a dangerous person, but the longer I began to know him, or the longer I was in the cell, the more I began to see the inside of him. Everybody else in the jail was basically afraid of him because they knew what he was, who he was."

While in Cell 210, Crutchley passed the majority of his days playing solitaire, reading books and magazines, and reviewing newspaper articles about his case. He spent much of the rest of his time talking on the phone with his attorney, Joe Mitchell, or his wife, Karen. And he continued to talk to Raub.

One night, Crutchley shared some information with Raub about his abduction of Christina Almah, a disclosure that also hinted at a darker past. As Raub recounted to Lt. Fair:

> I do remember him specifically saying that had he taken any more blood from this girl she would have died. Also, he broke down crying, he had tears in his eyes. He grabbed me by the hand, sitting on my bunk Indian style, looking me eye to eye. And he said, "You know, Greg, she would've been the last one. She was gonna be the last one." And I thought to myself, huh, that's always the same line everybody says in prison. This would have been the last drug deal or this would have been the last burglary. So I took it that he musta done this to other people. That's the only way I could've taken what he said.

As Raub continued to interact with Crutchley, he noticed how much Crutchley seemed to enjoy manipulating others. Crutchley did so with such ease and frequency that Raub came to believe that he had some type of mind-control ability, some supernatural power, like a vampire's hypnotic ability to entrance his prey.

Raub also noted that Crutchley believed himself to be considerably smarter than anyone at the Brevard County Sheriff's Office. In fact, he often bragged that he was so meticulous in getting rid of any evidence that investigators would never be able to link him to a single murder.

Joe Mitchell took Raub's deposition on April 14. During his deposition, Raub repeated much of what he had said during his interview with Lt. Fair, reiterating that Crutchley had told him that if he had taken any more blood from Christina "she would've died."

"If she wouldn't have gotten away on her own," Crutchley said coldly, "then she would never have ever gotten away."

According to Raub, Crutchley could not fathom how Christina had managed to escape. In his mind, her fate had been predetermined: she was "supposed to be like the others."

Raub testified that, despite how he performed in court or played to the media, Crutchley embraced his notoriety as the dreaded Vampire Rapist. Raub recalled how over the Halloween weekend Crutchley had obtained a set of fake vampire fangs, the plastic type that kids wear for trick-or-treating, commonly sold at costume shops. Crutchley enjoyed putting the fangs in his mouth and baring them with a hiss at passing jail officials or unsuspecting inmates serving as trusties for good behavior. According to Raub, the Vampire thought it was hysterical, but his victims were not amused and Crutchley's fun was short lived. It did not take long for the jail squad Sergeant to come to his cell and confiscate the fangs.

Leatherow joined Fair for the interview of Raub's girlfriend, Denise Wink. Wink told them that she first met Crutchley during one of her jailhouse visitations with Raub. Crutchley had quickly become obsessed with Wink, telling her how "sweet and pure" she was and how he wanted to "protect [her] from evil." He even talked to Wink about divorcing Karen so that he could marry her.

Wink had even lived at Crutchley's house for a week or so, at his invitation, while he shared a cell with Raub. Karen had been home the majority of that time, and one night, while Wink and Karen were playing board games, Wink opened one of the game boxes to get the directions. When she took out the directions, she saw that they were splattered with bloodstains. Although the bloodstains were so obvious that Karen could not have missed them, she did not mention them or even act as if anything unusual had happened. The blood spatter had been strange enough. Karen's nonchalant reaction to it had made Wink extremely uncomfortable.

Sensing the chance to get Wink to fully open up, Leatherow asked her about Crutchley's ability to manipulate others.

"We've had him described to us by other ladies who have known him as very, very intense, having a very powerful mind, almost like he looked through you into your mind, into your soul." Wink responded without hesitation.

"Yeah, he's scary. I feel like he knows exactly what I'm thinking. And he looks at me in such a way that it's like he can read my mind. And it scares me."

Wink was yet another person whose close contact with Crutchley had ended in fear.

Leatherow's interview with Wink also confirmed a promising lead through the identification of a new potentially important witness. That information came when Wink reported something to Leatherow that Raub had told her near the end of his time as Crutchley's cellmate.

According to Raub, while he had grown to know Crutchley

better during their time together, another inmate from Cell 210 seemed to have become particularly close to Crutchley while sharing the cell. One day, that inmate casually remarked to Raub that he could tell him things about Crutchley that would "make his hair stand up on end." That inmate's name was Patrick Dontell.

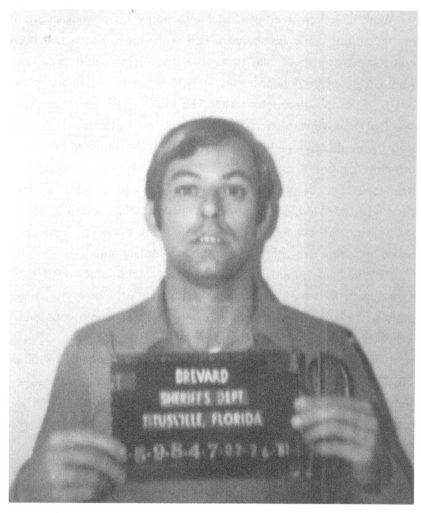

Booking photograph of Patrick Dontell, cellmate of Crutchley at Brevard County Jail

EIGHTEEN

Eyes like angels

P atrick Albert Dontell had been held in the Brevard County Jail since being transferred from an Orlando detention center the night of January 3, 1986. The forty-one-year-old Dontell was awaiting trial on a sexual battery charge in addition to a charge of solicitation of prostitution. A small man, Dontell stood barely five feet, six inches in height, and weighed less than 170 pounds, even after a heavy meal. Legally blind, his bluish-green eyes were usually concealed by thick glasses housed in a large, black frame. Without the aid of his heavy corrective lenses, he could only see out of one eye, and only about five inches in front of him at that. Despite this condition, he devotedly read the Bible every night, and meticulously kept a diary during his confinement, making almost daily entries.

On January 11, Dontell dedicated his diary entry to describing the living conditions in the Brevard County Jail.

This place reminds me of movies that I have watched showing scenes of Death Row. There are three of us in an eight by eight box, we have no room to move about. Besides the two beds and my mattress on the floor, we have a toilet, a sink, and a shower. The shower runs cold, the toilet and sink are so disgusting that a junkyard wouldn't keep them. Even the bugs walk around the toilet for fear they may catch something.

A month later, he recorded his surprise at how quickly he had forged friendships with his roommates in Cell 211 of the jail.

In the last few days I have gotten to know the people I'm now living with. It's so strange how fast you can understand and relate to people that just a few days ago were total strangers.

He detailed the habits of one "very unforgettable character" in particular.

Let me take a few lines and devote them to Walter. Mr. Walter Ellis, better known as Bubbles. That's right, Bubbles. Walter is about as gay as one can get. From here on out, I'll use the term "she" for it fits perfectly.

Walter is twenty years old and going on thirteen. She was arrested during a 7-11 robbery while dressed in drag. The judge had no sense of humor and sentenced her to six years.

Now Walter has a ritual that takes place every evening before bed. First, she showers for at least one hour. Then she shaves her legs and underarms. She greases her hair, clips her nails, and puts on five or six kinds of cream, after which time it's almost impossible to breathe. Then she flosses and brushes her teeth and primps around looking in the mirror to make sure all is well. Then she makes her bed, which is already made, and settles down for the night. By that time, it's 2:00 a.m. and everyone wants to kill Walter. This kid's worse than my ex-wife.

In the early afternoon of March 10, 1986, jail officials ordered Dontell to move from Cell 211 to Cell 210. Shuffling into his new accommodations, Dontell saw that three men were already occupying the four-person cell, but he happily discovered that none of them had claimed one of the two bottom bunk beds. Greg Raub had taken the other bottom bunk and Dontell could see him sleeping there. On the top bunk above Raub slept a young man about twenty years old named Lou Figarello. A slightly psychotic individual whom everyone called "Scarecrow" had staked out the top bunk directly above Dontell's bed, no doubt explaining why that particular bottom bunk remained unclaimed until Dontell arrived. Scarecrow lived in a world of his own. Convinced that the police had implanted a secret monitoring device in his arm, he repeatedly tried to make collect calls to federal authorities to report the egregious act, but the FBI and other federal agencies had long since learned not to take his calls. Thwarted in his attempts to appeal to a higher authority, Scarecrow sought relief by petitioning the jailhouse guards to bring in a metal detector so that he could prove once and for all the truth of his suspicion. The guards' continual refusal of his requests only served to reinforce his conspiratorial beliefs.

At around 3:00 p.m. on March 10, guards escorted another man into Cell 210. Since no more beds were available, the guards informed the most recent arrival that he would have to sleep on the floor. The new addition to the cell was John Crutchley.

Despite Scarecrow's eccentricities, Dontell's initial apprehension about moving to a new cell rapidly dissipated when he discovered that the men sharing the room with him were for the most part easy going and quiet. And they all generally kept to themselves. During the day, the men typically either slept, or read, or played cards. None of them watched television, which delighted Dontell as it afforded him ample time to meditate and reflect, a much-appreciated peace in which to read and write.

Several days passed in this manner with Dontell taking advantage of the relative quiet by silently studying his Bible. He spent much of March 13 like most of the other days he had passed in jail, primarily by reading and writing in his diary, but early that evening, while lying on his bed perusing a new passage in his Bible, Dontell felt an odd chill and shivered as if a ghostly presence had passed through him. As the strange sensation continued, he looked up and saw Crutchley standing like a specter beside him. His eyes fixed on Dontell's Bible, Crutchley spoke to him for the first time since coming to the cell three days earlier. He told Dontell that he had recently become a born-again Christian and asked if he could fellowship with him. Dontell stared at him in disbelief, momentarily shocked since, during the seven months he had been incarcerated, no one had ever asked to fellowship with him before.

Seeing that Crutchley appeared to be genuine and earnest in his request, Dontell managed a smile and answered that he would be happy to discuss the word of God with him. He and Crutchley studied the scriptures together for several hours that first night. In his diary, Dontell wrote of his delight in having someone of Crutchley's intelligence to talk to, since, up to that point, he had found the average brainpower in the Brevard County jail system to be "very close to that of a gold fish."

After that first evening, Crutchley and Dontell talked about the Bible for hours every night and they began sharing their backgrounds with each other. As of March 15, their fifth day in the cell, the two spent virtually all of their free time together. Their days were spent talking, fellowshipping about the Bible, and playing cribbage. Sometimes their conversations would stretch throughout the night, ending only as a new day dawned the next morning. Over the next two weeks, they would fellowship and talk for more than 300 hours.

For Dontell, the days with Crutchley comprised the most rewarding time he experienced in all of his months in jail. He slept only three or four hours each night, and spent the bulk of his waking hours with Crutchley. Although admittedly a strange way to feel in light of his confinement, Dontell thoroughly enjoyed the time he spent with Crutchley. In his diary, he wrote about the great happiness he felt to have "at last found someone who I can communicate and fellowship with."

Dontell was so happy about how close he and Crutchley had become in such a short duration of time that he never bothered to wonder why the erudite Crutchley, so much more intelligent and articulate than the typical inmate, had ended up in jail in the first place.

On March 25, Crutchley began to share some of his more "intimate thoughts" with Dontell, including personal things about his darker past.

George Hurley, Crutchley's Harris Corporation colleague who often visited him in jail and spoke with him frequently by telephone, expressed concern about how close Crutchley seemed to be getting to some of his cellmates. Hurley cautioned him not to tell other inmates too much about himself, but Crutchley cavalierly brushed off his concern.

"You don't know what it's like in jail," Crutchley told him. "Spending twenty-four hours a day with someone, you really get to know them well."

Not long after cautioning Crutchley to be on his guard, Hurley received a phone call from him. Crutchley wanted to borrow $500 for a retainer to procure a lawyer for Dontell. Exasperated at Crutchley for ignoring his advice and making such a request, Hurley quickly declined.

"It's only $500," Crutchley prodded.

But Hurley only grew more annoyed by Crutchley's attempt to guilt him into acquiescence. "You're stupid for trusting him," Hurley said, remaining steadfast in his refusal of Crutchley's request. "He's probably a snitch anyway," Hurley added, clearly perturbed.

After Crutchley tried to manipulate Hurley by playing on his religious faith, Hurley decided that he had had enough. He stopped accepting Crutchley's calls and letters altogether.

As much as he enjoyed Crutchley's company and conversation, Dontell did not approve of Crutchley's designs on Denise Wink, the girlfriend of their cellmate, Greg Raub. From the moment he met her, Crutchley had been obsessed with Denise, scheming how to get her away from Raub so that he could have her for himself. Crutchley had even talked Raub into letting Denise stay at his house for a while, hoping that, by letting her stay there, Denise would feel indebted to him, a feeling that he could then exploit.

As Dontell recalled, Crutchley constantly fantasized about Denise.

He related several times how he would enjoy the moment he could wrap his hands around her beautiful throat and watch her go to an unconscious state while making love. I knew in my own mind what he was planning. This was to be his next victim.

While Dontell did what he could to protect Denise, Crutchley continued to seek out his company and confide in him, and he introduced Dontell to Karen and Jason when they visited him in jail one weekend. After all of their time together, Crutchley's trust in Dontell had grown so much that on March 26, he let Dontell cut his hair despite knowing that the man with thick glasses could not see very well. Crutchley joked afterward that it had been the first haircut he ever received from a blind man.

On March 31, Dontell wrote a diary entry to express his thoughts about how the police had been handling their investigation of his new friend.

I mentioned to John that the sheriff's department realizes that he is not one of the usual morons they are used to dealing with. In fact, it is almost reversed here: they have spent thousands of dollars investigating vapor. They don't know where to look. As a matter of fact, they don't know what he has really done. As a tax payer that really upsets me. No wonder our taxes are so high. Maybe it's time to fire half the morons who claim to be detectives and donate their salaries to charity. At least our tax dollars would be spent constructively. I find it so hard to believe the money and man power involved in this investigation.

On April 1, guards opened the door to Cell 210 and ordered Crutchley to pack his things. When he asked where he would be going, they told him not to worry about it. Dontell helped a visibly stunned Crutchley gather his personal belongings together and then they said their goodbyes. Though they did not realize it at the time, the two would never speak or see each other again.

A few hours after Crutchley had been taken away, guards escorted Dontell to an attorney's conference room in another part of the jail. Leatherow and Fair were waiting for him inside. They motioned for Dontell to sit in an empty chair across the table from them, and then introduced themselves as police officers.

Fair studied Dontell's face for a few moments. Apparently satisfied with what he saw, but with his eyes still locked on Dontell, Fair began the interview.

"What can you tell us about John Crutchley?"

Growing more comfortable now that he knew why he had been brought before the two investigators, Dontell took a long breath and then exhaled slowly.

"I know a lot about him, but I could give you better details if I had my notes."

"What notes?" Fair asked gruffly.

"I mean my diary entries," Dontell explained. "They're back in the cell."

"Alright, go get them. Then be ready to talk. We'll give you ten minutes."

Dontell did not want to raise any suspicions that he might be a snitch, so he told his remaining cellmates that he had tried to see his attorney, but the attorney was nowhere to be found, so the guards had brought him back to the cell until the lawyer could be located.

A half hour later, Dontell strode out of the dim corridors of the jail and into the sunlight, enjoying the fragrance of fresh air and unobstructed sunshine for the first time in what felt like forever. Leatherow and Fair led him to their car and drove him to the Sheriff's homicide office in Titusville. They took him into an interview room, gave him a cold bottle of Coke, turned on a tape recorder, and began questioning him about Crutchley.

Dontell explained how he met Crutchley on March 10 when they became cellmates and how the two of them had quickly hit it off. According to Dontell, Crutchley was drawn to him because he believed Dontell to be an ordained Methodist minister, and Dontell had not seen fit to correct him. As they spent more and more time together, Crutchley began to open up to Dontell, eventually bragging to him that he had committed at least four or five murders in Brevard County as well as some others elsewhere in Florida. Crutchley told Dontell that investigators suspected him in about twenty-four homicides, but boasted that the actual number exceeded that figure.

According to Dontell, Crutchley also spoke of how he selected his victims, who he described as typically being of "average" attractiveness and "very plain looking."

He'd meet them by chance by picking 'em up hitchhiking, and uh, runaways, people with no known identity, no ties to the community, people that he believed wouldn't be missed. As soon as he sees a young lady that seems like she doesn't belong in a certain area or she's from out of town or she has no connections, bang, he feels that he can fit his fantasy in with the young lady.

Crutchley told Dontell that he came across many of his victims while driving to or from work. After picking up a victim, Crutchley would have sex with her, usually as part of a bondage and bloodletting session, before killing her by asphyxiation or blood loss, and then disposing of the body. Due to the enthusiasm in his voice, it was obvious that Crutchley enjoyed killing, particularly by strangling women until they passed out, allowing them to revive, and then strangling them again. Many of his victims had met their end in that fashion. Crutchley also described how he typically kept mementos of his victims, such as their driver's licenses or other types of identification cards. He said that, in addition to the identification cards that investigators seized from his home and office, he had other ones that the police never found—souvenirs from victims in Virginia, Ohio, Florida, and Washington, D.C.

Before moving to Florida, Crutchley had met several of his victims in Washington, D.C. and its surrounding suburbs through swing parties and sex clubs. In recounting his experiences, Crutchley had especially enjoyed telling Dontell about a young black woman he had dated in the D.C. area who worked in the computer field with him. Crutchley smiled as he recalled that she had been extremely smart and exotically attractive with a "white figure." However, like many others he had dated, Crutchley said that in the end "she didn't make it." They went out several times and then she suddenly disappeared.

"Don't you find that strange?" Crutchley asked, before breaking into a devilish giggle.

He bragged about his "trophy collection" comprised of the various mementos he kept of his victims, and claimed that he had put the collection someplace where investigators would "never find it."

"It's within a half hour of the house," Dontell told Leatherow, "and he said if you could see the place, you wouldn't believe it."

Leatherow knew that serial killers typically kept trophies in their home so they could relive the excitement they felt while committing their crimes, but it made sense that Crutchley would have relocated his prizes to prevent the police from finding them.

Crutchley admitted to Dontell that he had picked up Patti Volanski when he spotted her hitchhiking, and that he subsequently strangled her to death during sex. He also admitted killing Debbie Fitzjohn in Virginia by strangling her and then hiding her body in the woods. He used her own car to dispose of her body and then left the car in the Hunter's Lodge parking lot. Crutchley claimed that Debbie enjoyed kinky sex and liked to be strangled, revived, and then strangled again. However, the third time he strangled her, she did not come back.

"Unfortunately, she didn't make it in the end," he told Dontell with a knowing grin.

Crutchley said that he had learned an important lesson from the Fitzjohn murder, telling Dontell that it was the only close call he ever had. Since the police had come so close to catching him in the Fitzjohn case, after that experience he began targeting hitchhikers, prostitutes, and transients, rather than women he knew or dated, or to whom he otherwise had a traceable connection. He reasoned that such victims would not only be more difficult to link to him, but would also not attract significant police attention.

In his diary, Dontell described how Crutchley enjoyed following his case in the newspapers and reading about Leatherow and other investigators' efforts to link him to any murders.

He always knew that he was one step ahead of everybody. He figured he was too smart to get caught. That was the thrill of it all. He took pride in the fact that the police wouldn't solve the crimes. There was just no way because he had covered all of his bases. He took pride in the fact that there's no way in the world they can prove how the people were killed.

Crutchley did not share with Dontell any specifics about how he disposed of his victims' bodies, but he emphasized that they were not on or nearby his property. Indeed, he found it comical that the Sheriff's department kept searching the property with horses and dogs and sending divers into nearby ponds. During one of their lengthy conversations, Crutchley mentioned that a commercial incinerator could quickly get rid of a human body so that there would be no remains left to identify, but he did not elaborate any further.

He hinted that he had disposed of the body of one of his victims by burying it at the construction site of a shopping center near TGIFriday's on U.S. 192 in Melbourne. He told Dontell that he had at one time worked as an engineer in the construction industry, and he claimed that he could tell where sidewalks were being placed.

It would be so easy to dig down next to a wall where the dirt was soft and place a body or two in there, then cover it over and no one could ever tell. Then they would lay the cement over it and, guess what, there was a sidewalk. Buried forever and no one would ever know.

Crutchley told Dontell that a body buried that way would never be found because the police would not tear up an entire shopping center trying to locate it.

Crutchley's confident prediction proved true, as authorities never fully searched the site on U.S. 192. According to Norm Wolfinger, Dontell's testimony alone did not constitute sufficient evidence to justify the expense of excavating the area.

Crutchley also disclosed to Dontell that he had videotaped some of his victims, but the police had not found those videotapes. He had a special hiding place underneath the printer in his house, a secret space for stashing some of his trophies. He had hidden a notebook there that he referred to as his diary, a diary in which he kept records of every woman that he had killed, including how they died. He was astonished that investigators did not find the trophies or his diary.

"If the police had just lifted up the printer, they would have found everything," he told Dontell incredulously.

However, on the night of his arrest, during the initial search of his house, no one touched the printer, and after Crutchley bonded out of jail, he removed the diary and trophies, as well as other mementos that were still hidden around the house and property. Then he stashed them somewhere away from the house, someplace that the police would not find them.

"He told me that they were off the property. They were within a half hour of the house, and they were someplace that you'll never find in a million years," Dontell explained to Leatherow and Fair. "But he said that it's gonna be so funny when I see it because I'd be able to appreciate that it was so close, right under your nose, but yet you'll never be able to find it."

Crutchley told Dontell that the sexual fantasies which so frequently dictated his actions often arose from articles he read in *Variations* magazine. Once one of them took hold of his mind, he could not stop himself from making it a reality. He tried to perfect the fantasies by practicing them with girls he picked up hitchhiking. Crutchley's "ultimate fantasy," what he called the "ultimate dream," always involved rape ending with death. He claimed to have experienced the ultimate dream "many times."

At one point, Crutchley asked Dontell if he enjoyed fantasies and inquired about his sexual preferences. He told Dontell about his bisexuality and confided that he had slept with Jackie Horton.

"I said, 'Well, John, I appreciate that, but uh . . . I'm strictly interested in women," Dontell recounted. "I said, 'I prefer if we could just keep our relationship platonic.' And he respected that. He never, you know, dove into it again."

Crutchley also confided to Dontell that he had, on more than one occasion, entertained thoughts of killing his own wife, Karen. He almost followed through when he gave Karen enough pills to take her to the verge of overdosing, knowing that she would swallow whatever he gave her without question. Karen was totally submissive to him and would do virtually anything he wanted.

Crutchley had also discussed his interest in the serial killer, John Wayne Gacy. In addition to having read the Gacy biography, *Killer Clown*, he seemed to identify on a personal level with Gacy. He became fascinated with how Gacy had hidden his victims' bodies by burying them underneath his own house. Gacy's method of disposing of the bodies particularly intrigued Crutchley because he understood that by burying them under his house, Gacy had meant to demonstrate complete power over his victims, victims who he literally trampled under his feet. Although the boldness and meaning of Gacy's special burying grounds captivated Crutchley, he also knew that burying the victims on his own property had directly led to Gacy's arrest and conviction. Crutchley's cunning, calculating side made sure that he would not mimic that mistake.

Dontell made it a point to emphasize how much Crutchley enjoyed the publicity and media attention that he received as the Vampire Rapist, specifically mentioning how he found it infinitely amusing to introduce himself to people by referring to himself as "Count Malabar." He particularly enjoyed reading news accounts about police and prosecutors' inability to link him to any crimes other than the Christina Almah abduction. According to Dontell, Crutchley viewed the entire criminal investigation as a game, a game that he was winning. A game that he would always win. Crutchley showed no concern about getting caught. He seemed confident that law enforcement would never be able to muster enough evidence to support even a single charge of murder.

"He's one step ahead of everybody," Dontell told Leatherow, describing Crutchley's confident mindset. "He takes pride in the fact that he's beating you at your own game. There's no way in the world that you can catch him because he's too smart for that."

Crutchley's delight in the thought of outwitting the police sprang from the malignant narcissism that nurtured his psychotic personality.

"He thinks it's a joke," Dontell continued. "He thinks you guys are running around looking in the wrong places, and you haven't got enough evidence to convict him. And he says that what he has you'll never find, and there's no way you can put a case together. He's very confident in himself, believe me. This guy is a whiz kid. He's some kind of man that you read books about."

Beyond that, although Crutchley knew that he had broken laws, did not feel that he had done anything wrong.

"He believes that these are people that want him to hurt and rape them," Dontell remarked. "He said most of the girls that he meets are suicidal. They have this death wish and he's just the kind of person that's nice enough to carry it out. He's doing them a favor. So he's convinced in his own mind that these people want him to do this." Crutchley believed his victims welcomed it in the end. In his mind, he played the part of a necessary predator, and his victims served as his natural prey.

Christina Almah had just been the latest in a long line. She had presented him "a perfect opportunity to commit the ultimate rape and the ultimate fantasy" since she was from out of state and no one had seen him drive her to his house. However, he had been disappointed in the outcome of their encounter. Her failure to struggle or resist during their time together had nearly ruined the fantasy. Dontell did not know it, but he had described one of the hallmarks of a sexually sadistic serial killer: the need for violent eroticism to experience sexual satisfaction.

What Crutchley most enjoyed, what gave him the orgasmic, addictive rush that he felt compelled to seek over and over again, was the sense of power and control that he had over Christina and the others. He played with their lives like some bored demi-god toying with mortals merely for his amusement. When he drained Christina's blood, "he knew exactly how much blood to draw before passing out time occurred." When Dontell asked Crutchley what he would have done if Christina had not escaped, what would have happened if she had still been in the bathtub when he came home from work, Crutchley made it clear that he would have killed her. Crutchley said that if November 22 had not been a busy day at work and he had not needed to leave her alone at the house, then he would have never been caught. Instead, Christina would have become his most recent victim, disappearing without a trace. She would have vanished like the others, "one of many," he said.

Although surprised that the Brevard County Sheriff's Office did not find his hidden trophies or diary, Crutchley reserved special scorn for the Fairfax County Police Department, whose work on the Debbie Fitzjohn case he dismissed as "sloppy investigation." Reading between the lines of Crutchley's criticism of law enforcement's investigative efforts, Dontell speculated that deep down he had an unconscious urge to be stopped.

I feel that John wants to be caught. He indicated that when he left his trophy collection and his tapes in the house. He knew the police were going to arrest him when Christina escaped. He had time to hide all his things, but he didn't. When he was released on bond, he discovered that all was intact, and as he said, "They're just unprofessional morons." John wants to be outsmarted, but so far he has not found his match. He is treating this whole ordeal as you would a game of chess, and so far he has been placed in "check," but not "check-mate."

After finishing the interview, Leatherow and Fair took Dontell's notes and hurried to a phone to call Norm Wolfinger. They told the receptionist who answered the phone that they did not care what Wolfinger was doing or whether he was home in his pajamas, they wanted him at the homicide office *now.*

About twenty minutes later, Wolfinger appeared. Carrying Dontell's notes and his taped interview, Leatherow, Fair, and Wolfinger went into a nearby office and closed the door. An hour later, Leatherow and Fair emerged from the room, asked Dontell a few follow-up questions, and then drove him back to the jail, arriving shortly after 1:00 a.m. on April 2.

With the addition of Dontell's testimony, Leatherow moved another step closer to proving that the Vampire was something more than the typical rapist.

NINETEEN

More dangerous than Bundy

L ess than twenty-four hours after being returned to the Brevard County Jail, Dontell once again found himself being taken to the jail's attorney conference room. This time only Leatherow waited for him.

"Hello, Pat. I've been talkin' to the State Attorney about using you to help build a case against Mr. Crutchley. We're still evaluating how best to use you, but the State Attorney is certainly interested in the information you've provided, as well as any other information about Mr. Crutchley you can share."

Dontell handed him a piece of paper.

"This is what I need if you want my help." Leatherow glanced over the list and grimaced.

"You want a lot, don't you?" he said incredulously.

The list outlined eight items that Dontell wanted in exchange for his assistance, including that all charges be dropped against him, that his name be expunged from all police records, and that he be immediately released and placed under protective custody. The list ended with a blunt statement.

There will be no plea bargaining on my part. Either I start with a
clean slate or I go to jail. It's your choice. I am not a danger to
society. Can you say the same about Mr. Crutchley?

Dontell was bluffing to some extent, but earlier that morning, he
heard through the jail grapevine that he had been branded as a
snitch or a plant as well as a personal friend of the Vampire Rapist,
perhaps the most damning offense of all. He knew that being identified as any one of those could get him knifed in the exercise yard,
brutally beaten in the shower, or worse. If he was going to be a
state's witness against Crutchley, he would have to get out of jail.
Otherwise, he would not live another thirty days.

After his meeting with Leatherow, Dontell returned to his cell
and began writing a new section in his diary under the title "The
Real Story." He began the first entry by describing his state of mind
and explaining the nature of his relationship with Crutchley.

I find myself physically and mentally exhausted. I have lived with
a serial killer since March 10, 1986. Each day I wondered if the
conversations we had may have gone too far. I knew that John
Crutchley was by far more intelligent than myself and I felt it was
only a matter of time before he realized that I had a great deal
more interest in him than just reading the scriptures and sharing
personal conversations.

. . . .

John Crutchley was by far the most unique character I have
ever met in my entire life. It had gotten to the point that I was
obsessed with learning more about him. I knew that I was dealing
with a very dangerous person. But because of my Christian faith
and the fact that I am legally blind, I think that made John feel I
was not a threat. He needed someone to relate to and considered
me to be an ordained minister. Here at last he had someone to

confide in and anything he said would be kept in strict confidence.
As John said many times, I'm the brother he has always wanted.

In one section, Dontell wrote about Crutchley's relationship with his wife and son. Discussing Crutchley's dominance over his wife, Dontell detailed how she would do anything Crutchley asked her to do, including being tied down and hit with a whip or struck by a belt repeatedly to satisfy Crutchley's psychosexual urges.

Dontell described how Crutchley also lacked any emotional attachment to his four-year-old son. Crutchley had seen himself in his son's eyes and did not like the image that stared back at him.

He said he used to think of ways to kill the kid. John told me that he walked into Jason's room one night and watched his son in his crib. On the floor were a box of chocolate covered malt balls, which were Jason's favorite candy. John said that he thought how easy it would be to pick Jason up and let him eat a few so they would be in his stomach. Then he could place one in Jason's throat and put him over his shoulder and hold him until he choked to death. It would be so easy and no one would ever be the wiser. That was the one time I felt hate for John. I knew from that moment on that John was not only dangerous, but very sick.

His hours of conversations with Crutchley had convinced Dontell that his cellmate had multiple personalities.

John had three personalities that stood out once you had gotten to know him. One was the engineer and the computer whiz kid from Harris Corporation. Very level headed and quite intelligent. An upstanding, model citizen. Personality Two was the little child who would sit and cry for no apparent reason, and when you asked why he was crying he would say, "I'm just happy and filled with love." And he would put two pieces of a fork he had broken off in his mouth and jump up and down and play vampire. His third personality was the violent side, or should I say, fantasy side. He would talk of bondage, beatings, and strangulation with sheer enjoyment. He takes his fantasies and puts them into real life or death situations.

Dontell's diary suggested that Crutchley's psychotic blurring of fantasy and reality was already well underway when he was living in the Washington area.

He said that in the D.C. area the women were strange. For some reason, he kept meeting these girls that really wanted to die. He said they had this fantasy about being killed. John said it must be his personality. He attracts all the strange types. At times, he would make a gesture like a vampire.

He also reported what Crutchley told him about the "bones room."

John was taken at one point by the police to a room with several boxes with his name on the outside. Inside the boxes were remains of corpses. He said that some could have been his, but there was no way of proving that.

Turning to the Christina Almah case, Dontell described how Crutchley told him that he knew exactly how much blood he could withdraw from Christina without killing her.

He claimed the human body contained so many pints of blood and he knew from experience just how much to take before unconsciousness sets in. I got the impression that he was not new to this. After he felt that he had taken his limit, he realized it was Thursday and he needed to get back to work. If it was any other day, he could have taken off, but there were too many things that had to be taken care of at work. If it had been any other day but Thursday, Christina would not be alive today.

Dontell wrote about Crutchley's sexual acts with Jackie Horton after both had bonded out of jail, and how Crutchley had gathered up videotapes, "trophies," and the diary of his victims and then hidden them in a secret place away from the house.

John said someday in the future when we're both out and if and only if things totally die down, that he has a place to show me that is so neat. He claims my mind would really appreciate the beauty of how clever this place is.

He also added more details about how much Crutchley enjoyed all of the media attention he received.

John loves the attention of being called the Vampire Rapist. There isn't a day that goes by that he doesn't joke about it. He loves being in the limelight so to speak. He calls himself Drak of Malabar. At times when he calls Karen he'll tell the operator, "Make this collect from Count Drak." He took a plastic fork and broke off two pieces and uses them for fangs. He stands at the front door of the cell and jumps up at night to startle the guards. He even told Denise [Wink] to bring a camera to court and when he turns around to take a picture of his fangs. He would make sure she got the only shot and the paper would pay her top dollar for the shot.

Although Dontell thoroughly enjoyed Crutchley's company and

felt an almost brotherly bond with him as a Christian, he could not look the other way when he found out that Crutchley had committed murders. In his diary, he explained why he chose to tell the police what he had learned about the Vampire Rapist.

> *I must do what I feel is right. I do not want to hurt John's family. But I don't want John to cause any more hurt to anyone else. This is the hardest ordeal I have ever had to face, and as a Christian and a human being I feel I am doing the right thing. I hope and pray that John Crutchley receives the help he so desperately needs.*

Dontell had initially concluded his diary by describing the last time that he saw Crutchley, the day that Crutchley was moved to a different cell.

> *On April 1st, John was taken to a single cell. As he left, he grabbed my hand and said, "I'll see you at Malabar. Pray for our miracle in April. I love you brother." He had tears coming down his cheeks. I even had a little in mine. This was like an ending to a sad movie. I think this will be the last time I see John except in court. I just wish it could have been different. Under other circumstances we could have been best friends.*
> *May God be with him.*

After having the opportunity to think things through and further reflect on his conversations with Crutchley, Dontell appended the diary, disclosing more disturbing information about Crutchley's past and adding some alarming final thoughts.

> *The authorities handling the Crutchley case are convinced that they have another Bundy on their hands, and to some extent*

they're right. However, Crutchley is far more dangerous, and would make Bundy look like an amateur in many respects. Crutchley is a very intelligent individual. He may be sick, but he is still highly intelligent.

The police have no idea what they have stumbled onto. Crutchley is not involved in just a few homicides. His track record dates all the way back to his college years. John fulfilled his first ultimate fantasy in college. She was working her way through school, as he said, "On her back." He had the ultimate bondage session and "she didn't make it." After that, he would attend parties and have bondage sessions with young ladies he met, but never the ultimate, resulting in death. He saved that for drifters and no names so to speak where no connection would be made between him and the ones he picked up. Some he would take to motels, where he would wrap them up in a sheet and stuff them in his car, and as he said "just dump them off."

. . . .

After his first experience in college of the ultimate fantasy ending in death, all else seemed to be unfulfilling and not as exciting. As John said, it was changing from heroin to pot. The high just isn't the same. After his ultimate fantasy, he had sex with many women. He even tried a few men, but he found sex totally boring. He said he enjoyed sex, but he was not getting total satisfaction, his ultimate high. He said he tried it all.

John fantasized constantly and never forgot his first ultimate fantasy. He desired to reach that fulfillment again, and he did many times over. But after a period of time, he wanted more. After several sessions involving death, he wanted something different.

One of John's hobbies is photography, so he started making home movies of his sessions, some involving two women ending in death. John said it was like a merry go round that he could not get off of. And all of these girls he picked up had this death wish. He said it was really strange. But as he said he was giving them what they wanted and he was getting a kick out of it as well.

He has a "burial grounds" where he has placed many of his Florida drifters. Quote from John Crutchley, "Ashes to ashes, and dust to dust. Just like the Indians used to do." I asked him what he meant by that. He said, "Burn, baby burn."

. . . .

He has always prided himself in staying one step ahead of everyone else. He claimed that the only close call he ever had was in Virginia. He almost made a mistake by killing someone he had a dating relationship with and the authorities placed the both of them together.

He painted a sobering picture of Crutchley's extensive track record of killing.

During one of our conversations, I mentioned I had sold cars. John asked how many I sold on the average per month. I said fifteen to twenty. He laughed and said he has had that many people that didn't make it in one month. I said, "You mean as in your ultimate fantasy, they are no longer existent?" He laughed and said, "You get the picture." He has been involved in his ultimate fantasy for nearly twenty years. Lord only knows how many John has killed, and if it were not for his diary and trophy collection, as he said he would be unable to keep track.

. . . .

John Crutchley is not another Bundy. John is in a class all by himself. He is a very intelligent, sick human being. He has gotten away with murder so many times, he feels he's untouchable, and for the last twenty years he's proved himself right.

Dontell's final entry expressed his disappointment that the Sheriff's Office and State Attorney's Office had not actively pursued his aid in prosecuting Crutchley.

> *Let them keep me in solitary confinement and treat me like human garbage, and prosecute me for something I did not do in 1981, and I'll keep my memories to myself. It will make very interesting reading in the future, and as John said, "A great movie."*

TWENTY

Pride in not being caught

On April 3rd, Crutchley penned a letter to Ray Malone, a friend from his radio station days, enclosing some personal papers that he wanted Malone to have for safe keeping, and letting Malone know how close of a friendship he had forged with cellmate Patrick Dontell. Indicative of an effort to avoid screening or review by jail officials, the top of the letter bore the inscription, "Written 03 Apr 86. Mailed whenever I can get it smuggled out."

Dear Ray,

Enclosed is an envelope of some papers that are important to me and my family. I suspect a possible interception of them if I mail them soon – a letter I sent to my parents was intercepted at their place! I know I can depend on you – so, I'm sending this for you to HOLD until I call/write later and have you mail it. Please Do Not mail it, but put it in a safe place until you hear from me!

Pat Dontell may be renting our house for a while – I gave him your name and phone number and let him know of our relationship. He and I have so much in common just like you and I

do – He's more like you than me and I hope for a time in the future
that we can all get together!

   . . . .

May our Good Lord bless you, John

On the same day that Crutchley hoped for the help of an old friend, a new adversary sought assistance from George Hurley, Crutchley's former co-worker from Harris Corporation. Crutchley had been Hurley's supervisor when he first began working for the company and the two had developed a friendship based on shared interests in computers and motorcycles. During his interview of Hurley, Leatherow learned that on the morning of Thursday, November 21, the same day that he abducted Christina Almah, Crutchley had been given a poor job evaluation by his supervisor, Jim Pettus. Crutchley did not handle criticism well, and he had made no secret of his anger about the less than stellar evaluation. Crutchley had a meeting scheduled with the Department Director, Terry Casto, for Friday morning, November 22, to discuss the unsatisfactory evaluation.

That's why he had to leave Christina alone again at the house,
thought Leatherow. *If not for that meeting, she'd have ended up as*
another unidentified corpse, and Crutchley would still be out there
killing.

Every so often, truth really is stranger than fiction. In Crutchley's case, an unflattering job evaluation and something as mundane as a broken window lock had given Christina Almah a second chance at life, saving her from a shallow grave, and leading to the capture of a dangerous serial killer, a cunning vampire hidden in plain sight.

Later on the evening of April 3, Fred Pfeiff received a call from

Judy Riccitelli in Fairfax County, Virginia. Riccitelli was calling to report that she had lived with Crutchley for about a month in September 1979. She had been depressed at that time in her life because of a divorce that forced her to put her infant child up for adoption. Her depression had so dominated her mood that it had spawned serious thoughts of suicide by the time she met Crutchley. Like another of his former flames, Crutchley told Riccitelli that he could help her. He offered to drain her blood using surgical needles and told her it would be a peaceful, painless way to die. Although he almost persuaded her to do it, Riccitelli came to her senses before going through with Crutchley's proposed solution to her problems.

On April 4, emboldened by the new information from Gregory Raub and Patrick Dontell, prosecutors filed papers in court to add four new criminal charges against Crutchley: one count of sexual battery, one count of aggravated battery, and two counts of robbery, including one robbery charge for taking Christina Almah's blood. Based on the new charges, filed less than two weeks before the scheduled commencement of Crutchley's trial, the court pushed the trial date back to May 19. In his answer to the new complaint, Crutchley pleaded not guilty to all four additional charges.

"It's bizarre," Crutchley's attorney told a group of reporters, "I'm sure there's never been a case before in Florida – probably not the whole country – that says if you take someone's blood it's robbery."

The new charges against Crutchley were reported as far away as Thailand, with the *Bangkok Post* carrying the intriguing headline, "'Vampire' arrested on blood theft charge."

The next day, Crutchley wrote two letters attempting to further his plans for gaining Denise Wink's trust and affection. He addressed the first letter to Denise and her boyfriend, Greg Raub, in the guise of counseling them, as a concerned Christian, on how to have a happy marriage.

> *Dearest Denise and Greg,*
>
> *Greetings in the love of our Lord and Savior, Jesus Christ! My heart is made happy at the thought that you two are reunited at last!*
>
> *. . . .*
>
> *The following is a checklist of four Bible readings and four related questions. A solid, truthful "Yes!" to the first 3, and the right answer to the last question, will ensure the good foundation of the marriage you are planning to enter.*
>
> *. . . .*
>
> *For the conclusion, read 2 Corinthians 5:17 – "When someone becomes a Christian, he becomes a brand new person inside. He is not the same any more. A new life has begun!"*
>
> *May God Bless you,*
> *Brother John*

In his second letter, Crutchley's manipulative side wrote Raub's mother in a much different tone, attempting to convey the caring, positive self he had successfully projected to so many others.

> *Dear Mrs. Raub,*
>
> *This is an important letter regarding your son, Greg. But, first, let me introduce myself. I am 39, have a wonderful wife Karen, and a beautiful son Jason, who is 4 years old. I have a Master's degree, and for the last 3 years I was an engineering manager at Harris Corp. In November of last year I came across a Charles Manson follower who was in the wrong place at the*

wrong time. I committed adultery with her and, as a result, I wound up in jail.

I met Greg on February 12. On Feb 12, I was praying for someone to come into the cell that I could work with . . . as I finished, Greg was put into the same cell (#210) I was in.

. . . .

Between that time and now, Greg and I became close friends. He introduced me to Denise.

. . . .

Then, this week, agents Leatherow and Fair approached Greg with a "deal" to trade the few days remaining of Greg's sentence for testimony against me! It is conceivable that if he were to give testimony written by Leatherow or others, it could add years to a sentence I may receive.

Somewhere, in the free world, a wonderful woman and our 4 year old son will be deprived of their husband and daddy in a very unjust manner.

I am writing you, as one Christian to another, to ask that you convince Greg to be the Christian he says he is.

May God be with you,
John B. Crutchley

On April 8, Leatherow and Fred Pfeiff met with Patrick Dontell at the Brevard County Jail. Pfeiff had flown down from Virginia to interview Dontell regarding what Crutchley had told him about the Fitzjohn case. After they finished, Pfeiff took a tape recording of the interview with him back to Virginia to share with his supervisors at the Fairfax County Police Department, hoping to convince them to move forward with a case against Crutchley.

The next day, Ronald King, a former trusty at the Brevard County Jail, contacted Leatherow to inform him that, contrary to recent allegations, Gregory Raub and Patrick Dontell had not been planted in Crutchley's cell and were not otherwise working with investigators or the State Attorney's Office when they were placed there.

———

Two weeks after being interviewed by Leatherow and Fair, Dontell sat for a deposition taken by Crutchley's attorney, Joe Mitchell, with the agreement that after providing his deposition testimony, he would be moved to the Seminole County Jail for his protection.

During the deposition, Dontell repeated much of what he had disclosed in his interviews with Leatherow and Fair. He also stressed how confident Crutchley was that he would prevail in the court case concerning Christina Almah.

He told me that there was no way in the world that anybody was going to believe a second-generation Charles Manson child over an engineer from Harris Corporation. And that he had the best attorney money could buy and that he would just tear her apart on the stand. He believed that the charges were going to be thrown out of court and he was going to get an acquittal.

According to Dontell, Crutchley had absolutely no fear of being linked to any unsolved murders or disappearances. After all, as Crutchley had often told him, "a serial killer takes pride in not being caught."

TWENTY-ONE

Dead ends

After taking their depositions and hearing what they were prepared to testify about at trial, Joe Mitchell knew he would need to find a way to keep Patrick Dontell and Greg Raub's testimony from being admissible or, failing that, to discredit them in the eyes of a jury. He was well aware that if their testimony went unchallenged, it could be devastating to Crutchley's defense. He decided that the easiest way to undermine their credibility would be to claim that they were planted in Crutchley's cell by prosecutors to manufacture evidence or otherwise entrap his client.

Taking a preemptive approach, Mitchell told reporters that Raub and Dontell "misrepresented facts to get reduced sentences."

"I'm not saying I have any proof, but it's been known to happen before," he pointed out, insinuating that the State Attorney's Office had a habit of planting snitches in the jailhouse.

Both Raub and Dontell denied under oath that they had received any special consideration or made any deals with prosecutors in exchange for their testimony. To the contrary, Raub testified that he felt compelled to alert investigators about what Crutchley had told him in the jail cell because he had several sisters, and he considered what Crutchley did to Christina Almah to be unforgiveable and outright "sick."

Informed about their testimony, Crutchley claimed that the incriminating statements he had made to Raub and Dontell were just part of a game he orchestrated to make prosecutors and Sheriff's investigators "look like fools." Yet, only a few weeks earlier, while speaking with a reporter from the *Florida Today*, Crutchley referred to Dontell as his "brother" and said that the two of them were so close that he had told Dontell "everything" about himself.

While Joe Mitchell focused on damage control, Leatherow continued working to build a murder case against Crutchley. At a follow-up interview with George Hurley on April 15, Crutchley's former coworker informed Leatherow that Crutchley had an alias, "K.L. Risser," for which he had a separate phone number and listing in the phone book. Leatherow independently verified the phone number and listing, and began investigating potential other uses Crutchley may have had for the alias, but a subsequent state-wide search for safe deposit boxes or storage spaces under the name K.L. Risser turned up nothing. Hurley also claimed that Crutchley told him that he had taken the plastic garbage bag—the one Jackie Horton had described—and thrown it away in a trash can located in the lobby of the Malabar post office. Leatherow doubted that Crutchley had just tossed out his trophies like yesterday's garbage. It did not fit what he knew about Crutchley's personality and flew in the face of what he had learned about serial killers at Quantico. He had a hunch that Crutchley had fed Hurley that story to keep the police off his trail.

The following day, Leatherow visited Fountain Head Cemetery in Palm Bay in search of Crutchley's "burial grounds." He suspected that Crutchley might have resorted to a "double dig": finding a fresh grave where a recently deceased person had been buried, digging up the stillnew dirt, tossing the body of his latest victim in on top of the grave's rightful owner, and then refilling the grave. Aside from that possibility, one particular grave belonging to an Arthur Crutchley attracted Leatherow's interest. Although not related, Leatherow thought that Crutchley might have found it too tempting to forego using Arthur's grave to conceal one of his victims. It seemed just the sort of thing that would appeal to Crutchley's warped mind. He inspected Arthur Crutchley's grave and probed around the ground, but found no indication that it had been disturbed at any time in the preceding months.

While at the cemetery, Leatherow noticed that it had its own crematorium on site. The groundskeeper let Leatherow into the crematorium by sliding a small key into what seemed to be a particularly flimsy lock, and a look at the crematorium's furnace left Leatherow with the impression that it would be simple to operate. The control panel consisted of just three buttons clearly labeled as "on," "ignite," and "off." Leatherow felt certain that someone as clever as Crutchley could have easily entered the crematorium under the cover of night and fired up the furnace to dispose of victims' bodies. The crematorium's mortician assured him that someone would have heard the furnace if it had been operated without authorization, but the remote location of the crematorium raised doubts in Leatherow's mind about the likelihood of anyone hearing the furnace being used.

As he continued moving forward with the investigation, Leatherow began to be haunted by the plastic bag of "paraphernalia" that Crutchley had hidden while out on bond. Though recovering the bag remained a top priority, it seemed to have vanished without a trace.

"We've done everything," a forlorn Leatherow explained. "Air searches, ground searches, water searches, and dog searches. Is it still out there?" he wondered aloud, uncertainty creeping into his voice. "I just don't know."

Part III

UNANSWERED QUESTIONS

TWENTY-TWO

The time has come

I t did not take long for the information provided by Greg Raub and Patrick Dontell to bear fruit. On April 23, at approximately 7:00 p.m., Crutchley signed a negotiated plea agreement at the Brevard County Jail in Titusville, pleading guilty in the Christina Almah case to reduced charges consisting of one count of kidnapping and three counts of sexual battery. In exchange for his guilty plea, prosecutors dropped two counts of sexual battery, two counts of aggravated battery, two counts of robbery (including robbery of blood), and one count for possession of marijuana. State Attorney Norm Wolfinger explained the rationale for dropping the robbery of blood charge, a charge which had only recently been added and which had caused such a media furor.

"We're not here for the bizarre. We're here to put him in jail."

Wolfinger stressed that the plea removed a "very dangerous individual" from the streets, while sparing Christina Almah the trauma of reliving her ordeal by having to testify about the "most bizarre crime" he had ever encountered. He categorized the plea as just being the "tip of the iceberg" since police in Florida and Virginia continued to investigate Crutchley in connection with numerous unsolved homicides. Wolfinger assured reporters that the plea deal would prove to be "only the first chapter in the book about his activity."

And it certainly seemed like there would be more criminal charges to come. Aside from the strong suspicion of Crutchley's involvement with Debbie Fitzjohn's murder, the skeletal remains of four women had been found during an eleven-month period within a six-mile radius of Crutchley's Malabar home. He also had the distinction of being the prime suspect in the disappearance and presumed murder of Patti Volanski. The remains of another woman, forty-year-old Lynn Kay DeSantis, a former employee of Harris Corporation last seen on November 17, 1985, had also been found during the preceding year. However, Leatherow and other investigators ultimately ruled Crutchley out as having killed DeSantis because the cause of her death, severe blunt trauma to the side of the head, did not fit Crutchley's *modus operandi* or criminal profile. Other local unsolved disappearances or murders in which Crutchley served as a suspect included the July 6, 1983 disappearance of Tammy Lynn Leppert, a petite, eighteen-year-old aspiring actress with curly blonde hair, who was last seen at an Exxon gas station near State Road A1A. Leppert disappeared in an area known for prostitution, as did Nancy Kay Brown, who was visiting from California like Christina Almah. Due to the location where they went missing, their abductor may have assumed they were prostitutes, a group Crutchley had developed a preference for targeting as his prey. Crutchley also emerged as a suspect in the 1984 homicide of Cheryl Ann Windsor, a runaway from Orlando, and Diana Lee Casey, who disappeared on May 14, 1984, walking to a convenience store in Canaveral. As always, in each case authorities lacked a smoking gun, that damning piece of evidence to definitively tie Crutchley to the crimes.

Following the formal entry of his guilty plea on April 24, Crutchley held a press conference, despite the repeated objections of his attorney, Joe Mitchell. In the small dining room of the county jail, handcuffed and clad in an orange prison uniform, Crutchley sat behind a table covered with a red-and-white checkered tablecloth. His body looked pasty and pale, but his eyes remained bright and animated.

Crutchley had been following the television reports and newspaper articles about himself and obviously enjoyed the media attention. Before making a statement at the press conference or answering any questions, he turned to one of the reporters in attendance and admonished her, criticizing that every story she had written about his case had "glaring errors." Apparently, he liked being in the media spotlight, but wanted to have a say in telling the story.

Throughout the press conference, Crutchley came across as intelligent, well-spoken, and likeable, but at times his mannerisms and rambling responses suggested that he thought quite highly of himself and sought to manipulate those around him.

Attempting to cast himself in a positive light from the outset of the press conference, Crutchley announced that he had decided to enter into the plea deal primarily to spare the victim from having to endure an emotionally painful trial. He failed to mention that he did not believe he would fare well at trial, particularly in light of the expected testimony of Patrick Dontell and Gregory Raub.

He insisted that Christina Almah's sufferings should be attributed solely to the "old John Crutchley." The man sitting before them now was someone new, someone who had committed atrocities in the past, but who had since cast aside his evil ways and been spiritually and emotionally reborn.

"There's two people named John Crutchley," he maintained. "There's the John Crutchley prior to the last day of November last year, and there's the new John Crutchley who's growing."

Besides, Christina Almah was not the only one to be pitied. He himself had been a victim as well. The old John Crutchley had been led astray by pornography and X-rated adult stores, but he had rid himself of that mindset.

"The old me is dead," he insisted.

Crutchley attributed his brutal crime against Christina to a lack of fulfillment from life, a spiritual emptiness that had persisted in spite of all of the material success that he enjoyed.

"I did everything that everybody said I should," Crutchley remarked. "Everybody told me, 'get yourself a wife and kid, get a pool, you need a Jacuzzi, you need a stereo,' and on and on. But I had no reason to live, none at all."

Feeling that he had reached the end of his rope, Crutchley looked to pornographic magazines to add something meaningful to his life. They were what had fueled his perversely deviant behavior.

Crutchley attempted to convey the allure of the sexually explicit magazines, their offer of excitement to replace the emptiness, their promise of providing purpose and a more fulfilling life.

"Every story starts with 'I felt lost my whole life, so I tried different things . . . until I tried bondage' or 'until I tried whips and chains.' Until I tried all these different things," he explained.

Addressing the fateful day that led to his downfall, he described having seen Christina Almah by the side of the street when he stopped to let a truck turn at Weber Road.

"She was dazed and just standing there," he recalled. "She was lost, she was just lost," he said, his voice taking on the tone and tenor of something akin to pity.

He tried to convey how readily he saw himself in her since they were both spiritually and emotionally hollow. Instead of meaning and contentment, they knew only inanition and hopelessness.

"I know the feeling," Crutchley said somberly, "Nobody wanted anything to do with me. I never knew what it meant to be truly loved."

Crutchley's projection of himself onto Christina continued

during the sexual assaults and bloodletting that followed. In his mind, she had been given exactly what she wanted. In his reconstruction of events, he had been helping her find some twisted degree of affirmation, some strained quantum of happiness.

"Were the tables reversed and I was in her place, I would have wanted it to go on. What happened to her was happening to me at the time."

One reporter confronted Crutchley directly, clearly skeptical of his story.

"Were you going to kill Christina?" he asked.

Crutchley studied him for a moment.

"Let's put it this way. The old person that I was thought I could have."

Another reporter wanted to know how someone as intelligent as Crutchley, who seemed to have so much going for him, had ended up abducting and assaulting a teenaged girl.

"What about people out there who see an obviously well-educated person, a successful person, that ends up like this?" he asked.

Crutchley paused only a second or two before responding.

"It tells them a very big story. It tells them something very important. They look around and say, 'I'm good because I wear a threepiece suit and go to a job.' What they don't realize is that, if they look on each side of them, there's someone else like me, but they don't know it because that person also wears a three-piece suit."

Tears appeared on Crutchley's cheeks as he clutched a small photograph of his four-year-old son, Jason, whom he referred to as a "little kid that doesn't know about being hurt yet." He showed the photo to the group of reporters arrayed in front of him, and told them that he had not understood what it meant to love until recently. He explained that while he was out of jail on bail, Jason had approached him one day and asked for help with tying his shoes. He showed the boy how to do it and then they practiced several times, spending the next twenty or thirty minutes tying and untying the laces. When his son at last tied his shoes without any help, Crutchley marveled at the unabashed joy that he saw on his son's face. As his beaming son excitedly thanked him, Crutchley felt unconditional love for the first time in his life.

Trying to make the reporters understand the epiphany he had experienced, Crutchley continued his narrative of the event. "I looked into his face, and suddenly it was like looking into a mirror. That was my face there, only it was my face thirty-six years ago. It was me as a child."

Notwithstanding this supposedly life-altering event, moments later, in response to additional questioning by the reporters, Crutchley admitted having entertained thoughts about killing his son.

"I never *wanted* to kill him," he asserted, but then added, "I won't say those thoughts weren't there though."

Another reporter asked one of the final questions before two armed deputies ushered Crutchley out of the room.

"Do you think Sheriff's deputies will be able to link you to any other crimes in Brevard County?"

"No, Ma'am," Crutchley quickly replied.

Then, after the slightest of pauses he added, "Because there's no other crimes they can connect me to."

As the two deputies led him out of the room in shackles to be transported back to jail, Crutchley voiced a parting plea to the audience of reporters, beseeching them to get rid of the pornography stores that had so insidiously corrupted him before they led someone else tragically astray.

Two days later, on April 26, a sudden power surge occurred during a systems test at reactor four of the Chernobyl Nuclear Power Plant in Ukraine, Russia. The electrical surge caused an explosion and fire that sent a plume of dangerously radioactive particles high into the atmosphere, where they quickly spread across much of the western part of the Soviet Union, as well as a large segment of Europe. Ranking as the worst nuclear accident in history, the Chernobyl disaster would subsequently be linked to countless premature deaths caused by excessive radiation exposure.

On April 30, Patrick Dontell presented Leatherow a hand-drawn map of Crutchley's house and property, which Dontell claimed Crutchley had prepared and given to him. Dontell told Leatherow that when Crutchley gave him the map, he had hinted that it contained a clue. Crutchley said he would tell him more about it when Dontell called him from Crutchley's house after his release from jail. Dontell had annotated the map with a note:

> *Layout of John's house as drawn by John Crutchley. A few of his trophies are still at the house. He wants me to move them when I arrive at Malabar. He said he threw a clue in the picture and I'll understand later.*

Dontell subsequently passed a polygraph test about the map and what he claimed Crutchley had told him about it.

The same day, Crutchley wrote Ray Malone about why he had decided to enter into a plea deal.

> *Why the plea? Wolfinger added 5 more counts to the list of charges "to bolster the state's case." The chances of an acquittal were almost nil. With any conviction, under the point system of*

guideline sentencing, I would be looking at 40 years to life, and the seized property (car, TV, VCR, computer, etc.) would become the state's property under the RICO Act, and the mess with Jason's custody would continue indefinitely. After previous offers, their best and final plea bargaining offer was 9-12 years and return of all seized property, and dropping all Jason proceedings! Also, the judge can sentence outside that range, with good cause that he is required to state in his sentencing. The prosecutor is going to push hard for life I have been told because I am supposedly "very dangerous"!

   . . . .

It is possible that I may get a very light sentence, or just time served!! Also, historically in Florida, most people who behave have been getting released after doing only 1/3 of their sentence! So, there is hope!!

Hang in there –

John

The day before Crutchley's press conference, Norm Wolfinger, Leatherow, Fair, and nearly a dozen other Sheriff's personnel paid a visit to the old Malabar Cemetery. Located on a small hill beside the railroad tracks off of Malabar Road, and nearly hidden behind overgrown bushes and weeds, the old, neglected cemetery consisted of between one- and two-dozen graves dating back to the 1880s. The cemetery was located less than a fifteen-minute drive from Crutchley's house.

The group spent the better part of a day searching the cemetery grounds for fresh dirt or any other signs suggesting a disturbance of the graves. Although they were all grown men far removed from childhood fears of ghosts, more than one of them found it a bit spooky wandering through the graveyard, particularly when the sun began to set. By nightfall, they had probed around several suspicious graves, but unearthed nothing of value to the case. Rather than digging in the growing darkness, they decided to return the next day to continue their efforts.

On May 2, they came back and dug up two of the graves that looked to have been subjected to the most tampering, but the only thing they unearthed was a metal jewelry box that Fair coyly planted for Leatherow as a practical joke. When Leatherow went on a coffee run, Fair buried the metal box about four feet in the ground next to a faded tombstone encircled by a decayed wooden fence in the oldest section of the cemetery. After Leatherow returned, coffees and Danish pastries in hand, Norm Wolfinger suggested that he dig over by the old tombstone inside the wooden fence.

Leatherow dug for ten or fifteen minutes before making his discovery. When his shovel clanged against the top of the buried metal box, Leatherow felt a surge of adrenaline and hollered for his colleagues to come quickly, thinking that he had made the discovery that would help crack the case. Standing in a hole up to his chest, Leatherow reached excitedly down and pulled out the box like a kid finding buried treasure, eager to see what he had discovered. But when he pried open the metal lid, all he found inside was a piece of paper with a simple poem: *Dear Bobalouie, I wanted you to know that I did it. I killed them all, but you'll never catch me. Love you always, John Brennan Crutchley*. When he realized what had happened, Leatherow grabbed his shovel and chased after Fair, half-wanting to bash him in the head.

Although initially a bit miffed by Fair's practical joke at his expense, Leatherow shared his twisted sense of humor and eventually managed a laugh over his own unbridled eagerness. If nothing else, the prank had temporarily lifted the spirits of the group. But as darkness fell, the disappointed investigators departed without having found anything of relevance to the case.

Later that month, Norm Wolfinger wrote to the Director of the FBI, requesting that Special Agent Robert Ressler be permitted to appear and testify at Crutchley's sentencing hearing. As a result of his plea, Crutchley faced a maximum sentence of seventeen years in prison under the Florida sentencing guidelines in effect at the time, but Wolfinger wanted more. He planned on asking the court for a much longer prison term for Crutchley, and Ressler's testimony would be vital to support the imposition of an enhanced sentence.

As the date of his sentencing hearing loomed, Crutchley continued to enjoy his celebrity status, referring to himself as "Count Malabar" in conversations with other jail inmates, and relishing his popularity when touring groups of high school students or other curious jailhouse visitors ranked seeing him as their top request.

On December 14, Doctor David Greenblum conducted a psychiatric evaluation of Crutchley at the request of his attorney. Just prior to his examination of Crutchley, Dr. Greenblum interviewed Crutchley's wife, Karen, who advised that her husband had always been "a little weird," that he "never communicated his feelings," and that he had been "chronically depressed for years." During his evaluation of Crutchley, Greenblum noted that he "displayed no increase or decrease in psychomotor activity," maintained excellent eye contact, and spoke clearly and coherently. Crutchley described in great detail his abduction and sexual assault of Christina Almah, and Dr. Greenblum concluded that he was well aware of the wrongfulness of his actions at the time he committed the crime. However, Crutchley placed the blame for his behavior on the victim, claiming that she wanted a man to "take her" and do something "bizarre." Yet, he explained to Greenblum that he put masking tape over

Christina's eyes during the event because he felt like they were "drilling into the very bowels of his mind."

As the evaluation continued, Dr. Greenblum learned that Crutchley had seen a psychiatrist as a child, but he could not remember, or pretended not to remember, the reasons for receiving psychiatric treatment. Crutchley had suffered from severe depression in 1978— coinciding with Debbie Fitzjohn's disappearance— and had seen a pastoral counselor for several months during that time period. Crutchley also disclosed to Greenblum that he had been "fascinated with Satanism" since at least 1984 and that he had been plagued by "horrible dreams of a homosexual nature."

As a primary diagnosis in his efforts to penetrate Crutchley's personality, Dr. Greenblum found that Crutchley suffered from Sexual Sadism, largely because he provided a "long history" of fantasies that centered around inflicting psychological or physical suffering in order to achieve sexual excitement. Greenblum pointed to Crutchley's recurring tendency to blame the victim as further support for his diagnosis. He strongly recommended that Crutchley receive ongoing psychiatric treatment.

Dr. Greenblum's recommendation was exactly what Joe Mitchell wanted. He planned to ask the court for a reduced sentence due to the adverse influence of his client's abnormal psychological state. He would suggest that a relatively short stay at a state treatment facility could be the best way to rehabilitate Crutchley and exorcise the Vampire Rapist's inner demons.

TWENTY-THREE

Another sin
_____

U nder Florida's standard sentencing guidelines, Crutchley
faced between twelve and seventeen years in prison. Prosecutors filed papers with the court requesting that Judge Antoon
impose a sentence exceeding the guideline range, while Joe
Mitchell asserted that his client should be sentenced at the bottom
of the range or below due to the psychological problems underlying
his deviant behavior. Mitchell urged the judge to place Crutchley in
a facility designed to treat mentally disordered sex offenders, citing
Crutchley's emotionally and psychologically damaging childhood,
and a subconscious need for increased sexual stimulation, as key
factors driving his behavior. A written submission from criminologist Cloud Miller, hired by Mitchell on behalf of his client, echoed
the need for professional help, describing Crutchley's psychological
condition as "very disturbed."

The sentencing hearing in the case of *State of Florida vs. John
Brennan Crutchley* went forward on June 16, 1986. Leatherow
appeared in court as a prosecution witness and testified as to the
facts surrounding Crutchley's abduction and sexual assault of
Christina Almah, including details about the ghoulish blood

draining and drinking that had earned him his infamous nickname. Leatherow also testified about the facts of Crutchley's arrest and the incriminating evidence that had been recovered from his home and office.

The state also called Greg Raub as a fact witness. Raub testified about what Crutchley had told him during their time together in Cell 210, including Crutchley's statements that Christina would have died if he had taken any more of her blood and that if she had not escaped when she did, she would never have left the house alive. For reasons unknown, the prosecution did not call Patrick Dontell to testify.

The principal witness for the state was Robert Ressler, who appeared upon the personal request of State Attorney Norm Wolfinger. Ressler's lengthy and distinguished career focused on studying and predicting the traits of serial killers, and along with his colleagues at the FBI Academy, he had pioneered the art of profiling serial killers. Indeed, Ressler was so immersed in the study of serial homicide that it was he who had first coined the term "serial killer."

Early in Ressler's testimony, Joe Mitchell challenged his credentials, contending that the strange case of the Vampire Rapist was so extraordinary that Ressler could not legitimately claim to be an expert about the issues involved in it. As Ressler recounted several years later in his book, *Whoever Fights Monsters*, Mitchell asked him how many blood-drinking cases he had seen.

I gazed toward the ceiling for a moment and counted them in my mind before saying, "Oh, a half-dozen." People in the courtroom gasped . . . After that demonstration of my experience, I had smooth sailing.

Mitchell would later admit that he was impressed with the depth of Ressler's knowledge and his extensive experience.

Ressler described his area of expertise as criminal psychology and abnormal criminal behavior. He explained that he had been involved in criminal profiling since the early 1970s, and that the Behavior Science Unit he headed at the FBI studied crime scenes, using them to identify predictable characteristics of the criminals who committed the crimes. He had assisted in the investigations of some of the country's most notorious serial killers and spent hours interviewing incarcerated offenders such as Charles Manson, Ted Bundy, David Berkowitz, John Gacy, Edmund Kemper, and Richard Trenton, the Vampire of Sacramento.

Ressler testified that based on his experience Crutchley fit many of the characteristics of a serial killer categorized as an organized sexual offender, including (1) having average to above average intelligence (in Crutchley's case, *well* above average); (2) being socially competent and able to pass himself off as "normal" to society; (3) preferring skilled work; (4) experiencing inconsistent childhood discipline; (5) being married or living with a partner; (6) having mobility in finding victims; (7) frequently changing jobs or moving from areas where he committed crimes; and (8) following his crimes in the news media.

According to Ressler, Crutchley's match with the serial killer profile continued with respect to the traits of an organized serial offender's crime scene, as he: (a) planned his offenses; (b) typically targeted strangers as victims; (c) controlled the conversation and manipulated his victims to get them to vulnerable positions; (d) remained in control throughout his offenses; (e) demanded submissive victims and used restraints such as handcuffs and shackles to ensure his control over them; (f) transported and concealed his victims' bodies; and (g) hid weapons or key evidence used in his crimes.

Crutchley fit into the sexual psychopath category, Ressler claimed, because he exhibited characteristics of someone lacking a basic capacity for human empathy. Due to the defensive emotional detachment of his childhood, the biological circuits of Crutchley's brain failed to form the neural connections in his frontal lobe necessary to experience empathy. Instead of experiencing emotions or sharing sentiments of sympathy with individuals suffering misfortunes, he learned to fake sadness, compassion, and other emphatic feelings. In short, he had learned how to fake being human.

"A psychopath is basically a person with incomplete personality," Ressler explained in connection with his assessment of Crutchley. "They are devoid of super ego or conscience development. They have very little in the way of guilt, or remorse. They feel no responsibility to society. They tend to be, even in adult life, on the level with an immature teenager, adolescent in their state of mind."

Ressler continued by discussing how sexual psychopaths constitute the most dangerous types of sexual offenders, and he cited Edmund Kemper and Ted Bundy as recent examples. Asked to elaborate on what he meant by an "organized sexual offender," Ressler provided a description that could be readily applied to Crutchley.

> The organized offender would be an individual who has good intelligence, is bright, articulate, frequently holding good employment, able to deal with people, is a social outgoing type person, an extrovert, pretty good ego, very selfcentered, the type of person that can socialize in the community group.
>
> He could also maintain relationships with family, friends, and could be married . . . They can be sexually confident, they can be people who can handle themselves to the point of not bringing undue attention to themselves because of their appearance and their behavior within society; and, yet they have the capability of involving themselves in some rather bizarre sexual activity, some that include homicidal behavior.

The organized sexual offender would typically choose a stranger as his victim, rather than targeting someone he knew, Ressler explained, and being in control of the victim and the situation would be an essential part of the offense.

"The organized offender is very, very reliant on control and being dominant over his victim," Ressler asserted. "This is oftentimes reflected in the way the victim is controlled and restrained," he continued, "and frequently the person is freely interested in bondage and other elements of sadism like this particular activity."

However, unlike a true sadist, Ressler opined that Crutchley did not get sexual gratification primarily from inflicting suffering on nonconsenting sex partners.

"I don't think Crutchley derived as much pleasure from the pain as he did from treating the person as an object, which has far more serious implications. He was much more complicated than a sadist."

In conveying Crutchley's psychological state, Ressler painted a picture of an individual controlled by an indescribable emptiness. It consumed his thoughts, directed his behavior, and dictated his actions. For him, the need to kill had become as natural as the need to breathe. Only when he wielded absolute control over the life of another human being did he feel a sense of fulfillment, only then did he find relief from the emotional vacuum and boundless psychological abyss. But the relief never lasted long. The comforting sensation was always transitory. The emptiness always returned.

Ressler pointed out that an organized offender like Crutchley often kept mementos of his victims, small souvenirs such as jewelry, articles of clothing, or other personal items that have "considerable fantasy value" because they allow the offender to relive the experience and enjoy the kill over and over again. The souvenirs ultimately become "trophies of a sort."

Ressler also offered insight for Crutchley's insistence that the old John Crutchley was gone.

"This type of offender is very, very quick to come up with rationalizations and reasons why the person that is in court today or arrested today is a new person," he explained. "The rationalization that the behavior and crime is in the past, things of this nature, are very frequent for this type of offender."

He testified that Crutchley's contentions about Christina Almah willingly participating in the rape and bloodletting were not surprising. "That's a very clear pattern of testimony of the offender, saying that the victim really liked it, asked for it, really enjoyed it. And the victim would even come back for more because they liked it and found it so exciting. I've seen that [claimed] many times in many cases," Ressler attested.

Crutchley's claim that pornography should be blamed for his behavior also came as no surprise to Ressler.

"One of the characteristics of your psychopath is that they transfer the blame," he explained. "That goes back to early childhood, where they don't accept blame and they don't operate as an adult. They deflect the blame to all the people around them, society, institutions, et cetera."

In response to Norm Wolfinger's inquiry about Crutchley's belief that he was smarter than the police, Ressler elaborated how organized serial killers typically believe themselves to be above the law.

> Offenders of this particular category, the organized sexual psychopath, have grossly inflated their egos, and associated with that is often a high level of intelligence and perception, and they feel that they are above the law. This is the basis of feeling that they are somewhat untouchable and that the rules of society do not apply to them directly.
>
> Some of the things that they do in private may be harmless. But once the act is committed and they have stepped across the line where they actually act out their fantasies and their long term ideas, then that becomes very much a danger to society because now they have put themselves above the law and the police and they really believe themselves to be extremely clever, and they oftentimes are so.

As for Crutchley's disturbing taste for drinking his victims' blood, Ressler testified how that type of bizarre practice is usually engaged in by "your more psychotic individuals." He asserted that similarly repulsive behavior had occurred throughout history, but that without a modern understanding of psychological diseases of the mind, that type of unexplainable and repugnant behavior would have typically been attributed to supernatural sources such as vampires and werewolves.

Although Crutchley had attempted to place the blame for his behavior on pornography and drugs, Ressler rejected such excuses. According to Ressler, the "creation of people like Crutchley begins in early childhood," and Crutchley fits the classic case of a serial killer whose sexual violence has been caused by a confused past of sexual frustrations. Moreover, his history of physical and emotional abuse, including being forced by his mother to dress as a girl until he was five years old, had undoubtedly caused him permanent emotional and psychological problems that festered and worsened over time. He internalized inconsistent responses to important individuals and events in his life. For instance, at the same time that he developed resentment and hatred for his mother due to her emotional abuse and physical punishments, he also identified with her as the person in a position of power, a process of identification that fueled a life long need for wielding power and control.

In considering Joe Mitchell's suggestion of psychiatric treatment for Crutchley, Judge Antoon asked Ressler about the possibility of rehabilitating organized sexual offenders.

"My opinion," Ressler responded, "and I am speaking after some twenty years of experience, is that they are probably the lowest category for rehabilitative effort. They have resistant traits."

Ressler also elaborated about how the sexual fantasies of someone like Crutchley can evolve to the point that the person becomes a recurring sexual offender.

The pattern begins in preadolescence where there is a nonsupportive family environment or a lack of love in the home, and it continues to develop in the preteen years if the individual becomes socially isolated and introverted.

We find that the person is not being socialized properly to the point of being integrated within the adolescent communities and high school, and we find these fantasies to have taken a rather sadistic and dangerous turn.

About this time the person is into his later adolescence or early adulthood, a period where the fantasy development becomes extremely bizarre . . . where the person has stepped across the line and acted out his unusual fantasies by actually committing an offense, be it a minor, a medium, or a homicidal offense.

What we find here is that if the person is not apprehended or controlled by society, that does not satisfy him, and it becomes . . . a spiral of behavior, where they're getting away with the crime, getting to feel this omnipotence and self important, self-prized, and this fuels their fantasies and enhances the fantasies.

The fantasies then lead to other overt acts, and if they get away with it again or a second time, the pattern is repeated and then what we find is that oftentimes that is when you find a serial offender.

It is through this escalating pattern of deviant fantasy enactment, Ressler explained, that the organized sexual offender frequently becomes a repeat offender or serial killer despite knowing that what they are doing is morally reprehensible and against the law. According to Ressler's psychological assessment, Crutchley's encounter with Christina Almah simply constituted the latest episode of his experimentation. He would keep trying to find the most satisfying way, re-enacting and escalating his behavior, altering his approach until he could get it right. He had evolved into a calculating, lethal predator, compelled to hunt his prey with the same cold-blooded resolve as the primordial creatures stalking Florida's swamps in the black of the night.

Ressler did not find Dr. Greenblum's diagnosis of Crutchley as a sexual sadist to be adequate, opining that psychiatrists and psychologists without forensic expertise "are almost disabled in interviewing people like Mr. Crutchley."

After Ressler's lengthy testimony, Doctor Ronald Stern took the stand and testified that two-and-a-half quarts of Christina Almah's blood had been drained during her captivity. Dr. Stern opined that losing such a large amount of blood, nearly one-half of her body's total blood volume, would have killed her within 12 hours if she had not escaped and received urgent medical attention.

TWENTY-FOUR

What lurks behind the mask

The courtroom filled close to capacity for Crutchley's much-anticipated testimony. Everyone wanted to see and hear the infamous Vampire. As the time neared, the audience of onlookers assembled in the courtroom whispered anxiously among themselves, their excitement steadily building. The air was electric as they waited for the star of the show to arrive. At last he appeared, like the long-awaited headlining act of the concert of the century. He smiled when he saw the crowd. He was ready to perform. Wearing a blue, three-piece suit, Crutchley swore to tell the truth, the whole truth, and nothing but the truth, and then he settled into the witness chair.

After a prompt from his attorney, Crutchley began a lengthy narrative testimony, starting with a defense of his own character in an attempt to mitigate the prosecution's portrayal of him as a blood-thirsty monster.

Judge Antoon noted that Crutchley projected an "uncanny confidence" in the courtroom. He spoke confidently and seemed "boldly self-assured."

"I've had no trouble adhering to the rules of society," Crutchley told the judge and packed courtroom of onlookers. "I've been an exemplary citizen of this county for three or four years now that I've lived here. As a matter of fact, I have been so much of an exemplary citizen that I was asked to run for Mayor in the Town of Malabar."

But he admitted that underneath his "good citizen" façade, he felt utterly miserable. Despite having achieved considerable material success, he did not enjoy it. He wore the mask of a happy, well-adjusted professional and family man, but just below the surface lurked the real John Crutchley, fundamentally unhappy and bored with life, leading a hollow existence, "very lonely, very selfish, and very self-centered." Although he looked debonair and content, mimicking the motions of a happy and successful human being, in reality he found life to be stale and largely devoid of meaning. Where others felt satisfaction or contentment, he knew only moral and emotional emptiness that manifested as an overbearing feeling of hunger.

"In a technological world, I could solve any kind of computer problem and I had gotten everything that people said I should have, and I still wasn't happy."

Leading a "Godless life," he found everything "frustrating" and every day pointless and "boring." He could not escape the corrosive belief that "there was nothing to life for me then." There was always something missing, something not quite right, like a permanently lost piece of a puzzle.

Crutchley described an existence that had become increasingly isolated and self-absorbed. Communication with his wife had deteriorated to the point of being virtually non-existent, and when seized by one of his spiraling bouts of depression, he would go for a ride on his motorcycle or a solitary drive in the car to try to clear his mind.

"If it was raining or dark outside, I'd go and get in the car and drive and just unwind some of the frustration."

His words left many wondering whether his means of releasing frustration included hunting the local roads for potential prey.

Work, he claimed, had been the only thing keeping him from acting on his relentless thoughts of suicide. He had started a major computer project at Harris shortly before the incident with Christina Almah and he wanted to see it through to completion. But he claimed that he had made up his mind to bleed himself to death using the same surgical needles that he subsequently used on Christina Almah. In fact, he had recently drained two or three pints of his own blood to see what the process of dying would feel like.

Then he recounted how he had come across Christina on November 21, 1985.

> I was heading home to pick up a notebook. I didn't just pick her up. A white truck had stopped in front of me to make a turn. It was a rainy day and I was driving the car. It was sprinkling that day, and I asked the girl, do you need any help. She was standing at an intersection, and she just stepped into the car without saying where can you take me or whatever.

He had not been looking for someone like Christina, but "she had fallen into [his] world." At the time, he had been a compulsive reader of the pornographic magazine, *Variations*, which featured articles about extreme sexual fantasies. When he came across Christina, it seemed like a fantasy turned reality, manifested before him in the form of flesh and blood.

"The situation here, I had a girl who wanted to be taken and I had some time and it was like I was walking into one of those fantasies," he said.

When Christina told him that she wanted to do something kinky, he remembered having seen a videotape a week or so prior at the rental store entitled "Dracula Meets the Vampire." The memory of the images in that videotape sparked an irresistible impulse to reenact them and improve upon them, igniting an irrepressible desire to replace the banal drudgery of day-to-day life with more fulfilling fantasy.

"The vampire thing kind of popped into my mind," he explained. "I was not getting any sexual gratification whatsoever from the girl. It was like a nightmare. It wasn't like a videotape at all. The girl was not fighting, she wasn't saying stop; she wasn't screaming, she was just complacently laying there and quite obviously it was very disgusting."

The fantasy had failed to fulfill his erotic expectations, shattering like brittle crystal against the rock-hard inadequacy of reality.

Crutchley's testimony rambled on at times, and like the damned in Dante's *Inferno* forever blind to the depravity of their deeds, he refused to acknowledge any responsibility for his actions. Instead, he blamed the kidnapping and sexual assault of Christina Almah on the "lack of parental love" of his emotionally distant and unavailable parents as well as the difficulties at home with his wife and son. To top it off, he claimed that Christina had asked him to drain her blood and had insisted that she wanted him to be rough with her.

Confused by Crutchley's claim that Christina had been a willing participant in the dreadful ordeal that she had endured, Judge Antoon asked Crutchley why he had put her in the bathtub, handcuffed and shackled. Having anticipated the question, Crutchley had an inventive, if not necessarily believable, answer at the ready.

"The reason why she was in the bathtub was that she said she had a weak bladder and had to urinate a lot," Crutchley replied, "and she suggested, 'how about tying me up in the bathtub?' So that's what we did."

The frown on the judge's face conveyed his obvious skepticism. When the judge asked why Christina—if she was really there of her own free will—had crawled through the bathroom window to leave, rather than simply opening the door and walking out, Crutchley had an equally imaginative explanation.

We had a cat at the time, and she was making some noise and Christina anticipated that it was somebody else in the house. So I just let her fantasy play with that, and I said, "Well, I won't let anybody bother you. Just stay in the bathroom," I said, or something like that.

I also said something about having a brother. I just said, "My brother won't come in and bother you."

She said, "Don't let anybody see me, don't let anyone else touch me." She didn't want anybody else to be with her. She was very intense about that. So, in her mind there was somebody else in the house, so that's why she went out the window.

Consistent with the narrative he had been developing throughout his incarceration, Crutchley made a concerted effort to emphasize his religious conversion while in jail.

I was brought into the jail across the street and eventually they put me in cell number 204. I thought about hanging myself. I went so far as to even pull the shoestrings out of my shoes.

As I went to tie the strings around the bars, there was a bible there and I don't want to mention the bible or anything. I don't want anybody thinking I'm looking for an out, because that's not it. It gave me pause; it bothered me, and I didn't do what I had planned to do that night.

George Hurley, a very close friend of our family called up and wanted to see me, and they took me over to Cell 210 for visitation on a Saturday morning, November 30th. It was very vivid to me because there was a fellow there by the name of Jackie Lee Horton. He was a very spiritual kind of fellow and he explained what salvation was all about, and he answered what I didn't understand in the bible on that.

He continued the story of his spiritual renewal and rebirth by recounting how he had begun exploring the church after getting out of jail on bail.

> During the time I was out, the total of five weeks, I visited the Victory Christian Center, the Baptist Church, the Port Malabar Church of God, and the Way of Life Church up here. I had certainly felt for the first time that I had a place, that people were accepting me, that I was getting accepted.

In addition to describing his religious awakening, Crutchley testified about the emotional epiphany that he experienced on January 9 as a result of a memorable interaction with his son.

> I had never paid any attention to my child other than to make sure that he had food, diapers and those kinds of things. Well, the 9th of January, that morning he came to me and he asked me to tie his shoes for him. I taught him how to tie his shoes, and that child was 100 percent attentive, and he actually, at four years old, he actually learned to tie one of his shoes and tied it by himself.
>
> Then he stood up and he hugged me, and he said, "Daddy, I like you. Thank you."
>
> Judge, that was the first time the child had ever said that he liked me.

Tears appeared on Crutchley's cheeks as he continued.

"I looked at him and saw myself in his eyes. I looked in his eyes and they were my eyes, exactly. I realized here was a little four-yearold miniature of me."

This singular event, Crutchley claimed, amounted to the first time he had really felt what it meant to be loved.

While his spiritual and emotional regeneration had given him a new outlook on life, he realized that he needed healing in another area as well. He sought psychiatric help in Melbourne and Palm

Bay, and had his first appointment scheduled for January 10. However, on the January 9, Joe Mitchell called and told him that he had to turn himself in because his bond had been revoked.

Nevertheless, the new insights into his condition did not end after he turned himself in. Following his return to the Brevard County Jail, he had been given a copy of the book, *The Peter Pan Syndrome*, which he read voraciously, describing it as a "chillingly accurate portrayal of John Crutchley." Written by psychologist Dr. Dan Kiley, the book identified a typical individual suffering from the syndrome as a married, middle-aged man with steady employment and children, but clouded by a "bland despair that makes life dull and repetitious." The afflicted individual suffers from a myriad of psychological issues, including emotional paralysis, magical thinking, mother hangup, father hangup, and sexual hangup. The mother hangup involves anger and guilt that cause overwhelming ambivalence toward the individual's mother; the individual wants to pull free from the mother's influence, but feels guilty every time he tries. The father hangup concerns a feeling of estrangement from the individual's father; he wants to be close to his father, but is convinced that he can never receive the father's love or approval. The sexual hangup denotes a condition in which the individual's social impotence carries over into the sexual arena. During his teenage years, he is unable to attract a girlfriend despite desperate attempts to do so, and he typically remains a virgin until his early twenties. When he at last loses his virginity, he begins having sex with numerous partners to prove that he is sexually potent, but because of his sexual hang-up, he tends to become overly attached to the objects of his affection and he needs a partner that will be wholly dependent on him.

After reading the book, Crutchley diagnosed himself as suffering from the Peter Pan Syndrome. His social, emotional, and psychological conditions seemed to fit squarely within the parameters delineated in the text. Focusing in particular on the syndrome's symptoms manifesting as the mother and father hangups, Crutchley testified about the lack of parental love and affection during his childhood.

> Something that upsets me very intensely is when I look at my own self and know that I didn't even relate to people, not in my marriage and not to my parents.
>
> I was brought up to reject any open display of affection for male children, because it would weaken you.
>
> My father was a man that never did anything with me. I hated the man intensely until January of this year, until what happened with my son happened.

He continued to blame his parents for the situation he now found himself in. If he had been cast as a monster, his parents had played the essential contributing role of Victor Frankenstein.

In concluding his prepared testimony, Crutchley expressed regret at what Christina Almah had gone through and reiterated his belief that the two of them had been condemned to a similar existence of isolation and silent despair, tormented by the same feelings of senseless discomfort and inexplicable hopelessness. He called the sexual events with Christina Almah a "nightmarish thing."

Comparing Christina's clouded, confused state of mind to his own, Crutchley remarked, "I feel that she was lost in her own world. She told me that she was one of Charles Manson's followers. There is a lot of John Crutchley in her and quite frankly, I would like to sit down with her, but I understand that she is afraid of seeing me."

Asked to explain how he had first become involved in sexual bondage, Crutchley testified that Kathy Moseley, a "lost soul" as "self-centred" and "Godless" as himself, had introduced him to it shortly before he met his wife. During cross-examination by Norm Wolfinger, Crutchley emphasized how the "old John Crutchley," the one who had abducted Christina, had been destroyed and replaced by the spiritually reborn Crutchley, saved by the grace of his newfound Christian faith. He insisted that his new "ultimate dream" had nothing to do with sex or matters of the flesh, and instead centered on the spiritual desire to "talk with God."

But then he testified about his grave disappointment in the experience with Christina because she had never struggled or resisted and did not become sexually excited during the rapes. He could not understand why she had not been writhing in ecstasy as he had fantasized she would.

"So this young lady, this nineteen-year old girl, did not get aroused by the fact that you were taking her blood out and choking her?" Wolfinger asked.

"No, she just laid there as limp as a dishrag. I felt at that time up until the point where she said, 'ouch,' she was much like an object in my world."

"So, in rape you perceive the woman as enjoying it, right?" Wolfinger inquired.

"Yes, or at least there is some stimulation there. She was just lying there," Crutchley answered, apparently still bewildered by Christina's unresponsiveness throughout the encounter.

"So, this girl's being raped and she didn't enjoy it one bit, is that right?" Wolfinger continued.

"She was not very responsive, not one bit responsive. Whether she did or did not enjoy herself, she was just lying there."

Throughout the sexual assaults and blood taking, Crutchley had projected his own urges onto Christina and he believed that she willingly participated in what he did to her, that his fantasy merely reflected her own deeply rooted desires.

He admitted taking her blood on two separate occasions while he held her captive and he acknowledged that he had drunk her blood by sucking it out of her veins through surgical tubing. But he reiterated that the idea for drinking her blood had been implanted in his mind by a video he saw that showed "a guy biting people's necks and stuff like that." And he denied that he had ever drunk his wife's blood. When Wolfinger asked him why he told Agent Leatherow that he drank his wife's blood and had done so "hundreds of times," Crutchley had another ready-made response.

"For all intents and purposes, my life was over and I just wanted to get attention," he maintained. "I was just saying that, I was just babbling."

Wolfinger switched gears in his line of questioning to ask Crutchley why he had removed all of the identifying labels and lettering from his car. Crutchley testified that the various decals had corroded shortly after he purchased the car, so he had simply peeled them off.

"They looked so much nicer without the lettering on it, he explained, "and I happen to like things plain and simple."

In concluding his cross-examination, Wolfinger wanted to know why Crutchley had kept Christina's driver's license.

"Was it a souvenir, John?"

"Perhaps," Crutchley answered faintly, almost too inaudibly to hear.

"What about her wallet?"

"I guess I concede that is a souvenir or souvenir material," Crutchley replied.

He continued to insist that prosecutors and law enforcement were out to get him simply because of the notoriety of his case.

"They have a lot of unsolved crimes on their hands and no leads on any of them. Here's a chance for them to make a name for themselves."

Careful to maintain eye contact with the judge, Crutchley belabored his claim that poor judgment and bad decisions, and not any malevolent intentions or evil deeds, had led to his current condition.

"I picked up hitchhikers. I would get involved with people who put themselves in a high danger area. It was inevitable that when one of them died everyone would blame me."

Karen sat behind her husband throughout the over six-hour sentencing hearing, occasionally exchanging smiles with him, but never testifying on his behalf. She had been ready to testify in his defense, but then refused after hearing him detail their sexual practices to a packed courtroom. Like Mitchell, she had tried to talk Crutchley out of testifying, but he was adamant in wanting to take the stand. To appease her, Crutchley had agreed to limit the scope of his testimony and to keep it concise, but once on the stand, he felt compelled to tell his story, and did so for close to two hours.

During a recess in the hearing, Greg Raub, Crutchley's former cellmate, reiterated to reporters his belief that Crutchley suffered from a psychopathic personality and needed professional medical treatment. "He needs to go to the proper institution. I think he can be helped.

It's certainly worth a try."

Shortly before his sentencing date, Crutchley discussed his connection to Patti Volanski with a reporter from the local newspaper, the *Florida Today*. Crutchley admitted having given Volanski a ride on the day she disappeared, but claimed that he had asked her to get out of the car after about fifteen minutes.

"She got in the car and started talking about some motorcycle gang or getting into a fight with a motorcycle gang," Crutchley maintained. "She started asking me if I had any alcohol or drugs and started coming on to me real heavy duty. I stopped the car and told her to get out."

Crutchley said that he found Patti's wallet lying in the front seat of his car the next day. Not sure what to do with it, he took the wallet to his office, emptied out its contents, and threw it away. He wrapped Patti's identification cards in a plastic sandwich bag, put them in his desk drawer, and then subsequently forgot about them. However, under heated questioning, he could not explain why he took the wallet to his office in the first place or why he had thrown the wallet away after concealing its contents.

Crutchley also repeated the refrain that his five months in jail had utterly forged a new man. "The old John Crutchley, the one everyone wants to read about and talk to, is gone. He's dead. I killed him."

Although she decided not to testify at the trial, Karen expressed hope that her husband would get a lenient sentence. She felt sure that the police were being overzealous in their investigation of him. After all, the John Crutchley she knew had never been violent. Yes, his sexual tastes could be bizarre, and perhaps he seemed a bit eccentric at times, but she could not believe that he would ever intentionally harm anyone, and he certainly was not the psychopath the police and newspapers kept suggesting. When asked about Crutchley's statement to police that he had withdrawn her blood and drank it "hundreds of times," Karen claimed that her husband simply did not tell the truth.

"I've never seen him withdraw blood," she said adamantly. "He may have made that statement to exonerate himself or to try to be smart or fresh."

Karen asserted that a man with such a "brilliant mind" should not be shut away from society in a state prison. She assured reporters that her husband was no rapist or serial killer. He was, she said, "just a kinky sort of guy."

On June 22, Crutchley's attorney submitted a post-hearing Sentencing Memorandum to the judge, arguing that multiple mitigating factors, including the psychological conditions that Crutchley suffered from, supported a sentence at the bottom of the twelve- to seventeen-year sentencing guidelines. The memorandum cited excerpts of an interview with Walter Bennett, a co-worker of Crutchley's at TRW, who stated that Crutchley had always been "friendly, extroverted, and happy-go-lucky," never exhibiting "any type of behavioral problems" and always coming across as "mild-mannered" and "totally nonaggressive." Bennett added that he had gone to dinner with Crutchley shortly before his arrest and that "nothing seemed to be out of the ordinary." The memorandum attached several character reference letters as well, including one from Crutchley's father and one each from Ray Malone and Lisa Baker.

A letter from Crutchley himself, addressing the entire Brevard County community, served as the final attachment to the sentencing memorandum. In the letter, Crutchley continued to cast the blame for his behavior on external causes, including "pains of my childhood long forgotten" and the "path of neglect I had traveled." And he claimed that the circumstances giving rise to the depraved acts caused by his "emptiness and pain" should not be construed as a freak event. To the contrary, countless other individuals shared his baneful outlook on life, suffering the same state of emotional sterility and psychological malaise.

Dear friends and neighbors,

You remember my name because of the Vampire Rape stories. I have some answers to your questions. Will it happen again? Yes – by people who are well known and liked. It is not likely you will ever hear "vampire" associated with them. It will happen everywhere. Why? Please read on.

As a child my friends' dads played with and hugged them. My father never even played ball. They felt loved and important. I did not. I hated him because of it, but kept it to myself. Likewise, I resented my mother . . . no hugs or affection from her either.

. . . .

By this past year my 20 year engineering career allowed me to buy everything that people said I needed for happiness in life. I even had an attractive wife and beautiful child that people said would bring happiness. Outside, I learned to project a happy image to be socially acceptable. Inside I was selfish, self-centered, Godless, and miserable.

. . . .

My ever growing annoyance with life was also coming to a head. After my arrest, I was sure that the end of my pain was near at hand. My emotions and self-control let go completely. I no longer cared about what happened to me. The events of the following months would fill a book.

. . . .

Back in jail a forensic psychologist gave me a paperback book, "The Peter Pan Syndrome" by Dr. Dan Kiley. I read it. It hurt a lot because it described my hurt exactly and gave reasons and a name for it: affection understanding. I had never shared warm human affection.

. . . .

The book sums it up: "He's fun, charming, very often successful. But in a relationship he's frustrating, emotionally immature, and unable to handle love or responsibility. And he's heading for a crisis."

There are a lot more John Crutchleys around you than you think.

TWENTY-FIVE

Nothing of justice

Evil men understand nothing of justice
But those who seek the Lord understand all

\- Proverbs 28:5

On June 23, after considering the witness testimony and the parties' post-hearing written submissions, Circuit Judge John Antoon deemed Crutchley more monster than man, a creature in need of a cage. To protect the public, he sentenced Crutchley to 25 years in state prison. As grounds for exceeding the 12 to 17-year sentencing guidelines, Judge Antoon noted the grotesque nature of the crime, calling the recommended sentence inadequate for such "bizarre and outrageous" behavior that clearly demonstrated an "utter disregard for life." The judge also cited the severe physical and mental injuries to the victim, Crutchley's premeditation and excessive brutality in committing the crime, and the vulnerability of the victim throughout the crime due to her incapacitation and unconsciousness from the repeated choking and bloodletting.

In announcing the augmented sentence, the judge concluded that

Crutchley had "offered only transparent excuses and vague explanations" for his behavior. Furthermore, his crimes were not just crimes against Christina Almah, but "crimes against humanity."

In addition to a 25-year prison sentence, the judge imposed 15 years of probation for the second sexual battery count, 15 years' probation for the third sexual battery count, and 20 years' probation for the kidnapping count.

Crutchley sat stone-faced and silent as Judge Antoon recited the terms of his sentence. Remaining calm and composed throughout his sentencing, Crutchley's stoic appearance continued as deputies led him back to his holding cell. Whether an impressive ability to contain his emotions, or a refusal to register the reality of the situation, Crutchley's demeanor did not reflect a man who just received a sentence that far exceeded what he had expected. Crutchley had scheduled another press conference to take place after his sentencing; however, jail officials cancelled it because he "freaked out" in his cell once the reality of the sentence began to sink in.

"He went berserk," Joe Mitchell explained, "he was beating his head against the wall and had to be restrained." As a result of his unpredictable and self-destructive behavior, Crutchley was put on suicide watch in an observation cell where he could be checked every few minutes.

Crutchley's mother expressed deep disappointment in what she deemed to be an extremely harsh sentence. She believed that her son would be better off placed in a mental hospital to receive needed treatment.

"He really does need psychiatric help. I think that vampire stuff was all hallucinations and marijuana."

She showed no sympathy for the victim, calling Christina Almah a "tramp," and insisting that "you have to look at both sides of the story. She did get in the car. She's not lily-white."

Karen Crutchley did not attend the actual sentencing, but voiced similar disgust over what she perceived to be a grossly excessive sentence for her husband.

"I can't see why it exceeded the guidelines. It was a gentle rape, devoid of any overt brutality," she remarked, echoing her earlier characterization.

She spoke to her husband by telephone shortly after imposition of his sentence. He had not been in a good mood.

"He was very upset. He's disgusted that society would flush him down the toilet when he's got so much to offer."

She also mentioned that her husband had a few choice, unrepeatable words for Joe Mitchell, who he believed had betrayed him.

"You'd be upset too, if you were sentenced to three times more than what your lawyer had promised," she explained.

Told of Karen Crutchley's comments, Mitchell countered that he did the best he could with a "very difficult client." He attributed the extended sentence to the judge's evaluation of Crutchley's credibility and his obvious refusal to accept any responsibility for his actions. Apparently, the judge did not buy his client's story that the "old" John Crutchley was dead.

"Basically," Mitchell summarized, "he thinks John Crutchley is the same person he was when he committed the offense."

Mitchell added that if Crutchley wanted to appeal the sentence, he would need to get a new lawyer. Mitchell was done with the circus. He had already made up his mind that he would no longer represent the Vampire Rapist.

On the other side of the aisle, prosecutors were quite pleased with the sentence, pointing out that it "reflects the outrageousness and extreme violence of the acts" committed by Crutchley. As for the victim of Crutchley's depraved acts, upon hearing the specifics of the sentence imposed against him, Christina Almah expressed relief.

"I'd prefer the death penalty," she said, "but they can't give him that, so I guess 25 years is good enough."

Crutchley subsequently appealed the judge's decision, but on March 28, 1987, Florida's Fifth District Court of Appeal upheld the 25-year sentence. The appellate court did not issue a written opinion explaining its reason for upholding the ruling; it simply affirmed the sentence without comment.

On June 27, 1986, Crutchley began serving his prison term at Union Correctional Facility in Raiford, Florida. Union Correctional, or "Raiford" as it was commonly called, held Florida's most dangerous criminals. Filled with murderers, rapists, and habitual offenders, it housed the worst of the worst. Unfortunately for Crutchley, his notoriety as the Vampire Rapist preceded him in prison. As a convicted rapist, he would be targeted by many of the institutionalized inmates who abhorred child molesters and despised rapists. His bizarre acts of draining and drinking Christina Almah's blood served only to intensify the ill will other inmates held for him.

In a July 8 internal memorandum, Norm Wolfinger stated that Patrick Dontell would be allowed to plea to a reduced sentence for his crimes if he agreed to testify in court against Crutchley when the state had marshaled sufficient evidence to move forward with a murder trial. The next day, after agreeing to the negotiated terms, Dontell entered a plea to a lesser offense of battery, and he was released on bond from the Brevard County Detention Center with the requirement that he attend a sentencing hearing on August 28. However, when the August 28 hearing date arrived, he failed to appear for his sentencing, and instead fled the state, possibly being involved in the theft of an automobile and participating in a robbery along the way. It seemed as if something had scared him into changing his mind about testifying against his former cellmate.

Dontell's testimony would be forever lost when, in September 1987, he was found dead on the front porch of his mother's mobile home in Baltimore, Maryland. The lack of an autopsy raised suspicions in Leatherow's mind, but Dontell's death was quickly and officially attributed to a fatal heart attack.

Fairfax County Chief Prosecutor Robert Horan considered the loss of Dontell's testimony devastating to Virginia law enforcement's efforts to build a murder case against Crutchley. Although he acknowledged having "very strong suspicions" about Crutchley's role in Debbie Fitzjohn's death, Horan pointed to the "reality of criminal prosecution" as preventing his office from moving forward with a case against Crutchley due to a lack of direct evidence linking him to the crime. Justice would, at best, be delayed for the Fitzjohn family.

On August 5, Dr. Cloud Miller, the criminologist retained by Joe Mitchell to aid in Crutchley's defense, wrote to the warden of Union Correctional that Crutchley faced "considerable pressure from other inmates for homosexual sex" and that he had counseled Crutchley prior to his placement at Union that he would "more than likely be a target of sexual assaults from the more aggressive and bigger prisoners." He requested administrative confinement to separate Crutchley from the other inmates. The warden granted Miller's request, but Crutchley's personal safety concerns continued after being released back into the main prison population.

TWENTY-SIX

Evil spirits

Although Crutchley had been put behind bars and no longer constituted a threat for the immediate future, Leatherow continued sifting through the dry bones of the past, working diligently to unearth evidence linking Crutchley to one of the county's many unsolved murders. To date, he had not been able to find a smoking gun and the lack of conclusive physical evidence troubled him, but he remained determined to follow all reasonable leads and he vowed to devote whatever time it would take to fully investigate the case. The location of Crutchley's house in relation to the three sites where the bodies of Kim Walker and three unidentified women were found, combined with the similarities of the crime scenes, particularly the concealment of the corpses and their proximity to power lines, pointed strongly to Crutchley in Leatherow's mind.

In August, Leatherow led a search of the interior of the *former* Crutchley house on Hall Road, which had recently been sold for $108,000, much less than its appraised value. George Walters, a prominent Malabar real estate agent, disputed Karen Crutchley's claim that the reduced price resulted from the home being on a dirt road.

"There must have been another reason," Walters said, "that house was worth $129,000 easy."

Of course, the loss in value due to the stigma associated with being the Vampire Rapist's home did not concern Leatherow. His focus remained fixed on finding any trace of Crutchley's victims, whether in the form of a hidden memento or forgotten fragment of bone. The search team led by Leatherow concentrated on specific areas inside the house that had been depicted on the hand-drawn map by John Crutchley. While Leatherow supervised the search of the interior, about fifty deputies scoured the grounds outside via soil core sampling. Slowly, meticulously, they walked the property shoulder to shoulder. Their most significant find was an odd hole that had been cut into an area of the barn's concrete foundation. Circular in shape, the hole measured about a foot deep and a foot or two in diameter. Leatherow immediately noticed that it had been cut into the perfect shape and size for concealing a human skull, and the hole was positioned in such a way that it could have been easily covered with floorboards. As he examined the peculiar hole, Leatherow remembered something that Jackie Horton had mentioned during one of his interviews. Horton said that Crutchley claimed to have hidden Patti Volanski's head under the barn. It looked to Leatherow that the hole certainly could have been used to conceal Patti's skull, but if her head had been hidden there at one time, Crutchley had been careful not to leave any trace of it behind. Not even a single strand of hair remained.

View of Crutchley's house from the side

Skull-sized hole discovered in foundation of barn on Crutchley property after the barn was torn down by Sheriff's officials. Inmates who knew Crutchley told law enforcement that Patti Volanski's head had been hidden in the hole, but Crutchley allegedly removed the head after being released on bail.

In April 1987, when Patti would have been 31, Alta Pratt held a memorial service for her only daughter. Pratt had never wavered in her belief that Crutchley was responsible for Patti's death.

"From the first time I heard his name, I was pretty sure he had picked Patti up and killed her."

Pratt still spent countless hours walking through wooded areas of Brevard County searching for Patti's remains.

"I know she's dead and all I want to do is find her. If she was your daughter, you would be out there searching too," Pratt asserted, her eyes growing misty.

On the evening of April 23, a fifty-nine-year-old retired librarian in Palm Bay had a quiet dinner with his wife, washed the dishes, and then carefully put them away. Shortly thereafter, armed with a high-powered rifle, a handgun, and a hunting vest packed with bullets, William Bryan Cruse, Jr., embarked on a shooting rampage that left six people dead, including two police officers, as well as over a dozen injured. Three of the gunshot victims were pronounced dead at Holmes Regional Medical Center and three were found dead in store parking lots. Cruse's shooting spree started in front of his home after two boys began teasing him. He fired at the boys, jumped into his white Toyota, and drove to the nearby Sabal Palm Shopping Center, where he shot at customers in the Publix supermarket parking lot. A witness to the shooting remarked that Cruse "looked insane." After firing at customers by Publix, Cruse drove across the street to a Winn-Dixie, where he continued shooting before going inside and holding a number of customers and employees hostage. He shot at ambulances in the parking lot each time they tried to tend to the wounded who lay scattered across the parking lot. Over 200 police officers responded to the Winn Dixie, and after 2:00 a.m., a SWAT team squad dressed in flak jackets stormed the store while throwing flash grenades to blind and stun the gunman. They captured Cruse amid a tempest of smoke from the grenades and a downpour of water from the store's sprinklers activated by the grenades. Cruse did not go quietly and they had to subdue him in order to handcuff him before dragging him to a patrol car and taking him away. Later, a neighbor revealed that many in the neighborhood were afraid of Cruse. "I considered him off his head—crazy," said Eucal Grant. "He just acted crazy. No one talked to him, not even his next-door neighbors."

On June 18, the Brevard County Sheriff's Office sent the FBI three boxes of printouts from Crutchley's computer, along with a box of floppy disks that had been recovered from his office. The cover letter accompanying the four boxes mentioned that Crutchley had "intimated killing numerous women by decapitation and removing the heart while the victim was alive."

On July 1, 1987, Leatherow, Robert Ressler, and Norm Wolfinger traveled to Union Correctional Institute in Raiford to meet with Crutchley in hopes of convincing him to cooperate with their investigation of the unsolved homicides. Over time, prison had a tendency to loosen inmates' tongues, and they anticipated the same effect with Crutchley. As the three men waited for him in a prison conference room, they reviewed their strategy for conducting the interview. Leatherow had recently received a promotion to head the Sheriff's homicide unit, a tight-knit group of agents whose members treated each other like family, but Crutchley maintained a personal hatred of Leatherow due to the tenaciousness of his investigation, and the three men agreed that Ressler would take the lead in interviewing him.

After a few minutes, a large metal door at the end of the room opened with a resounding clang and then two guards escorted Crutchley inside. Clad in drab prison garb, Crutchley entered the room, hate clearly visible in his narrowed eyes, his hawkish gaze fixed firmly on Leatherow. Maintaining a fierce stare, Crutchley shouted at Leatherow with venom dripping from every word, repeatedly cursing him as "evil." As he continued making his way forward, Crutchley grabbed a nearby chair and hurled it across the room toward the startled investigator. The wooden chair smashed into the wall a few feet away from Leatherow, leaving everyone in the room momentarily stunned.

Within seconds, the two guards grabbed Crutchley and forced him into another chair across the table from the three investigators.

Ressler tried to defuse the situation by addressing Crutchley in a calming voice. "We just want to talk to you, John."

"I'm not saying a word with *him* here," Crutchley replied through clenched teeth, indicating Leatherow.

"Bob, maybe it'd be best if you waited over there," Wolfinger suggested.

"Sure thing, Norm," Leatherow answered stoically, before getting up and walking to the far corner of the interview room.

Satisfied that Leatherow was out of earshot, Crutchley leaned across the table toward Ressler.

"This whole case is based on nothing but lies," he asserted indignantly. "That man," he said, pointing at Leatherow, "has been making up 'facts' to manufacture a case against me. He's just hoping to make a name for himself. It's all bullshit!" Crutchley exclaimed spitefully.

"Then tell me what really happened, John," Ressler coolly responded.

"It's pointless, I know how all of this works," Crutchley replied sullenly. "They can't back down now, their careers are on the line. But I can promise you this. They won't get any further accolades on my account. I'm done talking with any of you."

With that, Crutchley terminated the interview, refusing to say another word.

After spending ten minutes unsuccessfully trying to get Crutchley to talk, an exasperated Wolfinger instructed the guards to take him back to his cell.

The two guards grabbed Crutchley by the arms and led him out of the room, while the stern faces of Leatherow, Ressler, and Wolfinger displayed the deep intensity of their disappointment.

Back in his cell, Crutchley completed a letter to his wife in which he suggested that his behavior could be traced to certain afflictions he had been suffering.

> *Dear Karen,*
>
> *I hear you asking, "Why?" Why is it that my life is so different than the ordinary person? Was it by chance that you took up participation in the nightmare that I am presently calling "life"?*
>
> *. . . .*
>
> *There has been a growing loneliness in me . . . The biggest problem is that as the loneliness increases, a defense mechanism of numbness also grows. The lonelier I feel, the greater the insensitivity to the world is.*
>
> *I'm unsure if there are such things as evil versus good spirits – but sometimes it feels as if evil spirits visit me and guide my actions and thoughts. The times this happens is when I'm lonely. I think that when I'm lonely and I become numb – I'm like soft clay and can be quite easily guided in any direction. For the first time I can remember, I've begun to pray for guidance from good spirits, if there are any listening. But I am not comfortable praying.*
>
> *. . . .*
>
> *As soon as you get here, there's a few important logistics to work out—first, is my "head." I don't know if I have a tumor, if I'm possessed, or what, but I am aware that something's wrong, and it has to be fixed somehow.*

In Virginia, two days before the scheduled convening of a September 15 grand jury, Robert Horan, the Chief Prosecutor for Fairfax County, announced his determination that the evidence gathered against Crutchley did not merit moving forward with a murder case against him in the matter of Debbie Fitzjohn's death.

Understandably disappointed by the decision, Debbie's grandmother voiced her dismay before reiterating her conviction of Crutchley's guilt. "Right from the beginning, I have always felt it was Crutchley because he was the last one to see her alive."

Debbie's father, Herman, could never come to terms with the lack of prosecution of Crutchley for his daughter's murder. He remained haunted by the last conversation he ever had with her, just five days before her disappearance.

"Debbie came home and told me that she had taken out a second insurance policy on herself," he recalled somberly. "I told her jokingly that she should make me her beneficiary. She laughed and said, 'Daddy, I'll outlive you.'"

On November 4, the Surfside Playhouse in Cocoa Beach presented the first of several performances of a new play entitled "The Trial of the Vampire Rapist." With an underlying theme focused on the exploration of Freudian issues, the play enjoyed a successful run on the Cocoa Beach stage before earning a special engagement in Manchester, England. The playwright, Jeff Johnson, said that he felt compelled to write the play after reading about the Crutchley case in the newspaper. Like so many others, he continued to be amazed that there had been a "real vampire in our midst."

TWENTY-SEVEN

A heart ever cold

In the spring of 1988, having explored all other avenues and increasingly desperate to recover her daughter's body, Alta Pratt wrote the first of several letters to Crutchley attempting to appeal to his humanity, hoping to persuade him to reveal where he had hidden Patti Volanski's body. On April 20, Crutchley penned his response, feigning ignorance of Patti's fate while trying to paint himself as the victim of an overly aggressive police force that had stooped so low as to orchestrate the improper seizure of his four-year-old son.

Dear Ms. Pratt,

Thank you for writing. I do not know you and may have never met you, but I understand your cry for help very much. I know because of another woman who became separated from her child. She suffered greatly when her four year old was brutally taken from her – right from her arms! She also saw the horror on the faces of another four year old and his parents, as the violent snatching of her son took place in front of them in the sanctity of their own home. I also heard that woman's gut wrenching sobs as she told me of how agents Fair and Leatherow told her that she would never see her child again unless she would go to court and swear a testimony to things which she knows are lies.

. . . .

The only thing I know about your daughter came via the men I mentioned above. If the men who abducted a mother's child in an attempt to extort testimony were the ones who gave you my name and address – you can rest assured they have no compassion whatsoever. I do not know your daughter, I do not know where she is, and cannot help you in locating her. If anyone told you otherwise, ask them what their motive is for torturing you in such a cruel way.

May our Lord enter into your life and bless you with His heavenly peace and comfort. Yours in Christ, John C.

Undeterred and emboldened by catching Crutchley in an obvious lie, Alta replied by letter dated May 18, pleading that he come clean so that she could give Patti a proper Christian burial.

Mr. Crutchley: John:

I must try to get across to you first that no one from the police department gave me your address, or are even aware that I have written to you . . . Also, any information I've learned about you is only from the newspaper – In which I might add, that you said to the newspaper reporter that Patti Volanski was with you and you made her get out of your car. And yet you said in your first letter, that you never knew Patti.

. . . .

Please, John, tell me about your encounter with Patti. Tell me where she is.

In his reply, Crutchley coldly ignored Pratt's plea, and failed to explain the discrepancy between his claim to her that he never met

Patti and his statement to the newspaper that he had picked Patti up along the road.

Meanwhile, the criminal investigation continued. A review of Crutchley's phone records and credit card statements revealed that in 1985, in addition to being out of town on November 21 when her husband abducted Christina Almah, Karen Crutchley had been out of town from March 15 to March 26, from August 21 to August 28, and for nearly the entire month of November. It looked as if she had been away for similar periods of time during the preceding year as well. Karen's absences had afforded Crutchley ample opportunities to look for victims, and Leatherow shuddered at the thought of how many women may have stumbled across his path during those prime hunting periods.

He struck quickly on March 15, apparently abducting Patti Volanski on his way home after dropping Karen and Jason off at the Orlando airport. Karen's trips also coincided with the timing of Miss Hollywood's demise since she had been dead for over three months before being found on December 15, 1985, and thus could have fallen victim to Crutchley in either March or August of that year.

After evaluating the number of unsolved homicides in Brevard County that could potentially be linked to the Vampire Rapist, Norm Wolfinger appointed a special task force composed of personnel from the Sheriff's Office and State Attorney's Office to focus on Crutchley's case. The first meeting of the task force took place on September 14, 1988 and included Leatherow, Russ Cockriel, Charles O'Neal, and Andy Casey. Over the next three-and-a-half months, the group met on eleven occasions to work the case, with Bob Carrisquillo and Mark Jones also joining the group at times.

On October 31, the FBI determined that the computer disks that had been removed from Crutchley's residence "very likely" contained "classified National Security data." In December, it began investigating whether to seek authority from the Internal Security Section of the Department of Justice to prosecute Crutchley for espionage.

On the morning of January 24, 1989, in a small, windowless room in the Florida State Prison in Starke, the State of Florida executed perhaps the most famous serial killer of modern times by strapping him to "Old Sparky," a three-legged wooden chair, and running 2,000 volts of electricity through him. Although authorities suspected that he had committed dozens of homicides spread throughout several states, Ted Bundy was convicted of only three and all of those were committed in Florida. When the nearly 500 people gathered across the street from the prison heard that Bundy had been pronounced dead, nearly all of them cheered the news. Many chanted "Burn Bundy Burn!" and others banged frying pans that they had brought along for the festive occasion.

While Crutchley served his sentence, earning 'gain time' for good behavior that would shorten the term of his imprisonment, investigators worked to build a murder case that could keep him permanently behind bars. On February 1, 1989, Leatherow and other members of the Crutchley task force interviewed George Hurley, who turned over Crutchley's IBM personal computer, which he had received from Crutchley's wife. At times during the five- to six-hour interview, the group suspected Hurley of being deliberately deceptive, particularly with regard to his account of what had happened to several missing components of the computer. However, the consensus among the group was that Hurley did not seem to have had any involvement in, or knowledge of, Crutchley's criminal activities.

On May 10, the special task force met with Norm Wolfinger at his office in Titusville. After an in-depth discussion of the status of the case, the group decided that Leatherow would devote approximately eighty percent of his on-duty time exclusively to the Crutchley case, with investigator Bob Carrisquillo assisting him from the State Attorney's Office. A few days later, on the recommendation of the FBI, Leatherow contacted the Texas Department of Corrections and requested the use of its cadaver dogs to search the Hall Road property formerly owned by Crutchley.

The following week, Leatherow viewed a videotape of *The Cat People*, an erotic horror film starring Natassja Kinski that had been released in 1982. Leatherow had received a letter from a recent cellmate of Crutchley's, alerting him to the potential relevance of the film, and explaining how he thought the movie may have influenced Crutchley's nefarious activities.

There are many things about this movie that make me think that John Crutchley identified with the character called "Paul." Below are some of the points I noticed. You may be able to find others.

1. *Bondage (especially at the end of the film where the female is tied to the bed in order to have sex).*
2. *Type of victim (reference is made to the fact that he purposely selected prostitutes, runaways, and other derelict females as victims).*
3. *Body parts (in the basement scene it is noted that he kept some body parts and buried others on his property).*

4. *Photographs his victims (at least once Paul photographs a victim in a cemetery and later kills her and devours some of her flesh).*

5. *Sexual dysfunction (in the aforementioned scene, Paul has a problem with erection. You will recall that John also had some difficulty performing without erotic stimuli, bondage, etc.).*

6. *Incest (Paul attempts to force himself on his sister in a couple of scenes. I recall some evidence of incest in Crutchley's history).*

7. *Indian lore (I recall some reference made to the fact that Crutchley studied ancient Indian rituals. The cultism portrayed in this movie has roots in this type of behavior).*

8. *I think it is also significant that Crutchley chose the theme music from this film as the background for his own pornographic video production [with Karen].*

Maybe I'm off base, but I really believe that Crutchley was influenced by some of these scenes. Since the film came out in 1982, he had plenty of time to see it before some of his escapades. Watch it and see what you think.

As Leatherow learned while watching the film, the lead female character, Irena, meets her older brother Paul, in New Orleans, after they have been separated for most of their lives. Paul eventually tells her that they come from an ancient lycanthropic family of werecats, and that all werecats are incestuous. The werecats are similar to werewolves, but become leopards after having sex with a human being, rather than transforming into wolves when the moon is full. Having morphed into a leopard, the werecat must kill a human in order to regain its human form. Paul kills several people during the story, but is eventually shot and killed. Meanwhile, Irena falls in love with one of the zoo's caretakers, and ultimately chooses to remain a leopard rather than killing him to regain her human form.

While viewing the film, Leatherow immediately noticed Crutchley's close physical resemblance to the film's character, Paul. Both had similar facial features and haircuts, and they shared the same body frames and builds. Moreover, just as Paul had a hidden, dark side, transforming into a savage creature that preyed on unsuspecting women, Crutchley changed from an unassuming, apparently harmless computer engineer into a vampiric predator stalking the streets for victims. The fact that Crutchley had named his fictitious homicidal brother "Paul" when warning Christina Almah to keep quiet while confined in the bathtub was not lost on Leatherow either. And the parallels did not end there. In the movie, when confronted with evidence of the seemingly docile Paul's murderous acts, his sister responds with a combination of denial and disbelief: "It couldn't be my brother. My brother would never do those things." News of Crutchley's malevolent activities drew the same reaction from his wife, mother, and co-workers. None could believe what he had done.

On May 23, Leatherow, Carrisquillo, Cockriel, and other investigators searched the former Crutchley property with the aid of specially trained cadaver dogs handled by Sergeant Bill Smith of the Texas Department of Corrections. To check for the presence of decomposed bodies, they also took core samples from the ground in the northwest area of the property to conduct chloroform testing. The next day, to follow up Patrick Dontell's tip from several years earlier, the group took the cadaver dogs to the TGIFriday's location at the Promenade Mall on State Road 192 in Melbourne. Unable to detect anything at that location, the dogs were taken to the corner of

McCain Lane and Hall Road, where they alerted on one area in the northwest corner of the former Crutchley property.

Invigorated by the prospect of finding the remains of one of the Vampire Rapist's victims buried on his property, Leatherow and the other investigators excitedly began digging at the spot shortly after 9:00 a.m. They continued digging for the entire day until darkness forced them to stop, and then they resumed digging the next morning. To aid the excavation, they enlisted the aid of a backhoe from the county road department, but the only thing unearthed by the intense digging was the badly decomposed carcass of a dog that the current property owner had buried there.

The "big dig" continued on May 26, focusing on two areas marked with an "X" on the hand-drawn map that Crutchley had given to Patrick Dontell in 1986. Still nothing of relevance to the investigation could be found.

Despite growing frustrations, on June 1 and 2, Leatherow and other members of the investigative team undertook yet another search of the former Crutchley house, this time using fiber optics to look inside the interior walls and the attic. They even drained the home's septic tank, but the search effort still came up empty. If any bodies or body parts had been hidden on Crutchley's property in the past, he had long since removed them, likely while out on bond.

On June 8, Leatherow interviewed Linda Souders, a Malabar resident who knew Crutchley and his wife for a short period of time prior to his arrest. Souders told Leatherow that at times Crutchley had "demon looking eyes," and that Karen had told her that she was scared of leaving their son, Jason, alone with him. Indeed, Karen would not let her husband babysit Jason because she feared that he might harm the child. Karen also confided to Souders that she was scared of her husband and had wanted to leave him on several occasions, but each time something held her back. Karen believed that her husband possessed "some power over her" that kept her from leaving him.

On June 17, Leatherow and Carrasquillo made the fourteen-hour drive to Quantico, Virginia for another meeting with Robert Ressler. On June 18, they spent the entire day with Ressler preparing an affidavit to authorize a search of encrypted files on Crutchley's personal computer. The following day, they again met with Ressler, as well as Fred Pfeiff from the Fairfax County Police Department, to discuss the latest developments in the case.

Later on the afternoon of June 19, Assistant State Attorney James Graham took Ressler's deposition to preserve his testimony for potential use in future criminal proceedings against Crutchley. During his testimony, Ressler discussed how Crutchley's sexual behavior most likely evolved from kinky sexual experimentation and bondage to more violent and destructive acts. During the later stages of this aberrant development, Crutchley would have begun treating his victims more like objects than people.

> When an individual goes through these rituals where in fact they inflict dominance and control power, tying up the individual, holding the person more or less in the palm of their hand from the standpoint of their safety. What we see here is, in fact, what he is doing is escalating his fantasies to the point of becoming more and more dangerous.

According to Ressler, Crutchley wanted to keep Christina Almah alive for a period of time in order to prolong his feelings of dominance and control, whereas his earlier victims may have been killed quickly before he learned how to control his impulses and increase the length of his sexual fantasies.

> What you'll see over a period of time is conscious effort at keeping the victim alive longer and longer. Frequently these types

of individuals will get their thrills from again holding that person's life literally in their hands . . . taking that person right to the moment of death, then letting them revive. This is the ultimate power over a victim. Life or death is in their hands.

Crutchley's repeated pattern of choking Christina to unconsciousness, and then reviving her, and his care to drain only an amount of blood that would not kill her—his deliberateness in keeping Christina alive—convinced Ressler that Crutchley's encounter with her had not been his first-time engaging in such behavior. Ressler was confident that if Christina had not escaped, once Crutchley had milked her for all of the pleasure that she could provide him, he would have killed her just as he had killed his previous victims.

"When a person carries on this long, experiments this long, keeps the victim alive that long, it indicates to me a pattern that you see with people who have killed many times before."

On June 21, Leatherow and Carrisquillo interviewed Karen Crutchley in Silver Springs, Maryland. She was attending law school at the University of Baltimore and purportedly planning on divorcing her husband, though she had not yet done so. During the interview, Karen disclosed that she had at one point asked Crutchley whether he had any involvement in the disappearance of Debbie Fitzjohn, but she said that he had quickly "cleared up" her questions about it. She described their marriage as a "fairly happy" one at the time they made the move from Virginia to Florida. Up to that point, although Crutchley had occasionally asked her to do sexual things that were "somewhat kinky," there had not been anything too peculiar. However, after the move, his sexual requests started becoming stranger. He became an avid, even obsessive, reader of *Penthouse* and more hardcore pornographic magazines, he began leaving her letters about his bizarre sexual fantasies, and he "didn't seem to enjoy sex unless it was kinky." She eventually refused to indulge his sexual desires because he "just seemed to be only into bizarre sex." Yet, other than her husband's deviant sexual interests, Karen felt that they had a "pretty good life" together.

At some point in 1985, Crutchley became "disconnected" and depressed. He often became short-tempered with her and frequently flew off the handle over trivial things. Karen began to fear him during the times when he lost his temper because he became "so irrational, it was scary." He started accusing her of doing things that in reality he had done himself, and she found it increasingly difficult to reason with him.

In November, she had taken Jason to visit her parents for several weeks so that her husband could concentrate on an important project at work. Then, one night shortly before his arrest, Crutchley called her and told her that he loved her. He said that he had something to tell her, but that he would explain everything when he picked her up at the airport in a few days. The next time she heard from him was the night of his arrest.

She told Leatherow that the only reason her husband pled guilty in the Christina Almah case was because their attorney, Joe Mitchell, refused to take the case to trial and he promised that Crutchley would only get a three or four year prison sentence if he agreed to plead.

As the interview came to an end, Karen mentioned the Nissan Stanza that Crutchley had used to pick up Christina Almah. She called it the "Generic Car" because it was "completely clean and no one would know what brand it was" since Crutchley had covered up or removed the Nissan logos with black tape. Although she thought it a little strange that her husband had altered the car in that fashion, she had never been alarmed by it. She just chalked it up to another instance of his quirkiness.

Leatherow and Carrisquillo returned to Florida on June 24, and attempted to interview Crutchley at Union Correctional Institute the next day. However, when Crutchley entered the small interview room and saw who wanted to talk to him, he instantly became enraged and refused to speak with them. They tried to get Crutchley to cooperate by bluffing him, telling him that they knew all about Debbie Fitzjohn and everything else that he had done and that they had more than enough evidence to tie him to the murders he had committed. But he just sat and stared at them with angry, untrusting eyes. The interview ended within ten minutes, and Crutchley continued to rant on about Leatherow's misdeeds as guards led him away.

In July 1989, the FBI learned of a possible link between Crutchley and Richard Sherman, a former CIA employee living in McLean, Virginia, who was still working for the CIA on a contract basis. The FBI sought to ascertain whether Crutchley ever solicited any classified information from Sherman during the time that the two had shared a working relationship. The FBI described Crutchley as a "sophisticated computer engineer," but a "most bizarre individual." A memorandum to the FBI Director from the special agent in charge of the investigation pointed out that "it is believed that [Crutchley] is a serial killer," and that experts from the FBI's Behavioral Sciences Unit "have noted that [he] closely fits the profile of a serial killer."

Due to dwindling leads and an ever-increasing caseload, work on Crutchley's case came to a virtual standstill for the next few years. Although Leatherow and his team had gathered considerable evidence, they could not piece together the complete puzzle. In some cases, such as the Kimberly Walker murder, they had bodies, but no evidence linking the bodies to Crutchley. In other cases, such as the Patti Volanski disappearance, they had evidence tying Crutchley to the victim, but no body to establish in the eyes of the law that a crime had actually occurred.

Across the Atlantic, on November 9, 1989, crowds of jubilant Germans cheered as a somber symbol of communist oppression and a ruthless, tyrannical police state came crashing down. The demolition physically manifested the culmination of the destruction of a system that had been steadily decaying from within, a decay hastened by Ronald Reagan's challenge to the reformist-minded, recently elected Soviet leader Mikhail Gorbachev to "Tear down this wall!" The fall of the Berlin Wall signaled the beginning of the end of the decades-long Cold War, the roots of which had taken hold shortly after World War II, and the effects of which would last for many lifetimes.

The January 22, 1990 airing of the television show, *Inside Report*, featured a story on the Vampire Rapist in which Crutchley discussed how shocked he had been when Christina Almah said "ouch" as he stuck her with a needle to drain her blood. In what seemed to be a slip of the tongue, apparently inadvertently alluding to previous victims, he explained that "nobody had ever said 'ouch' before."

TWENTY-EIGHT

Missed opportunities

On July 22, 1991, police on patrol in Milwaukee, Wisconsin, picked up a frightened young man who was running frantically down the street with handcuffs dangling from one of his wrists. The man told police that he had escaped from an apartment where a man tried to handcuff him. After some time to collect his thoughts and steady his nerves, the frazzled young man led police back to the apartment. After knocking and announcing themselves as police officers, a man fitting the description of the apartment's owner answered the door and allowed the officers to come inside. They arrested him after discovering a ghastly assortment of body parts scattered around the dwelling, including a severed head that was being stored in the refrigerator.

Convicted of committing fifteen murders during a killing career spanning from 1978 to 1991, Jeffrey Dahmer received a sentence of fifteen terms of life imprisonment.

On November 24, 1994, Dahmer was beaten to death by a fellow inmate. Upon hearing the news of his death, Dahmer's mother lashed out at the media: "Now is everybody happy? Now that he's bludgeoned to death, is that good enough for everyone?"

On the ten-year anniversary of the disappearance of her daughter, sixty-five-year-old Alta Pratt felt immensely saddened and depressed by the prospect of Crutchley being released on parole.

"I would hate the thought of that creep ever getting out of prison and being on the streets again," she said. "I don't want him dead; I just want him behind bars."

A decade's time had done little to deaden the pain of losing her daughter.

"She was my buddy," Alta explained. "We did things together all the time. I still feel the pain of losing her today."

As the Vampire Rapist's parole date approached, media interest in his case rapidly rekindled, steadily building to levels on par with that of his original arrest and trial proceedings. One series of news stories shed some light on the potential extent of Crutchley's killing career.

On April 11, 1995, the *Florida Today* reported that law enforcement now considered Crutchley a suspect in thirty-two murders in Florida, Maryland, Ohio, Virginia, and Washington, D.C. Private investigator James Wilt, who tracked Crutchley for more than six years in an effort to link him to the murder of Debbie Fitzjohn, was not surprised at that figure.

"Anyone who would do the kind of things this guy has done in his life is capable of pretty much anything. The guy is a monster," Wilt asserted.

Contacted as Crutchley's parole date in Florida drew ever closer, Virginia Commonwealth Attorney Robert Horan admitted that the evidence strongly suggested Crutchley's involvement in Fitzjohn's murder.

"If one believes all of the fingers that point at him on different matters, he is truly a bad guy," Horan acknowledged. "And there are lots of indications to back that view."

Fairfax County police shared Horan's opinion and enlisted the aid of Robert Ressler in their efforts to link Crutchley to Fitzjohn's murder with sufficient evidence to charge him with the crime.

Lt. Dennis Wilson, head of the Fairfax County Police Department's cold case unit, candidly disclosed his department's perspective. "In our minds, we know Crutchley did it," he said.

Fred Pfeiff, the detective who worked the Fitzjohn case for more than a decade, readily concurred.

"For the time being, he's gotten away with it," Pfeiff remarked regretfully. "Will he get away with it forever? That remains to be seen."

The April 14, 1995 edition of the *Florida Today* reported that, as part of the plea deal floated by his attorney approximately a decade earlier, Crutchley had been prepared to confess to twelve murders that he had committed in Florida, as well as perhaps twenty others committed out of state. The newspaper went on to advise that Crutchley would have led investigators to the burial sites of his Florida victims in exchange for the State Attorney's Office agreeing to the imposition of multiple life sentences as his punishment, rather than pursuing the death penalty. Crutchley's life would be spared, but he would spend the rest of that life in prison, and the families of his victims would be given something extremely valuable: a sense of closure and the ability to properly bury their loved ones.

In researching its story about the aborted plea deal, the *Florida Today* had contacted Crutchley's former attorney, Joe Mitchell. Mitchell told the paper that, based on what he knew about his client, investigators would never be able to solve the murders. As for the possibility of Crutchley ever confessing, Mitchell believed that window permanently closed when the plea deal fell through in 1986. In Mitchell's mind, any chance to make headway in the unsolved Brevard County homicide cases vanished when investigators put Crutchley in the bones room. The FBI's idea had backfired. Instead of breaking down in a blubbering confession, Crutchley had barricaded himself behind impenetrable psychological walls, burying the truth just as resolutely as he had hidden the bodies of his victims.

"I don't think the police will ever solve the murders," Mitchell bombastically declared. "He's too smart and savvy. I don't think he'll ever confess."

State Attorney Norm Wolfinger downplayed the 1986 plea offer, saying that the negotiations never really got started and a concrete offer had never been put on the table.

Due to the increased media attention and the resulting public outcry and pressure, Brevard County Sheriff Jake Miller reopened his office's investigation of Crutchley on April 24. Miller explained his reasoning in an internal memorandum to Sheriff's personnel.

Although this is an old conviction, the future prospect of [Crutchley's] release, coupled with speculation about other crimes in which he may have been involved, suggest that a review of all known facts and evidence should be undertaken.

Having heard of Crutchley's early release, Robert Ressler contacted the Brevard County Sheriff's Office. Ressler, whose testimony during Crutchley's original sentencing hearing had been pivotal in convincing the court to impose a sentence beyond the guideline range, wanted to share some ideas he had for "keeping Crutchley in prison."

On May 10, Leatherow interviewed "jailhouse lawyer" William Omasta, an inmate at Union Correctional. A con man who impersonated a lawyer and a U.S. Marshal during the course of his criminal career, Omasta had assisted Crutchley with various legal filings over a period of nearly two years. During his interview, Omasta told Leatherow that, despite his claims of being a new man, Crutchley still harbored a fetish for blood, often sucking his own blood and hiding the puncture marks under his watchband. Omasta offered to help Leatherow gather incriminating information about Crutchley if Leatherow would agree to get his criminal record expunged.

On May 11, Leatherow and Agent Scott Armstrong returned to Union Correctional Institute, hoping to gather additional evidence on Crutchley by interviewing other inmates who had interacted with him. The next week, one of the inmates they had interviewed, Frederick Smalley, wrote a letter to Armstrong, attempting to strike a deal in exchange for his assistance in gathering evidence against Crutchley. Smalley advised Armstrong that after the May 11 interviews "much animosity surfaced towards Drak" among the prison population. Apparently, the inmates did not appreciate being interviewed by the police and they blamed Crutchley for being subjected to the investigators' intense interrogations. Indeed, according to Smalley, Crutchley should consider himself "fortunate to be alive as there are many here who express a desire to cut his heart out." Smalley also wrote about Crutchley's involvement in the Occult and indicated that Crutchley's criminal acts had been influenced by his interest in the supernatural. Smalley seemed to believe that Crutchley had experienced some sort of demonic possession.

The Vampire has named active circles (Covens) and talked about rituals of Descent, sacrifices, and the catching of spirits. Most details he referred to in a coded language, but I think I can tell you how some of the girls died. What the Vampire did cannot be pardoned. He needs to be destroyed and the Demon within him must be banished.

The next day, Leatherow received a call from Judy Riccitelli. She had seen news reports on T.V. about Crutchley's upcoming parole date. Now she felt compelled to divulge something that she had not mentioned when Leatherow originally interviewed her back in 1986. She told Leatherow that in 1983 Crutchley informed her that he had killed a woman in Northern Virginia years earlier and hid her body in the woods.

On May 23, still hoping to locate Crutchley's "burial grounds" or the hiding place where he had stored his trophies, Leatherow and Cockriel searched the property surrounding the Port Malabar Church of God. Finding nothing there, they also searched the church and grounds of the First Baptist Church of Malabar, located within ten minutes of Crutchley's former residence. Once again, the frustrated investigators found nothing of relevance to the investigation.

Unable to shake his suspicion that Crutchley had buried some of his victims or their belongings near his home, Leatherow undertook still another excavation of the former Crutchley property in June 1995. This time investigators used new ground-penetrating radar equipment to survey the property. Over the four-day period of June 12 through June 16, they conducted an exhaustive reconnaissance of the property, including tearing down the barn located behind the house so that they could search beneath it. They searched within the concrete pads that formed the foundation of the shed and dug where the barn formerly stood. And yet, despite all of the demolition, excavation, and extensive searching, they again turned up nothing.

Leatherow eventually came to believe that Crutchley had given Dontell the hand-drawn map of his property with several "X"s marked on it merely as a decoy to throw the police off his trail, to send them on a wild goose chase so that they would not find where he had really buried his victims.

Around the same time that Leatherow and his fellow investigators were undertaking their latest search of the former Crutchley property, the *Florida Today* obtained a copy of an internal law enforcement document reflecting that, beginning in the year 1977, Crutchley had been investigated in twenty-six homicide cases in four states and Washington, D.C. The document seemed consistent with Patrick Dontell's testimony that Crutchley informed him that he had been involved in approximately twenty-four homicides with "at least four or five" in Brevard County. The story also quoted Joe Mitchell, Crutchley's former attorney, who said it "wouldn't surprise me" if Crutchley killed more than two dozen people in an eight-year period spanning 1977 to 1985. "Based on all the information presented to me while I was representing John Crutchley, it was obvious to me that he was involved in a number of homicides," Mitchell remarked without going into any specifics.

On June 27, Frederick Smalley sent another letter to Armstrong, advising that Crutchley had been closely monitoring newspaper articles about his case, and that the "demon" occasionally mentioned how he had dismembered bodies. Smalley followed up his earlier correspondence to Armstrong with another letter on July 11 expressing his frustration that no one from the Sheriff's Office had contacted him in response to his first letter. This time, he revealed that Crutchley had mentioned "flying in small aircraft and the convenience they provide," and he included a cryptic statement: "I think some of the evidence you're looking for is underwater, far out at sea. To quote John – 'plop, plop, fizz, fizz. Oh what a relief it is!'"

Leatherow and Armstrong came back to Union Correctional on July 24. One of them, Charles Davis, professed a belief in Devil worship and claimed to be an active practitioner of the Occult. He informed the investigators that he and Crutchley had spoken several times about those topics and that Crutchley showed signs of being actively involved in Satanism.

That summer, in hopes of gaining additional information that might assist in identifying the skeletal remains that had been found in 1985 at Savery Road, the Florida Department of Law Enforcement assisted the Palm Bay Police Department in having noted forensic anthropologist William R. Maples examine the body. Following an extensive analysis, Dr. Maples concluded that the victim was female, likely white, approximately five feet, three inches in height, and between twenty-five to thirty-five years old. He determined that the victim's left leg had been separated from the torso by cutting it, most likely with a hacksaw. Dr. Maples opined that, after the saw had sliced through most of the femur, the separation had been completed by bending the leg and snapping it off, undoubtedly a particularly bloody technique.

On October 1, in anticipation of his approaching parole, the *Florida Today* ran the first of a four-part feature story on Crutchley. Recounting Crutchley's abduction and rape of Christina Almah, the paper noted the general belief in the law enforcement community that she would have become the latest of Crutchley's many victims, but she had been "lucky" enough to escape. The paper estimated the number of Crutchley's victims as between four and more than two dozen, and noted that prosecutors "are anxiously looking for a case that will keep him behind bars." In a tone conveying disbelief, the article advised that despite "mountains of suspicion and circumstantial evidence," Crutchley had not been indicted for a single murder, largely because no fingerprints, weapons, or other "smoking gun" direct evidence could be linked to him.

In the days that followed, Florida Department of Law Enforcement agents met with investigators from the Brevard County Sheriff's Office to discuss what assistance the FDLE could provide with regard to the unsolved homicide cases in which Crutchley remained a suspect. Sheriff's investigators advised their FDLE counterparts that a thorough review of the Crutchley case had been undertaken and that no further investigative efforts were possible. Based on that representation, the FDLE closed its file on Crutchley following the meeting.

On October 4, the front-page headline of the *Florida Today* screamed "NOT GUILTY" in announcing the jury's verdict in perhaps the most publicized criminal trial of the century, the murder trial of famous African-American athlete-turned-actor, O.J. Simpson. Shockingly, following a trial that had taken eight months, the jury reached its not guilty verdict in less than four hours. In a racially polarizing proceeding, O.J.'s acquittal in the double murder of his ex-wife Nicole Brown and her friend Ronald Goldman—both white—prompted cheers nationwide from the black community, while bewildered whites were left to ponder how justice had been so clearly denied. Although the notoriously jealous O.J. had an obvious motive for the murders, and his DNA placed him squarely at the scene of the crime, a perjured police detective and a glove that did not seem to fit were enough for the predominantly black jury to produce an acquittal. Visibly relieved after the announcement of the verdict, in a statement reminiscent of Crutchley's assertions of his own innocence, O.J. stated, "I can only hope that someday, despite every prejudicial thing that has been said about me publicly, both in and out of the courtroom, people will come to understand and believe that I would not, could not, and did not kill anyone."

Lead prosecutor Marcia Clark, sensing the widespread national outrage over the jury's verdict, pleaded with whites across the country not to become disillusioned: "Please don't let this make you lose faith in our system." But for many it did just that, exacerbating an already rampant cynicism toward the nation's criminal justice system.

Although the O.J. verdict dominated the news and commanded most of the front page, another story shared the prime spot of the paper. At the bottom of the front page, just below the article on the O.J. trial, appeared the last part of the paper's four-part feature story on the Vampire Rapist. With Crutchley's parole date looming ever nearer, media interest in the case had mushroomed. The final chapter in the *Florida Today* series entitled "The Never-Ending Investigation," chronicled investigators' efforts to link Crutchley to one of the many unsolved homicides they suspected him of committing.

The paper reported that in addition to the Fitzjohn, Volanski, and Walker homicides, as well as the three unidentified Brevard County victims, Florida investigators considered Crutchley a suspect in the disappearance and death of several other women in the county. The other cases mentioned in the story included Nancy Kay Brown, a twenty-five-year-old Illinois resident last seen alive on June 9, 1983, while walking in Cocoa Beach. Her skeletal remains were found near a lake in Canaveral Groves on March 8, 1984. Another possible victim, twenty-year-old Diana Lee Casey, disappeared on May 14, 1984, near Canaveral while walking to a convenience store to use the phone. Her body was found three weeks later near the side of a dirt road on Merritt Island. Others that Crutchley may have encountered included Cheryl Ann Windsor, a runaway from Orlando who disappeared from Merritt Island while hitchhiking in April 1984, and whose body turned up on Merritt Island in a creek on May 1, 1984; and Tammy Lynn Leppert, an eighteen-year-old Rockledge resident, who disappeared on July 6, 1983, while walking in Cocoa Beach by State Road A1A near an Exxon gas station. All of the women disappeared during the time period that Crutchley prowled the area and all fit within his *modus operandi* of victims chosen from hitchhikers and women he passed while driving along the road.

In the same article, the *Florida Today* reporter asked Leatherow to evaluate his agency's investigative efforts in the case. Leatherow answered that the Sheriff had instructed him not to leave any stone unturned and that is what he had attempted to do, methodically exhausting each lead and following every potential clue to its end.

After reflecting on the full extent of the Sheriff's Office's investigation, Leatherow added, "I think we've gone beyond what most agencies would do."

TWENTY-NINE

Day by day

The Vampire's first taste of prison had not been pleasant, and it did not improve with time. Each day in prison merged into the next, each day excruciatingly the same as the last. Only the number on the calendar changed.

For Crutchley, a typical day in prison began at 5:30 a.m. with the morning wake-up call, when he would get up, get dressed, and go to breakfast in the prison cafeteria. After finishing breakfast, he returned to his cell for the morning head count at 6:30. Immediately after head count, he reported for work. From 6:40 to 11:30 a.m., he worked at the prison's recreation department, spending much of the time checking out basketballs, baseballs, and other recreation equipment. At 11:30, he returned to his cell for another head count, and then had lunch at noon. At 12:30 p.m., he returned to his cell for the third head count, and then it was time to return to work. The workday would end at 4:30 p.m., at which time he would return to his cell to clean up. Dinner was promptly at 5:30 p.m., and then he had free time, under supervision of the guards, until dark. A fourth head count took place at 7:00 p.m., after which he could meet with his attorney or other visitors, read, or play board games. Lights out came at 11:00 p.m., followed by the fifth and final head count of the day at 11:05 p.m. Occasionally, he would be awakened during the dead of night, anywhere from 1:30 a.m. to 4:30 a.m., for random drug tests or to take various medications. The next day would be substantially the same. As would the next, and the next.

The isolation and boredom of solitary confinement had proven to be particularly difficult for him to endure. White fiberglass had been placed in the cell windows to block inmates' views out of their isolation cells, but some windows still allowed sunlight to enter for a short period of time each day. Crutchley had learned to savor that daily time period and he had become adept at abiding by the prison rules. Indeed, several officials at Union Correctional called him a "model inmate," and he only had one serious disciplinary incident during his ten years of imprisonment. The incident occurred in May 1991, when he was placed in solitary confinement for attacking another inmate who had mockingly called him the Vampire Rapist and snickered.

Crutchley applied himself to learning various trades while serving his prison term. He developed a particular interest in welding and cabinetry since they allowed him to use his hands and natural mechanical abilities. He also excelled in graphic arts and received several commendations for his work in creating posters for the prison's psychological services department.

The years in prison rid Crutchley of his love for the media. He no longer reached out to the newspapers or television stations and he began refusing interview requests. Although he claimed to have been offered "big bucks" for his story, Crutchley declined the opportunity to tell it. He submitted an Inmate Request form to the prison superintendent on June 1, 1996, stating, "I decline *all* media requests for interviews. Period."

Investigators visited Crutchley several times during his imprisonment, hoping that he would eventually break down and confess his crimes. However, prison did not effectuate any such transformation.

"We've hoped time would soften him up, but so far we've had negative results," said Lt. Bill Thompson of the Brevard County Sheriff's Office.

Although he had been sentenced to twenty-five-years in prison, Crutchley's actual incarceration time grew shorter every year. Automatically given a 3,000-day reduction in his sentence as soon as he walked through the prison doors in July 1986, his sentence was also reduced fifty days for good behavior during the first five months of his incarceration. A further reduction of twenty days a month began in 1987, for a total additional reduction of 1,960 days. Another 176 days were deducted from his sentence for time served while awaiting trial in the Brevard County Jail. Applying all of the credits and adjustments, Crutchley received a total reduction in prison time of 5,250 days. As a result, from the June 23, 1986 commencement date of his sentence until his expected release date of August 8, 1996, he would serve only 3,699 days of his 9,125-day sentence. Sentenced to twenty-five years, he would be released after serving only ten. Amounting to forty percent of his original sentence, the reduced time roughly equated to the percentage of blood that he had drained from Christina Almah.

On November 23, 1995, Leatherow received a letter from William Omasta, who had recently transferred from Union Correctional Institute to Sumter Correctional. In his letter, Omasta wrote that a recent conversation with Crutchley had convinced him of Crutchley's guilt in relation to a number of murders.

The purpose of this letter is to let you know that I'm now totally convinced of Mr. Crutchley's guilt. Since John and I have been

close friends, I now find it hard to accept his guilt. I have been
working with John on both his civil and criminal cases for almost
two years. And it was not until two weeks ago, after a two hour
conversation with John, that I became convinced of John's guilt.
John is one of the most intelligent persons in prison that I have
ever met. In fact, it is not uncommon for inmates to tell me all
about many crimes that they have committed, yet John has held
out longer than any other inmate, and has only provided limited
information.

Again, this letter is for the purpose of supporting your
convictions of John's guilt. I'm sorry that I had not agreed to a
wire in this matter since I must now live with the truth. (I have
never wanted to kill anyone, and I find it hard to accept someone
taking a life, and harder when there were so many involved).

On the morning of December 3, serial killer Gerard John Schaefer
was stabbed to death in his cell in Raiford, the same prison housing
the Vampire Rapist. Although convicted of just two murders, Schaefer, a former Martin County, Florida deputy Sheriff, had repeatedly
boasted that he killed more than thirty women and girls.

On December 12, Leatherow conducted another interview of
William Omasta, who was now housed at Sumter Correctional.
Omasta offered to return to Union Correctional wearing a wire to
attempt to obtain incriminating statements from Crutchley;
however, the offer was never accepted or acted upon. Leatherow
had negative experiences when dealing with Omasta in the past,
and no one at the Sheriff's Office had a high opinion of him.
Omasta's history of a lack of veracity prevented Leatherow from

ever seriously considering his offer of assistance in the Crutchley case.

On January 3, 1996, Agent Bill Bevil of the Brevard County Sheriff's Office cold case squad met with retired CIA agent Andy Casey as part of his supplemental investigation of the Crutchley case. In speaking with Casey, Bevil learned that several potentially relevant witnesses, including Carl Von Bane, Helen Olive, and a female known only as Annette, had not been interviewed during the initial case investigation. Bevil found the information about Carl Von Bane, the man Christina Almah had been visiting at the time of her abduction by Crutchley, particularly interesting. It turned out that Von Bane's mother, Suzanne Von Bane, had been working at Harris Corporation at the time in the same building that Crutchley worked in.

And the connections between Carl Von Bane and Crutchley did not end there. Andy Casey also informed Bevil that in 1985 Carl Von Bane had been a biker and a known associate of a local motorcycle gang, while Crutchley was a "wanna be biker" pursuing an interest in adopting the biker lifestyle. It was certainly plausible that Crutchley and Von Bane knew each other prior to Christina Almah's abduction, and it was possible that Von Bane had told Crutchley about Christina's visit. Yet, police had never interviewed Von Bane and he subsequently left the area sometime after Crutchley's November 1985 arrest. Upon running a criminal history check of Von Bane, Bevil discovered that he had multiple aliases and a thirty-five-page arrest history.

On January 5, Bevil interviewed Helen Olive, now going by her maiden name of Helen Picconi. Picconi advised that she had met Von while working as a bartender in November 1985 at Buzzy's Pub, a biker bar in Melbourne. Von introduced her to Christina

Almah shortly after Christina arrived from California. After that, since Von Bane worked during the day, he dropped Christina off at Picconi's house several times so that she would have someone to hang out with while he was working. For some reason, on November 21, he had simply left Christina home alone.

The same day he met with Picconi, Bevil interviewed Annette Krasky, who advised that she had also met Von at Buzzy's and that he later introduced her to Christina Almah as well. Krasky told Bevil that, when Christina was released from the hospital following her escape from Crutchley's house, Krasky had been the one who picked her up. During the drive home, Christina told her that while she was being held captive at Crutchley's house, he had shown her several identification cards belonging to other women, and that he told her the identification cards had come from other girls "like you."

On February 2, Bevil flew to California to interview Christina Almah. Christina told him that one of the reasons why she had initially been reluctant to prosecute Crutchley was because she had been so sexually naïve in 1985. At the time, she thought that what happened to her had somehow been her fault, and she feared having to testify against Crutchley in the public forum of a criminal court proceeding. Bevil asked if she would be willing to undergo hypnosis to see if there was anything new she could remember about the abduction and sexual assaults that might help connect Crutchley to one of the unsolved cases. Although hesitant at first, eventually, reluctantly, Christina agreed to be hypnotized. However, as the hypnotist started his work, she became visibly upset, trying unsuccessfully to fight back tears.

"I've spent all of these years trying to forget what happened to me, and now you want me to relive all of the things that I've tried to forget. I can't do it!"

Although the hypnotist explained that Christina's reaction indicated that she had forced many of the details of the crime deep down into her subconscious mind, Bevil decided to terminate the session rather than risk causing her additional emotional or psychological harm.

On February 6, Andy Casey told Bevil about one other lead in the case that had never been fully explored. During the original investigation, along with all of the other evidentiary items, Leatherow had recovered two microcassette tapes from Crutchley's office at Harris Corporation, but in the midst of everything else going on with the Crutchley investigation, no one had ever listened to the tapes. Casey eventually tracked down the tapes and reviewed them. On one of the tapes, Crutchley could be heard ordering a video camera, the same one that he later used to videotape his rape of Christina Almah. During the taped conversation, Crutchley could be heard telling the salesperson that he wanted the camera by March 13, 1985, and needed it at the latest by March 15. And it seemed more than mere coincidence that Crutchley's March 15 deadline corresponded to the date that his wife and son went to Maryland, the very day that Patti Volanski went missing.

In March 1996, Agent Bevil traveled to Ohio to interview Crutchley's long-time friend, Ray Malone, hoping to learn something that could help keep Crutchley in prison. Malone recounted to Bevil how he had engaged a friend to fly him from Ohio to Florida in March 1985 so that he could stay with Crutchley for a weeklong visit. Everything seemed fine until the second night of the visit when, shortly after midnight, Malone suddenly woke up, petrified with fear. He said that he felt like a little kid scared of the dark, terrified of something he could not see. As he lay in bed too afraid to move, one thought dominated his mind: he had to get away from Crutchley. After a mostly sleepless night, he informed Crutchley the next morning that he needed to return home, careful to tell

Crutchley outside of the house because he did not feel safe doing so inside. Since his pilot friend did not expect to fly Malone back until the end of the week, he had to stay at a Palm Bay motel that night, and then he flew back home the following day. The experience had been so strange that, even years later, Malone could not put into words why he had been so fearful in Crutchley's house. He could only try to convey the overriding sense of horror that had temporarily consumed him.

After that night, he realized that he needed to stay away from Crutchley. Although Crutchley wrote him from prison and tried calling him from time to time, Malone told Bevil that he did not read any of the letters and just stuck them in a dresser drawer. Now he no longer had any of the letters. He claimed that his ex-wife threw them all out after their divorce, but Bevil found it hard to believe that Malone had never read any of Crutchley's letters. He pressed Malone specifically about a letter in which Crutchley had asked him to hold onto an unidentified personal item.

"But you don't remember the letter that he wrote to hold a certain item?"

"I, I, I never read it," Malone stammered in reply, clearly surprised that investigators had obtained a copy of the letter. "I just wanted away from him. And I didn't want to believe he'd done it, y'know? I, I felt like y'know, why didn't I, why didn't I know that? That he was that kind of a person and capable of that, was I that bad in judging character?"

He had a hard time accepting the fact that Crutchley had maintained a Jekyll and Hyde persona, able to so completely hide his darker side from someone who had been his closest and oldest friend. Malone took no comfort in the fact that he was just one of many who Crutchley caused to question their ability to judge human character; one of many fooled by the elaborate deceptiveness of his external mask.

The interview abruptly ended when Malone realized that he

might be endangering himself by talking to the police about Crutchley. Fear of Crutchley or of being implicated as some sort of accomplice set in and his cooperative tone suddenly turned combative.

"If you don't succeed in keeping him in prison and he finds out I'm helpin' you, what is my life worth if he walks?" he demanded before refusing to speak any further.

On April 3, 1996, FBI agents approached a small wilderness cabin in the mountains near Lincoln, Montana. As they cautiously and methodically crept closer, one agent called out to the cabin, "Ted, are you home?" For a few moments, the only response was silence. Then the wood door of the rustic dwelling creaked partially open. A man's disheveled head slowly peeked out. Posing as employees of a mining company, the agents asked Ted Kaczynski if he could point out his property boundaries for them. He told them that they would have to wait a minute while he looked for his deed. He started to close the door, but before he could secure it, one of the agents grabbed his wrist, yanked him outside, and placed him under arrest. One of the longest manhunts in recent American history had ended without resistance, almost anticlimactically, with the Unabomber peacefully subdued in handcuffs.

In May, increasingly concerned about the mounting public outcry in reaction to his approaching parole, Crutchley tried to assure the citizens of Florida that they had nothing to fear from him.

"I'm old. I'm beat. I'm tired," he insisted. "I've been beaten down.

It's healing time. We've played the vampire game long enough."

Robert Ressler did not believe him. Based on his extensive

experience with serial killers, Ressler knew that Crutchley remained a danger despite having spent the past ten years in prison.

"The best predictor of future behavior is past behavior," Ressler remarked to a reporter who had contacted him about Crutchley's case. "A person who forcibly abducts, rapes, and bloodlets people doesn't have a record of being a safe citizen." Ressler urged Florida law enforcement to find a way to keep the Vampire Rapist from being freed to kill again.

THIRTY

Releasing the beast

O ne more day, Crutchley thought, *just one more day and I'm free.*

For Florida Department of Corrections Inmate Number 103067, a decade felt like forever. The years in prison had given him a new appreciation for the notion that time is a relative concept. He had eventually adjusted to the prison rules and constant supervision, if not fully acclimating to the confinement. He had generally kept to himself, managing to stay out of trouble for the most part, but he had never become fully institutionalized, an inmate who felt most at home behind bars. Preferring to avoid drawing attention to himself, Crutchley had conducted himself in prison in the same unassuming fashion he had followed before his arrest.

Still, the time in prison produced profound physical changes in Crutchley. Years of stress and prison food dropped his already light bodyweight by nearly twenty-five pounds, and he had noticeably aged. His hair had greyed and his complexion was more pasty and pale, but the physical changes did not particularly surprise him. After all, prisons were meant to punish, designed to deter, and intended to reform.

He did not dispute the first function. He had felt first-hand the punitive force of a life behind bars, and was convinced that no one could consider it pleasant. The goal of deterrence presented more of a problem. He wondered how the threat of prison could be a deterrent to someone who refuses to entertain the notion that they will eventually be caught. He certainly never thought that he would be, and his ability to elude the authorities, even after the colossal mistake of the Debbie Fitzjohn matter, had only emboldened this sense of invincibility. Indeed, the possibility of being caught had never seemed real until the day he returned home and found out that Christina Almah had escaped, and even then he believed that he would avoid any charges.

As for the goal of reforming the criminal offender, that was an endeavor worth emphasizing. Out of everything his experiences in the criminal justice system had taught him, the value of showing remorse would be one of the most important lessons. If you could show everyone how sorry you were for what you had done, you were halfway home. If you could also convince them that your prison time had somehow changed you for the better—the proverbial "I found Jesus" phenomenon—then you were well on your way. He had recognized this truth early on and had so consistently played the role of the repentant, born-again Christian, the lost soul rescued from damnation by God's divine grace, that he almost believed it himself.

Now that he had nearly served his time, another problem presented itself. As his August 8, 1996 parole date neared, the issue of where Crutchley would be released to serve his fifty-year probation was yet to be resolved. He initially requested to transfer his probation from Florida to Bridgeport, West Virginia, where his mother still lived, but West Virginia authorities denied the request in the face of objections from local residents, citing safety concerns both for Crutchley's mother and the community. Police in nearby Clarksburg, West Virginia, where Crutchley grew up, echoed their

Bridgeport colleagues' concern, stating that all of Crutchley's mother's neighbors "have been very upset about the possibility of him coming here."

Mildred Crutchley said she felt devastated by the news that her son would not be able come to West Virginia. On June 6, in an interview with her local newspaper, she compared her despondent state of mind to how she and her husband had spent their fifty-fifth wedding anniversary.

"On the night of our anniversary, we were watching the news and we saw the story about John's conviction," she told the reporter. "We just sat there and cried in each other's arms."

Due to the denial of Crutchley's request for release in West Virginia, Florida Department of Corrections officials had to scurry to find another location for him. They eventually settled on the *Christ Is The Answer* mission in Melbourne, Florida—a halfway house for transients, reformed drug addicts, alcoholics, and ex-convicts—as a suitable site. The mission's founder had agreed to accept Crutchley after being contacted by a probation officer from Orlando, but Brevard County Sheriff Jake Miller vehemently disagreed with the new location.

"We don't have a choice," Miller said angrily. "If we did, we definitely would rather he relocate to another state. He's not welcome here."

Melbourne Chief of Police Keith Chandler voiced his deep-seated disapproval as well. "I can't be convinced that he's not going to do it again," he said. Chief Chandler pointed out that, in light of the community's fierce hostility toward Crutchley, "I'm not sure we can guarantee his safety if he comes here."

On August 5, the City of Melbourne rejected the plan to house Crutchley at the *Christ Is The Answer* mission, and the mission's founder confirmed that both the Chief of the Melbourne Police and the City Manager asked him to withdraw his offer to allow Crutchley to stay at the mission. But city officials were not the only ones who had been encouraging him to change his mind. He also received calls from numerous members of the community urging him to do so and stating in no uncertain terms that failing to do so would forfeit their much needed financial support. He had even received some bomb threats.

"It's in our hearts to help this man, but if the majority of residents don't want him, then I have to go that route," the mission's founder explained matter-of-factly.

The mission's rejection of Crutchley sent state corrections officials once again scrambling to find another site for him. Since *Christ Is The Answer* proved not to be the answer to their dilemma, corrections officials contacted the *Resurrection Ranch* mission about the possibility of placing Crutchley there. However, the *Ranch* summarily rejected him.

On Tuesday, August 6, the *Florida Today* featured a cover story on Crutchley's parole and the Department of Corrections' attempts to find a proper location for his release. As part of the story, the paper included an insert urging Brevard County residents to call a hotline to share their thoughts about Crutchley's release. A large number of residents had already voiced their feelings on the matter.

"He's a blood-drinking, girl-killing demento," Danni Nichols stated angrily. "He ought to be locked up forever or killed."

Malabar resident Gary Crane agreed in less aggressive language: "I really feel what he did was a heinous crime. This is just not the kind of person we need in our community."

The next day, newspapers across the country chronicled Crutchley's parole woes. Papers as diverse as the *USA Today*, the *Akron Beacon Journal*, and the *Los Angeles Times* carried stories with titles such as the *Times'* "No One Wants the 'Vampire Rapist.'"

While newspapers nationwide reported Crutchley's parole problem, his local paper sought input from citizens to help shape the story. On August 7, the *Florida Today* printed a front-page box item, titled "Let's talk," in which it invited county residents to a

"Community Conversation" panel discussion to be held on August 8, the same day as Crutchley's parole date, to discuss where felons should live after their release from prison. State senators, State Attorney Norm Wolfinger, and other elected public officials were slated to participate on the panel, and the paper noted how "hundreds of people" had "expressed anger to officials and to the newspaper about the release of John Crutchley."

Meanwhile, with his release date only a day away, prison officials raced to find a suitable location for Crutchley to serve his probation. James Freeman, a senior ranking probation officer at Union Correctional, fielded countless calls from newspapers, television stations, and law enforcement agencies about Crutchley's pending release. The law enforcement agencies were unanimous in conveying in no uncertain terms that the Vampire Rapist would not be welcome in their jurisdictions.

If the Department of Corrections could simply release Crutchley without accounting for his whereabouts, the release would have been much less problematic, but that was not an option. As the Department's spokesperson pointed out in discussing the dilemma of being required to release Crutchley while also finding an appropriate place for him to serve his probation, "we certainly can't let him out the front door and not know where he's going."

Legally required to release Crutchley on August 8, the Department of Corrections found a last minute location, the only one that would agree to take him: the Orlando Probation and Restitution Center. Situated on seven acres near an industrial property in northwest Orlando, the Center reluctantly agreed to take Crutchley with the understanding that his placement there would be temporary, lasting only until he could get a job and find a permanent residence. Moreover, while residing at the Center, Crutchley would be required to attend a sex offender counseling program, after first completing a one- or two-week orientation period. He would also be required to stay inside the facility unless accompanied by a corrections officer, and he would be under constant surveillance and supervision. While the average stay at the center was about four months, Crutchley's circumstances were such that he was approved to stay up to 364 days if necessary to secure a job and permanent residence.

Relatives of the Vampire Rapist's victims expressed deep disappointment and outrage over his release.

"My daughter and I think he should have gotten life," Christina Almah's mother commented. "We're scared. He says he is a changed man, but I think he is a sick man. And I don't think he can ever change."

Christina's mother said that her daughter still had not recovered from the abduction and rape that had occurred a decade earlier.

"She's scared to go outside," her mother said, the sadness in her voice clearly audible. "She's become a hermit. She's married now, but says she will never have children because she is afraid of what might happen to them."

Patti Volanski's mother, Alta Pratt, conveyed a similar sentiment, "I dread to see him get out of prison. I don't want him to hurt anybody else, but I believe he will."

Herman Fitzjohn, the father of one of Crutchley's first victims, voiced his anger and bewilderment as well. "They're just going to let him out on the public. What the hell do they think he's going to do there? You mark my word. It'll happen again. He'll do the same thing again. Why sacrifice another woman for this person?"

In Maryland, private investigator James Wilt received a telephone call from a reporter at a Florida television station. Wilt had heard about the local community's outrage over Crutchley's parole, and the reporter wanted to know what he thought about Crutchley being released. The station sent a limo to pick him up and shuttle him to the set of a local news program addressing the parole. Wilt appeared on the show as part of a remote panel, with the Brevard County Sheriff and a professed expert on vampires appearing via satellite from other locations.

Having spent years trying to link Crutchley to Debbie Fitzjohn's murder, Wilt made no secret of his feelings about Crutchley's pending release.

"I believe he killed her," Wilt told the panel moderator, "but he'll probably get out and do the same thing to someone else."

Out of concerns for his safety, corrections officials kept Crutchley's mode of transportation and route to the Orlando probation facility secret. Showing the effects of his decade of incarceration, the forty-nine year-old Crutchley left Union Correctional Institution in the early morning hours of August 8 for the three-hour drive to his temporary home. He arrived at the Orlando center without incident, stepping out of a white Department of Corrections van with darkly tinted windows, wearing a baseball cap and carrying a small box containing his belongings.

Orange County Sheriff Kevin Beary was quick to express his indignation over Crutchley's relocation to his county.

"I'm not a happy camper," he growled, "I think the system screwed up."

At a news conference held to speak out against the parole arrangement, Beary strongly condemned the decision to dump Crutchley into the community of "theme parks, fun, and family."

Deputy Chief Charlie Wright of the Orlando Police Department echoed Beary's impassioned disapproval, emphasizing that Crutchley "is not your average, everyday person who goes through the system." Wright pledged to tightly monitor his whereabouts.

Beary continued his condemnation of Crutchley's release by pointing out his close proximity to particularly vulnerable potential victims. "To put him in the vicinity of a school, hospital, and several neighborhoods is like putting a kid in a candy store," Beary announced. "That is not acceptable." Perhaps aiming to enflame the passion of the public, Beary shrewdly added that "having a heinous criminal like this getting out fifteen years early and coming back into the community" should be considered a "slap in the face for every woman in this state."

Beary vowed to be vigilant, promising that Crutchley's picture would be posted in every Orange County police car.

"If he violates the law, we'll be there to stick his sorry tailbone back in prison," he promised emphatically.

Most residents living near the rehabilitation center voiced cautious concerns or outright fears about having the Vampire Rapist as a neighbor. Disney World lab technician Leroy Rogers criticized a criminal justice system that could be so dysfunctional as to ignite widespread fear among the public, causing many to feel as if the system was "putting the public in jail."

Another resident, Tulie Phillips, started a phone and fax barrage aimed at local lawmakers, proclaiming "we will do anything we can within the law to get him out of here."

Vera Wright, who lived just down the road from the Center, perhaps best encapsulated the overall mood of the majority. "People just don't feel safe with him around," she said expressing the essential mood of the community.

The public criticism did not confine itself to a verbal medium. It flowed into a written forum as well. Orlando City Council members, Orange County commissioners, and Florida's Governor received scores of letters from citizens of Orange County voicing their disagreement and dissatisfaction with the determination to house Crutchley in the Orlando area. Not content to confine his anger to a verbal arena, Sheriff Beary dispatched a letter to Governor Lawton Chiles on August 8.

Dear Governor Chiles:

I am outraged. A violent sex offender is being released into my County, and I found out about it on the radio.

As Sheriff of Orange County, my primary responsibility is to protect our citizens and visitors. When the safety of my jurisdiction is deliberately and purposely violated by the State of Florida, I should at the least receive some advanced notification.

The Florida Department of Corrections made a decision to release John Crutchley based on an opinion that he is rehabilitated. Governor Chiles, John Crutchley is not only not rehabilitated, he is non-rehabilitable. Less than one percent of violent sex offenders are ever rehabilitated. Corrections knows this, Probation and Parole knows this, and we here in Orange County know this.

We are not happy, and John Crutchley is not welcome here.

I ask that you find other accommodations for this violent individual, preferably prison, as soon as possible.

Letters to newspaper editors at the *Tampa Tribune* and *Orlando Sentinel* joined the growing chorus of public displeasure, repeatedly referring to Crutchley as a "monster" and branding his crime as "horrendous." The swelling surge of letters engulfed public officials in an overwhelming flood of criticism, clearly conveying a community's outrage.

The story of the Vampire Rapist's parole also monopolized the airwaves. It quickly became the dominant topic for local radio talk-show hosts who spent the day debating the issue and trading sarcastic jokes about vampires. Most of the hosts and their listeners seemed to be against Crutchley's release, but at a doctor's office next door to the parole center, Yvonne Abrams opined, "Hey, this man's paid his dues. Everybody deserves a second chance." And Leroy Stewart, a former guard at Union Correctional during Crutchley's tenure there, described the infamous inmate as a "neat, polite" prisoner who generally kept to himself, obeyed the rules, and did not talk much. Stewart added another observation about Crutchley, one that touched on the strength of his mental discipline. "Most of the inmates will tell you what they did, but he wouldn't talk about it. He just smiled all the time."

As for Crutchley himself, the man many knew only as the Vampire Rapist expressed optimism and high spirits during his first day of freedom. During a telephone call with his mother, he said that he liked the facilities at the Orlando probation center and that everyone was treating him well there. He looked forward to spending time with his mother, reconnecting with his now fourteen-year-old son, Jason, and starting a new life somewhere in South Florida. Miami, with its diverse population, eclectic South Beach scene, and abundant nightlife, held a particular attraction for him. He hoped to be able to blend into the community once the media mania subsided and people began to focus their attention on other things.

However, his newfound happiness would prove to be short-lived.

THIRTY-ONE

Back again

On Friday, August 9, just one day after his release from prison, Department of Corrections officials announced that Crutchley had violated the terms of his probation by smoking marijuana the night before beginning his parole. According to corrections officials, when Crutchley arrived at the Orlando Probation Center on August 8, he had been informed that he would have to take a drug test, a requirement commonly applied to new residents at the facility. As Crutchley prepared to take the test, he told the supervising probation officer that he had smoked marijuana during a farewell party thrown for him by the other inmates at Union Correctional.

It did not take long for officials to secure a warrant for Crutchley's arrest. Brevard County Judge Edward Richardson signed the warrant around noon on August 9. A little over two hours later, eight Orange County deputies and Orlando police officers arrested a visibly shaken Crutchley and placed him in the back of a patrol car. Less than thirty hours after Crutchley arrived at the probation center with what seemed to be a new lease on life, the State of Florida had him back in custody.

And now he faced the prospect of a life sentence.

Mildred Crutchley found the timing of her son's probation violation to be entirely too coincidental. She summarily condemned his rearrest as a set up. Given the massive public outcry that had been raised against her son's release, her suspicions were not unreasonable.

"It's too obvious," she insisted. "Everyone knows you wouldn't do that. You wouldn't risk not getting out."

But Burton Green, a Melbourne defense attorney, believed that Crutchley might have purposely sabotaged his own parole. In Green's view, Crutchley had to have known that smoking marijuana the night before his release would put him right back in prison. After ten years behind bars, Green reasoned, Crutchley might have become comfortable there and consciously or unconsciously chosen to stay in familiar surroundings, rather than facing a life of uncertainty in a society that would be hostile to him and where he would struggle to survive. Green speculated that Crutchley could have concluded that "everyone, including himself, might be better off if he's in prison."

Terry Casto, the Director of Crutchley's department at Harris Corporation, also theorized that Crutchley might not have wanted to get out of prison. After all, his homosexual tastes could be easily indulged among a captive population of sexually frustrated men. Indeed, many of the inmates housed with him alleged that he had demanded sex in exchange for granting them special recreation privileges. Or perhaps he purposely smoked marijuana the night before his release because he knew what macabre activities he would resume if he regained his freedom.

Regardless of the reason for Crutchley's re-arrest, Christina Almah's parents were ecstatic upon hearing the news.

"That's wonderful," her father exclaimed, "I know she'll be relieved. They need to keep him in there."

Orange County Sheriff Kevin Beary, who had been so vocal in

his opposition to Crutchley's release to the Orlando probation center, could not contain his giddiness.

"This has definitely made my day," he said excitedly. "This is one for the community, one we all won. The people responded and I'm very proud of them," he proclaimed.

Of course, the absurdity of the entire situation was not lost on Leatherow. He could not help being amused by the notion that one marijuana cigarette might accomplish what investigators in four states had been unable to do: put Crutchley in prison for the rest of his life.

Detective Buck DeCoteau of the Palm Bay Police Department similarly celebrated the news. As the homicide investigator working the case of the skeletal remains found in January 1985, he had long since concluded that Crutchley was the unidentified woman's killer. Upon hearing of Crutchley's arrest for the violation of probation, a jubilant DeCoteau declared, "the citizens of Brevard County and myself will sleep better tonight."

Sheriff Jake Miller also joined in applauding the news, pronouncing Crutchley's arrest a "stroke of good luck."

Since Crutchley's underlying crimes that had given rise to his probation occurred in Brevard County, Orange County police turned him over to the Brevard County Sheriff's Office for transport back to the Brevard County Jail. Cellblock 300 of the jail's maximum-security section became his temporary home until a hearing could be held on the parole violation charge.

Blaise Trettis, Executive Assistant Public Defender for Brevard County, expressed doubt about the legality of the probation violation charge since the alleged violation had occurred while Crutchley was still been in prison.

"You can only violate probation once you begin it. If he took drugs while in prison, he may have violated prison rules, but not probation."

Joe Mitchell agreed, and suspected that his former client had been set up.

Similar thinking came from an unlikely source. Despite having spent years trying to tie Crutchley to Debbie Fitzjohn's murder, and though happy to hear of Crutchley's return to custody, James Wilt shared Mitchell's belief.

"I think it was all set up," said Wilt. "The community was in such a tizzy when he came up for parole, they had to do something. Everybody was scared to death about him being released. They were looking for anything to keep him in jail."

During Crutchley's intake process, Brevard County Jail officers discovered that he had numerous body piercings, including 12 silver rings through his penis and scrotum, and one ring on his navel. One large teardrop-shaped ring through the tip of his penis even had a small padlock on it. Crutchley explained that he had chosen that particular piercing as a way of demonstrating to his wife, Karen, that he would be chaste while in prison. Mark Riley, the jail's Operations Commander, remarked that Crutchley's piercing constituted the "most bizarre thing I've ever seen in regard to self-mutilation," and he could not help noticing that Crutchley seemed "very happy to show it, almost boastful."

After looking into the matter, jail officials determined that guards at Union Correctional had noticed the extensive piercings when they were preparing to transport Crutchley to the Orlando Parole Center. However, due to Crutchley's early morning departure time, Union Correctional Superintendent Dennis O'Neill did not learn of the piercings until Crutchley was already en route to the parole facility. After Crutchley arrived in Orlando, Department of

Corrections officials "at a higher level," perhaps aware of a potentially greater offense, instructed O'Neill to let the matter drop.

On Tuesday, August 13, 1996, a grey-haired, ghostly-thin Crutchley, slightly stooping from being shackled, and wearing a red prison jumpsuit reserved for the most dangerous inmates, appeared in front of Brevard County Judge Ken Friedland to receive a hearing date on his violation of probation charge. The meek, "mousy" looking Crutchley ran a hand through his short, sandy hair several times, and then adjusted his glasses before informing the judge that he could not afford his own attorney. Judge Friedland scheduled Crutchley's violation of probation hearing for October 7 and appointed an attorney to represent him.

On August 17, the *Orlando Sentinel* published a letter to the editor from Orlando resident Margaret Gust. In her letter, Gust expressed her bewilderment and disbelief about how Crutchley's situation had been handled by Florida's criminal justice system. She found the circumstances of Crutchley's original sentence, parole, and re-arrest absolutely asinine.

> *Some people have served more time for possessing or selling a small quantity of a controlled substance or stealing a car than Crutchley did for torturing another human being. How ludicrous that he is sent back to his rightful place – prison – for smoking marijuana and perhaps violating his probation. Our "justice system" is apparently more outraged at marijuana use than it is at rape and torture of another person.*

On September 6, correctional investigator Keith Adams of the Department of Correction's Office of Inspector General released his report concerning Crutchley's violation of probation. Adams found that, shortly after arriving at the Orlando Probation Center, Crutchley admitted to correctional officer Herbert Zucker that he had smoked marijuana on the night of August 7 during a "going away party" that other inmates at Union Correctional Institute held for him in his cell in Building 65. However, Crutchley did not identify the names of any of the inmates involved in the party. According to the report, in response to Crutchley's admission of marijuana use, all eighty-four inmates in Building 65 were submitted to drug tests on August 9. Thirty-five of them tested positive for drugs, a figure significantly higher than normal.

The report detailed that, on August 21, Adams took a taped statement from Gary Sult, Crutchley's cellmate at the time of the alleged party. Sult advised that Crutchley had been in the cell packing his personal items from the time of the 8:00 p.m. head count until about 10:30 p.m. when Sult went to bed. Sult denied that Crutchley smoked marijuana in the cell, and he denied that any kind of party had taken place in the cell or anywhere nearby. He recalled that during the course of the evening some inmates had dropped by the cell at various times to wish Crutchley good luck, but none of them had smoked marijuana. Sult insisted that he did not use drugs and did not allow anyone around him to use drugs. Relevant evidence seemed to support Sult's contentions, as he had tested negative for drugs on August 9 and August 13.

Adams's report also recounted the results of a taped statement taken from inmate Dwayne Hilliard on August 23. Hilliard had advised that at approximately 7:30 p.m. on August 7, a large group of inmates in Building 65 watched a television program that featured a disturbing story on Crutchley as the "Vampire Rapist." After seeing the program, many of the inmates became upset about Crutchley and talked about "jumping on him," prison slang for severely beating him or otherwise causing him great bodily harm. Hilliard stated that later that night he approached Crutchley with the intent of physically harming him, but Crutchley convinced him that witnesses for the prosecution had lied about the case against him. Crutchley also gave Hilliard two marijuana cigarettes called "pin joints," which Hilliard took to his own cell and smoked. Hilliard swore that he did not smoke any marijuana in Crutchley's cell and stated that he had no knowledge of a party in the building.

Inspector Adams took the statement of Correctional Officer James Heard on August 26. Heard had been the officer on duty in Building 65 on August 7. He stated that sometime after the start of his 4:00 p.m. duty shift, he heard inmates discussing a television show about Crutchley. Shortly after 7:30 p.m., the show *Hard Copy* featured a story about the Vampire Rapist, and after the program many of the inmates seemed agitated and upset. He overheard some of them talking about hurting Crutchley. Officer Heard advised that he made a conscious effort to keep an eye on Crutchley afterward by checking the area around Crutchley's cell periodically, at which times he saw Crutchley packing up his personal belongings in preparation for his release. Heard further stated that he observed several inmates stopping by Crutchley's cell during the course of the night, but he did not see or hear anything resembling a party or other gathering.

The remainder of Adams's report discussed his findings with respect to Crutchley's piercings, including detailed descriptions of a pencil-sized silver ring about the width of a silver dollar pierced through his penis, and two smaller rings situated in the skin between his scrotum and anus.

By now wholly suspicious of the court, Mildred Crutchley hired Melbourne attorney Michael Bross to defend her son rather than trusting the court appointed public defender. Local lawyers joked that Bross "never met a mirror he didn't like," and most figured that he took on the Crutchley case more for the publicity than for whatever money Mildred managed to pay him. As his first act after being retained, Bross requested a postponement of Crutchley's violation of probation hearing. Bross informed Judge Tanya Rainwater, the judge assigned to preside over the hearing, that he needed the additional time to finish taking depositions of witnesses still incarcerated at Union Correctional prison. He advised the judge that he intended to argue that Crutchley's alleged parole violation had been a set-up, pointing out that shortly before his release date, prison officials knowingly transferred Crutchley, a nonsmoker throughout his incarceration, from a nonsmoking area of the prison to a smoking section of the facility that was wellknown for rampant inmate marijuana use.

"We want to know why he was set up," Bross exclaimed, "and we will subpoena the necessary people to find out." Bross asserted that he would also argue that the alleged marijuana use could not constitute a violation of probation because it occurred before his client's release while he was still serving his sentence in prison.

On September 25, Bross took the deposition of Herbert Zucker, the Senior Probation Officer at the Orlando Probation Restitution Center. Zucker testified that after Crutchley arrived at the Center, he informed Crutchley that he would be tested for drugs as part of the Center's normal intake procedures. Zucker stated that Crutchley did not object to the test, but told him that he would test positive for marijuana because he had smoked marijuana at a going away party in his cell between 9:00 and 10:00 p.m. the night before his release. Following Zucker's deposition, Glenn Jay, one of the probation officers supervised by Zucker, testified to substantially the same version of the facts as Zucker.

The following month, George Gallo, an inmate at Marion Correctional Institution, wrote a letter to Special Agent Dennis

Fischer of the Florida Department of Law Enforcement's Gainesville Field Office, advising that he knew another inmate, William Omasta, who had assisted Crutchley in preparing various legal documents while in prison. Gallo claimed that Crutchley had revealed information about his crimes to Omasta, and asked to meet with someone from the FDLE to discuss the information. A few days later, Agent Fischer interviewed Gallo at the prison. Gallo informed Fischer that Omasta told him that he had learned significant information about Crutchley's crimes, including the location of the bodies of some of Crutchley's victims, but that Omasta had been saving the information in case he ever needed to make a deal with prison officials or other law enforcement.

After concluding the interview and returning to his office, Fischer reviewed his files and discovered that he had interviewed Omasta on February 1, 1996, while Omasta was incarcerated at Sumter Correctional Institute. During that interview, Omasta advised Fischer that he had previously talked to detectives from Brevard County, but had not provided them with any information concerning Crutchley because they had not been willing to make a deal with him in exchange for his help.

On November 19, Judge Rainwater received a letter from John and Ann Blanton of Cocoa, Florida, requesting leniency for Crutchley.

Dear Judge Rainwater,
    We have watched with great concern the
    lopsided views of the media concerning John Crutchley. Why has this man been singled out?
    . . . .
    We have gotten acquainted with John through ministry, letters, and phone conversations. We have come to love this sweet man

God has changed – the man he is today. For 9 years we have
known him and he has shown an attitude of great remorse and
sorrow for his past, concern for those who have been hurt because
of his actions, care and concern for all he meets today that are
hurting, and a genuine desire to be a model citizen.
> *PLEASE GIVE HIM THAT CHANCE!*

The next day, Robert Bache, a classification officer at Union Correctional, testified at deposition that Crutchley had maintained an "exemplary record" throughout his time there. Bache expressed surprise about the allegation that Crutchley had smoked marijuana the night before his release because Bache had never seen, or even heard of, Crutchley smoking while he had been incarcerated there. Indeed, Bache testified that Crutchley had never failed a drug test while in prison.

"He had an exemplary record with us. He was a good worker. It just surprised me," he told Bross.

Gary Sult, Crutchley's roommate in cell 102 at the time of the alleged probation violation, testified at his November 20 deposition that Crutchley did not smoke the marijuana that triggered his re-arrest. According to Sult, after watching a television program about Crutchley's case that aired the night before his release, several of the larger black inmates with bad intentions started talking about doing something to him. Sult talked them out of physically harming Crutchley, but later in the evening three inmates came to his cell and blew "shotguns" at Crutchley, meaning that they smoked marijuana cigarettes, held Crutchley down, and made him inhale the smoke. Due to the small size of the eight feet long and two feet wide cell, it had not been hard for them to restrain him.

"They cornered him in the corner by the toilet," Sult testified, "and they were blowing smoke in his face."

During his January 15, 1997 deposition, Lamar Griffs, the Administrative Lieutenant at Union Correctional, could not explain why Crutchley had been moved from Building 2 to Building 5 a few weeks before his release. On the same date, Lieutenant Alfonso Robinson, the officer who supervised the southwest unit housing complex that included Buildings 2 and 5, testified that in August 1996, Building 2 had been a non-smoking building, while Building 5 was used to house inmates who were smokers. Bross asked Robinson why Crutchley, a known non-smoker, had been moved from Building 2 to Building 5 so close to his release date. Robinson could not provide an explanation.

"The only thing I know," Robinson said, "is that approximately I guess about two months ago the major – Major Dickson asked me if I had received a request on Inmate Crutchley to move him to Building Five, out of Building Two. I told him no. Now as far as him going to Building Five I don't know the real reason."

A week prior to the hearing on his violation of probation, Crutchley stumbled into a prison interview room, handcuffed and shackled. He told reporters that he was a changed man, and he continued to blame pornographic magazines for fueling his sexual fantasies to the point of kidnapping and raping Christina Almah. Crutchley admitted that, at the time of the sexual assaults and bloodletting, he interpreted the fact that Christina did not resist as her *wanting* him to rape her and drain her blood, but now he understood the extent of his erroneous thinking, telling reporters that "now I realize she might have just been scared to death, too afraid to move." And he swore that he would never harm anyone again if given his freedom.

"I hurt one person very, very bad, and I will never hurt anyone again in my life," he promised. "I'm worn out, drained. But my eighty six-year-old mother needs me; my teenaged child needs me. I need to be there for them to make up for some of the pain that I've caused in their lives."

The hearing to determine whether Crutchley violated the terms of his probation went forward on January 27, 1997. During the first day of hearing testimony, Gary Sult warned that Crutchley would be killed by other inmates if he returned to prison.

"If he goes back there," Sult asserted, "he won't live the day."

Sult's testimony supported Crutchley's out of court contention that he had only confessed to smoking marijuana to avoid implicating other inmates because they would viciously retaliate against him if he identified them to the authorities. Sult repeated what he had said during his deposition as to what had actually occurred on the night of August 7. Crutchley had not intentionally smoked marijuana. Instead, several inmates deliberately got Crutchley high by blowing smoke in his face.

"There were a bunch of people coming in and out that night. A couple of guys came in and pushed him over by the wall and started blowing shotguns in his face."

While Sult's testimony corroborated Crutchley's claim that he had not voluntarily inhaled marijuana smoke, it remained to be seen whether the judge would find Sult credible.

During the second day of testimony, the prosecution played an audiotape of Crutchley that had been recorded at the Orlando Probation Center after he told a probation officer that he had smoked marijuana. On the tape, Crutchley admitted that he had smoked marijuana, but he explained that he had been in his cell packing when a group of inmates started banging on his door saying that they wanted to party. Since they would not take no for an answer, he reluctantly invited them in "to placate them." He said he smoked a marijuana cigarette that someone handed him because he hoped that it would help get rid of anxiety that he had been suffering due to nervousness and excitement about his pending release from prison.

He tried to explain to the judge how agitated his state of mind had been.

"It's like you're in a sardine can and you can hear somebody yelling 'help' outside and you can't get help," Crutchley said. "I know what a caged animal in the zoo feels like. You see that lion in the zoo pacing back and forth, back and forth, and I will never go to the zoo again in my life. This experience—those poor animals, I know what they feel like."

After the prosecution presented its case-in-chief, the defense put on its case, recalling Crutchley's cellmate, Gary Sult, to establish that Crutchley had been set up. Sult testified that Crutchley had been moved from Building 2, a non-smoking building, to Sult's cell in Building 5, a smoking building, less than two months before his release date. Crutchley had been transferred into Sult's cell during the middle of the night, which Sult characterized as being considerably "out of the ordinary."

Sult described the cell they shared as eleven feet long and eight feet wide with a two-man bunk bed at the end of the room opposite the door. The cramped cell contained two footlockers, a small writing table, a sink, and a steel toilet. A solid steel door with an eleven-inch by four-inch glass view port was the only way in or out of the cell. Sult stated that he never saw Crutchley smoke *anything* during the time they were cellmates, and that Crutchley had at times chased away other inmates who were smoking cigarettes in the room because smoke of any kind irritated his bronchitis.

He testified that on the night of August 7, several inmates came to Crutchley's cell with marijuana, but Crutchley did not intentionally smoke any of it. Instead, the other inmates forced it on him. They pushed Crutchley over by the toilet and blew shotguns in his face to force him to get high. Sult would not name the inmates involved because, like Crutchley, he feared retribution if he did so.

Sult further testified that after Crutchley tested positive for marijuana use, the warden had put all of Building 5 on a restrictive status, and the inmates blamed Crutchley for the punishment. Sult made it clear that if Crutchley went back to the prison, his life would be in danger.

"It's in real big jeopardy," Sult insisted. "If he goes back there, he won't live through the day."

After Sult, it was Crutchley's turn to take the stand. Crutchley explained that he had been housed in Building 2, a smoke-free building, for a lengthy period of time because he suffered from congenital bronchial problems and could not be around smoke. He testified that "several weeks" prior to his scheduled release date, he was moved against his will to Building 5, a smoking building known to house large numbers of inmates with drug problems.

On the night before his release date, he had been packing up his personal belongings when several inmates came to his cell and announced that it was "party time." They tried to hand him a marijuana cigarette, but he refused to take it, so they pushed him into the corner by the toilet and said, "Come on Crutch, you want to smoke some of this—we'll party you up a little bit." Then they shot-gunned him. One of them took the cigarette, lit it, put the lit end in his mouth, moved over a few inches from Crutchley, and then blew out through the cigarette so that the smoke went into Crutchley's face. While one of them blew the smoke, the other inmates pressed against his chest and told him to hold the smoke in. They repeated the process over and over again for five or ten minutes, each time forcing Crutchley to hold the smoke in his lungs.

When asked by his attorney why anyone would want to try to get him in trouble by forcing him to smoke marijuana, Crutchley testified that some inmates wanted to get even with him for not doing them favors when he was the clerk in charge of the prison's recreation activities. He said that the majority of the inmates at Union Correctional were serving life sentences with no hope of ever getting out. Some of them were jealous that he was going to be released, so it was not surprising that they would try "jamming" his time by getting him into trouble.

Crutchley also explained why he failed to inform the parole officer at the Orlando Probation Center that he had been forced to inhale the marijuana smoke by other inmates.

"If you talk about other people's activities in prison, you have to watch your back because your back is going to get opened with a shank. It's that simple. You don't talk about other people's activities in prison or you become extinct. It's just life in prison. You learn that real quick up front."

Crutchley pointed out that, after being clean in prison throughout his ten years of incarceration, it would have been completely irrational for him to do any drugs on the eve of his release.

"I'm facing perhaps the biggest moment of my life and going out and being with my wife and son and my mom, and the last thing I wanted to do is get high."

After the defense rested its case, Judge Rainwater announced that in her deliberations she would disregard Crutchley's testimony about being forced to inhale marijuana smoke. She simply did not find his account of events to be credible.

"I disregard his testimony today. He's had five months to come up with this story that it was forced on him. Clearly, the statements that he gave to the officers the day after, and two days after, the ingestion of the marijuana is a much more believable and much more coherent story as to what happened."

Before deciding whether to send Crutchley back to prison or to permit him to serve time on probation, the judge allowed Crutchley to address her one last time.

From the defense table, Crutchley expressed remorse for what he had done to Christina Almah and claimed his life had simply snowballed out of control, describing it as some sort of a "cross between Forrest Gump and a Stephen King movie." He stressed to the judge that he had received psychological treatment by completing a Mentally Disordered Sexual Offender Program while in prison, and he needed to get out so he could help take care of his mother and son. He steadfastly maintained that his vampire days were far behind him.

"Everybody knows John Brennan Crutchley, the big vampire. I'm so sick of the word vampire," he insisted.

After Crutchley finished, Judge Rainwater took a few moments to reflect on all of the testimony. Then she stoically announced her decision, sentencing Crutchley to life imprisonment for violating the terms of his probation. In imposing a life sentence, the judge adopted the factual findings that had been made by Judge Antoon during the original sentencing hearing, ruling that they justified an upward departure from the sentencing guidelines. The judge identified as "key" findings that, at the time she arrived at Holmes Regional Medical Center, Christina Almah (1) had lost 40 to 50 percent of her total blood volume, (2) was experiencing hemorrhagic shock at or near a level likely to result in death, and (3) would have died if she lost more blood prior to receiving medical treatment or if she had not received any medical treatment. Although the recommended guideline sentence was twelve to seventeen years, Judge Rainwater found "clear and convincing" reasons to depart from the guideline range, apparently convinced that the accused was more monster than man. The judge concluded that the facts established beyond a reasonable doubt that Crutchley used "excessive brutality" in the commission of his crimes of kidnapping and sexual battery and that his acts were premeditated.

With a life sentence now imposed, it appeared that Crutchley's one-day probation had cost him his freedom forever; however, Crutchley showed little emotion while the judge pronounced his sentence. Later, he told a reporter that he was not surprised by the judge's action given the massive public outcry when he had been released on parole. "The judge bowed to the media pressure and hype," he said resignedly.

Crutchley's attorney, Michael Bross, dispassionately expressed his disappointment in the judge's ruling, while Crutchley's mother blasted the sentence as unfair, furiously insisting that her son had become a new man after finding God in prison.

Conversely, the relatives of Crutchley's victims celebrated and welcomed the news of his life sentence. Patti Volanski's mother exclaimed "Hallelujah!" when told that a sentence of life imprisonment had been imposed. "I just know he was dying to get out to start doing it again," she said with obvious relief.

Christina Almah's younger sister called the sentence a "miracle," and said that her sister would be "ecstatic" because "it's exactly what he deserves."

In an interview with the media shortly after his sentencing, Crutchley continued to deny being involved in any murder, but a curious inconsistency arose as he explained how he came to have Patti Volanski's identification card in his office desk at Harris Corporation. He claimed that the identification card ended up in his desk because a motorcyclist whom he had picked up along the road left it behind in his car. When he noticed the laminated card, he put it in his desk drawer with the intention of calling Patti to let her know that he had it. However, back in 1986, Crutchley had told a reporter that he picked up *Volanski* as she was hitchhiking, and that it was Volanski herself, not some unknown motorcyclist, who left behind the identification card after he made her get out of the car.

The controversy surrounding the significant shortening of Crutchley's original prison sentence due to gain time reinforced the need for considerable changes strengthening the state's sentencing laws. Florida's laws in effect in 1985 had required, among other reductions, an automatic grant of 3,000 days gain time. As Governor Chiles pointed out in his reply to Sheriff Beary's August 8 letter of outrage, the Crutchley case "illustrates why we worked hard to change the sentencing law to require prisoners to serve 85% of their sentence before they are released." Had such laws been in place at the time of Crutchley's original twenty-five year sentence, he would not have been eligible for parole until at least 2007, by which time he would have been over 60 years old.

THIRTY-TWO

Human cruelty

Human cruelty and treachery surpass all understanding.

– John Crutchley

B ack in prison after a brief taste of freedom, Crutchley began his life sentence by serving a stint in solitary confinement. Having lied to jail officials by claiming that he could not remove his penile piercings, Crutchley received a disciplinary report and was placed in administrative confinement on February 5, 1997. The truth came out during his intake strip search when Earle Petty instructed him to remove the ringed piercings.

"I can't take them off," Crutchley calmly told him. "I can't remove them."

Petty did not hesitate with his reply. He glared at Crutchley, cracked a slight smile, and shouted to no one in particular, "Somebody get me a pair of pliers!"

After realizing that Petty was serious, Crutchley had a sudden change of heart. He quickly removed the rings himself, needing minimal effort to do so.

A poetic essay composed or copied by Crutchley, and bearing the title "A Life Means Nothing Here," provided a glimpse into his state of mind as he began his second round of imprisonment, while also casting doubt on the sincerity of his spiritual rebirth.

> *Prison is where you exchange the dignity of your*
> *name for the degradation of a number.*
> *Prison is where you live from visit to visit . . .*
> *If you're lucky enough to have a visitor.*
> *Prison is where you learn the counting of life:*
> *You count the years, seasons, months, weeks, days,*
> *hours, minutes, & seconds.*
> *Prison is where you hope and pray not to die.*
>
> *Prison is where you're lucky if you never have to kill*
> *some fool over bullshit.*
> *Prison is where therapy & religion are not looked*
> *upon as beneficial in themselves.*
> *They are looked upon as beneficial in a parole board*
> *report.*

After completing his administrative confinement, Crutchley returned to the regular prison population and spent much of his free time working feverishly to find a loophole to reinstate his parole. On April 16, 1998, he wrote to his mother, urging her to keep up her efforts to secure his release, warning her that "If I don't get effective help soon—I will die here. . . . It's getting frighteningly close to the end of all hopes of you ever seeing me home."

In another note, he wrote more about that loss of hope.

"In all my years, I've never felt lost—not truly lost. Frightened, yes. Sometimes confused & bleak. But always I had a map in my mind of where & what I'd do the next day, week, month, year . . . but now my map seems to have been surrounded by mirrors of doubt."

On May 1, he drafted another letter to his mother, this time expressing his yearning for the "soft, gentle pleasure of resting my head on a real pillow on a soft bed with clean sheets in a quiet, peaceful room." Later, in the same letter, he discussed an "unusual dream" in which he had somehow exchanged his male body for that of a woman. He reported that he had found the experience to be a pleasant one, explaining that the "difference in gender did not startle me at all – it just felt as natural as having four fingers and a thumb on each hand." He wondered whether other men had dreams of a similar nature.

As the days became weeks and the months morphed into years, he recorded extensive narratives exploring the idea that "no man is so entirely masculine that he has nothing feminine in him." One such passage suggested an attempt to sort out his own conflicting feelings and inability to find satisfaction and contentment.

As orgasms shuddered through both bodies for the second time of the evening, the fact dawned on Bill that this indefinable state of consciousness and feeling he had entered exceeded the intimacy one could experience with a woman to such an extent that there could be no true comparison simply because no woman can ever be inside a male body and know the feeling of exquisite pulsing release of one's passions coursing through one's hard dick. When a woman pleasures a man, she can at best only imagine what the man feels, but when a man brings another man through orgasm, both know what the other is feeling through experiencing it in their own body. This experience was one to savor.

Still laying there, Bill pondered the evening's events. The revelation swept over him like the sun suddenly appearing from behind a cloud: the truth behind the fear men have of intimate contact with another man comes from the instinctive knowledge that, like sex, once the boundary is crossed, the intense pleasure to be found there can never be removed from memory.

Bill reflected that he had finally experienced the fullness of his own self. Its existence had always been there – but soundly asleep. Now it was awake. More aware. More receptive. He'd found the unique balance which only can be savored with someone whose mind and body match his own. Feeling the supreme ecstasy of orgasm pumping full circle was beyond mere dizzying recreation: it brought a happiness to his heart he never would have dreamed of.

However, reflections on his sexual identity and homosexual inclinations were not the only thoughts occupying his time. He also wrote about long nights spent thinking about "past stupidities," things so inherently shameful that he tried to deaden the pain of their memory by self-mutilation, sometimes biting his arms hard enough to leave tooth-shaped bruises that were visible for weeks afterward. On a sheet of paper listing several items that he wanted to discuss with his sister, Crutchley included the cryptic notation: "The girls: I wonder how many."

Unbeknownst to Crutchley, he ended up in the same prison as Greg Raub, his former cellmate from the Brevard County Jail, who had testified against him years earlier during his original trial proceedings. Although the prison housed approximately 1500 inmates, Raub was afraid that Crutchley would find out that he was there. With anxiety approaching agony, he feared that Crutchley would put a hit out on him or try to attack him himself. Joseph Burke, Raub's cellmate at the time, decided to play a practical joke on him. He caught up to Crutchley in the prison yard one day and asked for the Vampire Rapist's autograph.

Crutchley let loose a loud laugh and his face broke into a broad, toothy smile.

"That was a long time ago," he said, "I've found God. I'm a different man now."

"I'd still like an autograph, if you don't mind," Burke replied, handing Crutchley a pen and paper.

"Sure, why not. What's your name?"

"Greg," Burke lied.

Crutchley wrote, "To: Greg. From: The Vamp – John Crutchley," and then handed the paper back to Burke.

That evening, Burke proudly presented the autograph to a clearly startled and considerably annoyed Raub.

Throughout his time in prison, Crutchley remained tight-lipped about his suspected crimes, refusing to confess or divulge any information about the location of his victims' bodies. In an undated letter to his son, written sometime while serving his life sentence for the violation of parole, Crutchley came close to confessing, but explained why he could not.

My son, Florida has a curious law. This one is called the Son of Sam law. In it, the state seizes all rights to writings a convicted person makes about his crime. The philosophy behind such a law is simple: strip the profit motive from such things as diaries, movie rights, etc. from the felons so they can't commit a crime, and then, while they are being supposedly punished for it, they can't make a fortune by selling a juicy story about the crime.

   . . . .

Because of that law, if I were to write you an account of my crime, the writings would be fully protected under the 1ˢᵗ Amendment of the U.S. Constitution, but Florida boldly steps all over that and taxes those selected thin slices of writings. Taxes them at a 100% level.

Now, in operation, what this law . . . has done is stripped the citizens of a source of information about what went on in the mind of someone who broke a law . . . Who, in their right mind, can honestly pick up a newspaper story, or watch a TV account, and REALLY BELIEVE that they are getting a truly accurate report of all of the facts about that event? Really, now.

. . . .

Since the Son of Sam law could conceivably be used against you by the state, as a vehicle to seize something I've written, I shall avoid including those details regarding my crime which the SOS law taxes.

And so the years passed and the vampire remained silent, refusing to talk about any of his suspected victims, declining to discuss his involvement in so many suspicious disappearances and unsolved murders.

THIRTY-THREE

Better off dead

S hortly after midnight on March 30, 2002, James Elders returned to his cell in Hardee Correctional Institution in Bowling Green, Florida, after having spent some quiet time reading alone, or at least the closest thing to quiet an inmate can find in prison. For the past several weeks, Elders had shared a cell with John Crutchley. Although the cell was dark as he entered it, he could see the fifty-five-year-old Crutchley sitting upright on the top bunk bed, leaning against the wall with his back propped up on a pillow. Elders figured that Crutchley had fallen asleep.

"Hey, you need to move! You're gonna fall off the bunk in the middle of the night and wake me up!" Crutchley did not stir.

Elders tried banging on the bottom of Crutchley's bunk, but he still did not move. *Damn, this guy is a heavy sleeper,* Elders thought to himself.

Growing slightly annoyed, he nudged Crutchley and poked him on the shoulder, but Crutchley still did not respond. Now Elder's annoyance gave way to alarm. He began to suspect that something might be wrong.

Moving closer to the bed to get a better look, Elders noticed that

Crutchley seemed to be leaning to one side and he had something covering his face. In the dim light of the cell Elders saw a plastic "Country Hearth" bread bag pulled down over Crutchley's head and face. A red rubber band held the bag in place around Crutchley's neck. Inside the bag was a white handkerchief wrapped around a partially full Albuterol inhaler.

Crutchley wore only white boxer shorts, which had been pulled down to the middle of his thighs. His mouth was hanging open and his eyes were rolled upwards.

Elders yanked the plastic bag off Crutchley's face and shook him vigorously, trying to revive him. When Crutchley still did not respond, he felt for a heartbeat at Crutchley's wrist and neck. Finding no trace of a pulse, Elders yelled to the guards for help.

Members of the prison medical staff responded to the scene and tried in vain to revive Crutchley. The Vampire Rapist, the man who had terrorized a nineteen-year-old girl and stolen her blood just as ruthlessly as he had stolen her virginity, the monster who had murdered untold numbers of women without a modicum of remorse, was pronounced dead at 12:43 a.m.

———

In an affidavit signed later that day, Elders stated that he and Crutchley had been talking outside their cell at around 10:00 p.m. on March 29. At 10:30 p.m., Elders went into the cell to pray, while Crutchley went to the day room so that Elders could have some privacy. According to Elders, this was part of their nightly routine. At 10:50 p.m., Elders finished praying and left the cell to call his wife. When he could not reach her, he returned to the cell and engaged in general conversation with Crutchley, who had also returned. After a few minutes, Crutchley went to the day room to read the newspaper and Elders went to the shower area to read a book because it was the most illuminated area that was available to inmates at night. When the 12:00 a.m. count was called, Elders returned to the cell and discovered Crutchley sitting lifeless on the bed.

Crutchley's body was transported to the Medical Examiner's Office at 5:45 a.m. on March 30, and the medical examiner conducted an autopsy a few hours later. Upon completing the autopsy, the examiner concluded that Crutchley's death had been accidental as a result of autoerotic asphyxia.

A sexual practice in which heightened pleasure is produced by reducing the supply of oxygen that normally reaches the brain, autoerotic asphyxia induces a semi-hallucinogenic state that, when combined with sexual orgasm, can generate an intensely pleasurable rush comparable in power to that produced by cocaine. Practitioners of autoerotic asphyxia typically engage in the practice as a solitary act while masturbating, and common ways of producing the hypoxia, or state of reduced oxygen flow to the brain, include self-hanging, strangulation, choking, and suffocation, often with the use of a plastic bag. However, due to the risks inherent in the act of autoerotic asphyxia, practitioners usually employ a safety mechanism to prevent accidental death in the event that unconsciousness occurs.

Elders told prison officials that six months earlier he and Crutchley had discussed an article about using oxygen deprivation to enhance sex, and they had both agreed that engaging in such a practice would be nothing short of stupid.

Wesley Pope, who had been Crutchley's cellmate before Elders, signed an affidavit on April 9 stating that he shared a cell with

Crutchley from November 2000 to March 2001. During that time period, he had seen Crutchley masturbating, injecting needles into his penis, and inhaling spray inhalers for sexual purposes. According to Pope, one night around 3:00 a.m., he heard a choking sound and saw Crutchley sitting in a lotus position masturbating with a black belt wrapped around his neck. Pope requested a cell change shortly afterward.

If autoerotic asphyxiation indeed killed him, then Crutchley's quest for the "ultimate experience," which continually pushed him to seek more intense, more stimulating sexual encounters, and which drove him to murder Debbie Fitzjohn, Patti Volanski, and untold numbers of others, ultimately ended in his own destruction. Locked up, unable to get sexual satisfaction from strangling anyone else, in the end Crutchley may have had to settle for suffocating himself.

As Norm Wolfinger put it, Crutchley's "appetite for the bizarre just continued. One thing led to another, to another, until it finally killed him. He was the ultimate sex fiend."

In its investigation report dated June 17, the Florida Inspector General's Office arrived at the same conclusion as the medical examiner, ruling Crutchley's death accidental. Senior Inspector Daryl McCasland reported having examined Crutchley's body at 2:40 a.m. on May 30, at which time he noticed semen seeping from Crutchley's penis and onto his leg. He noted that a tan rod approximately one-quarter inch in diameter had been pierced through the head of Crutchley's penis, and a one-inch long metal electrode on the end of it was embedded about a half of an inch at the base of the penis.

McCasland inspected Crutchley's cell and observed no obvious signs of a struggle. He reviewed Crutchley's medical history, which included substance abuse, bronchitis, and Hepatitis C, along with two admissions for suicide observations in May 1987 and July 1997, as well as various diagnoses including Schizoid Personality, Compulsive Personality Disorder, and Sexual Sadism. Crutchley had been seen by the prison's Mental Health Department on March 21 in connection with the February 28 death of his mother, but it had been determined at that time that he did not exhibit any suicidal tendencies and did not need further counseling. McCasland noted that suicide had been definitively ruled out as inconsistent with Crutchley's psychological state and behavior in the weeks leading up to his death. In addition, prison officials reported that in the days before his death Crutchley's behavior had not undergone any noticeable changes, and he was "always smiling." A review of recordings of his telephone calls in the weeks leading up to his death revealed that he had spoken to his son and two friends, but nothing suggested that he was upset or depressed. If anything, he seemed excited about the prospect of his case being reviewed by the Supreme Court.

Some thought it just that the cause of death of Crutchley's final victim – himself – was the same as his first, but not everyone was convinced that Crutchley's death was accidental. Gregory Raub, Crutchley's former cellmate, believed that Crutchley had been murdered. Raub knew from first-hand experience how rapists are often targeted in prison, and Crutchley's notoriety as the Vampire Rapist only amplified such feelings of ill will among some of the prison population.

Bob Leatherow also believed it feasible that Crutchley had been "helped" to his death, perhaps by a jilted prison lover.

Crutchley's family claimed his body on April 1. Shortly thereafter, Dr. Jose Silva, a respected psychiatrist with an interest in the neuropsychiatric origins of serial homicide behavior, received a phone call from Carolynn Crutchley. She wanted to know whether he would be interested in having her deceased brother's brain. Although Silva never took possession of Crutchley's head, he later worked with Carolynn in preparing a study, "The Case of John Crutchley 'The Vampire Rapist' From the Perspective of the Neuropsychiatric Developmental Model," which he planned to present at a conference held by the American Academy of Forensic Sciences. In undertaking his analysis of the case, Silva ruled out Asperger's disorder as a cause of Crutchley's deranged acts and diagnosed Narcissistic Personality Disorder as a contributing factor. However, he never presented his findings because he began to suspect that Carolynn suffered from a mental disorder herself and he did not feel comfortable working with her any longer.

Ultimately, the mortal remains of the Vampire Rapist, the man who hinted at having burned some of his victims' corpses to ash, were incinerated at 1800 degrees Fahrenheit in the purging flames of a crematorium. Unlike his many victims, Crutchley received a proper funeral and his remains were laid to rest in a well-marked, meticulously maintained burial space. After a short service, his ashes were placed alongside his mother's in a columbarium in the peaceful memorial garden of the Christ Episcopal Church in his hometown of Clarksburg, West Virginia. In death, as in life, the debauched genius would never be able to gravitate far from his mother's influence.

| Ash remains of Mildred Crutchley and her son

In a similar fashion as his life, Crutchley's demise commanded widespread media attention with news channels and newspapers reporting the story nationwide. In Brevard County, the *Florida Today*, the paper perhaps most familiar with Crutchley, devoted the front page of its April 2 edition to coverage of his death. The article highlighted how Crutchley had been a prime suspect in dozens of murders, and stressed that he may have been "one of the deadliest serial killers in the nation."

The April 6 airing of NBC's popular television show, *Saturday Night Live*, tried to inject some humor into the news of Crutchley's death, albeit inaccurately as to the manner of his demise. Comedian anchors Tina Fey and Jimmy Fallon addressed the news in a "Weekend Update" skit.

Tina: "John Crutchley, known as the Vampire Rapist, committed suicide this week at a Florida prison, where he was serving a life term."

Jimmy: "Oh, man, that's terrible."

Tina: "What? No, no, it's not. He raped people and drank their blood."

Jimmy: "Oh, I thought he was called the Vampire Rapist because he raped vampires."

(Studio audience erupts in laughter)

Jimmy: "That would be a good thing, you know?"

Tina: "No, no, I'm glad we cleared that up."

Jimmy: "Well anyway, we'll miss you Vampire Rapist."

Tina: "No, we won't."

Michael Bross, the attorney who represented Crutchley during his 1996 violation of probation hearing, felt saddened by the news of his death. Unlike Norm Wolfinger, who pointed to the Vampire as proof that "evil people do exist," Bross came to know another side of Crutchley, the side that Lisa Baker and others had known, the side that could be witty, charming, and polite.

"When I met him, he was a caring, witty, intelligent person," Bross recalled. "I thought he would have been a good, law-abiding member of our society," he said with a hint of regret. Bross remembered his client as being "uniquely intelligent, very articulate," "well-behaved," and "calm" throughout the time that Bross represented him. However, he also recalled Crutchley's strange sense of humor, such as the time Crutchley cracked himself up, cackling hysterically after changing whatever the topic of conversation had been by announcing in an altered voice: "Well, in another *vein* . . ."

Lisa Baker, who lived with Crutchley for five years in Indiana and Virginia, recalled him as a "happy man" throughout the time that she knew him. She expressed genuine sorrow about what had happened to him, lamenting the fact that someone who had once been a happy, healthy human being "seemed to be a broken man when he died." Baker still could not believe that Crutchley committed any of the crimes for which he was convicted or that he had been involved in any murders.

"He was a good person in spite of his actions, if in fact, he did commit any crimes. I'm not sure he was guilty of what he was accused of. I guess no one will ever know what really happened."

Like most law enforcement personnel involved in working Crutchley's case, Former Brevard County Sheriff Jake Miller did not harbor any doubts about his guilt, and he did not feel even a sliver of sadness when informed of Crutchley's passing. He would always think of Crutchley as a creature of darkness.

"I've worked about every kind of deviant behavior case in law enforcement. This man was just evil throughout. He represented evil in everything he did."

Miller echoed Leatherow's belief about Crutchley's guilt in other unsolved homicides.

"There's no question in my mind that he fully intended to drain Christina Almah's blood until she died. And then he'd put her in a shallow grave somewhere just like the others."

Phil Williams, another former Brevard County Sheriff, called Crutchley one of the two worst criminals that he had ever encountered in his twenty-seven years of law enforcement. Crutchley shared that distinction with admitted serial killer Gerald Stano, who confessed to killing forty-one women.

"I'm not a superstitious person and I'm not easily spooked," Williams said, "but when you were in Crutchley's presence, it literally made the hair on the back of your head stand up. That's the worst I've ever seen."

Williams, a prosecutor in the State Attorney's Office before he became Sheriff, found Crutchley "fascinating as a criminal," and developed a firm conviction that Crutchley "committed a lot more crimes, more heinous crimes" than the Christina Almah abduction.

While far from disappointed about Crutchley's death, he regretted that it prevented investigators from learning the full extent of his criminal acts.

Norm Wolfinger, who had been intimately involved in Crutchley's prosecution, did not beat around the bush in conveying his feelings about Crutchley's death.

"He was the most bizarre defendant, by far, that I ever prosecuted," Wolfinger pronounced. "As much as I hate for anybody to die, society is better off with him gone. He was always looking for something more forbidden, more bizarre. He finally found it, and the world is better for it."

THIRTY-FOUR

A question of why

I n the years following Crutchley's death, questions about the disturbing nature of his crimes continued. How the little boy who had so tenderly cared for a baby duck became a deranged sociopath lacking any empathy for others, killing for sexual pleasure and disarming his victims with his unassuming appearance and reassuring smile, continued to puzzle and perplex. How that little boy's bitterness about an isolating home environment and lack of parental affection transformed him into a modern day monster, one who entertained thoughts of murdering his own son, continued to beguile and bewilder. How the well-dressed, articulate, attractive man who seemed so friendly and harmless concealed the Vampire Rapist, a psychotic killer whose indifferent cruelty shocked a nation, continued to confuse and confound.

With his former client forever silenced, Joe Mitchell bemoaned the fact that his attempts to strike a deal with prosecutors in 1986 had been turned down. According to Mitchell, it had been Crutchley himself who had suggested making the plea offer. He had floated the idea to Mitchell shortly after being interrogated in the "bones room." As Mitchell recalled, although Crutchley continued to seem confident that law enforcement would not be able to link him to any murders, his experience in the bones room had actually "scared him to death." He had been willing to make a deal to avoid the death penalty and save his own neck, but with the caveat that he would deal solely with the State Attorney and not have any more contact with the Sheriff's Office. So in the end, while the staged gamble of the bones room had burned any bridges of dialogue between Sheriff's investigators and Crutchley, it had not wholly backfired. According to Mitchell, it would have bore fruit but for the State Attorney's failure to pursue Crutchley's offer of a plea deal.

Tom Fair corroborated Mitchell's claim. As Fair recalled, Mitchell had been willing to cut a deal and his client was willing to make the deal with Fair because of the trust and professional friendship that Mitchell and Fair shared. They had developed a friendly, mutually respectful relationship over the years, a relationship that began in connection with a 1978 case in which Assistant State Attorney Michael Hunt's brother, Richard ("Dickey") Lee Hunt, had disappeared. After wearing a wiretap to gather incriminating evidence against Clarence Zacke, a local drug smuggler who had solicited Dickey to murder a customs agent, Dickey vanished. Although Dickey himself was never found, parts of his car were recovered in junkyard car shredders along the east coast of Florida from Daytona Beach to Fort Pierce. In 1984, Fair took over the case and contacted Mitchell, who represented the drug smuggler. Fair told Mitchell that he wanted to interview his client, who was serving a lengthy prison term, and in response Mitchell told Fair that his client would probably tell Fair to "go fuck himself," but that he was welcome to give it a try. On the agreed upon interview date, Fair and Mitchell rode together for the over-three-hour trip to the prison, and the two made several subsequent trips together as well. With each trip, Fair built up his relationship with Mitchell further. As it turned out, Mitchell might not have ended up representing

Crutchley but for Fair's conversation with Crutchley the night of his arrest.

Due to the depth of their relationship, Mitchell had felt comfortable approaching Fair about a potential plea deal. Late one night back in early January 1985, Fair received a phone call from Mitchell.

"You're right," Mitchell exclaimed, "he's a serial killer. You need to come to my house right away."

Fair drove to Mitchell's house as quickly as he could, arriving shortly after midnight. After exchanging pleasantries, Fair sat down across from Mitchell and asked him what was going on.

"You were right," Mitchell said," "he is a serial killer, but I'm not going to let you put him in the electric chair. I'm not going to represent him through never-ending death penalty proceedings and appeals. I will only represent him through the current rape case. After that, he belongs to the public defender. So your time is short."

"What do you want for a plea?" Fair asked, trying to hide his surprise.

"One life sentence."

"What are the numbers?"

"He'll plea to twelve," Mitchell replied.

"Were all of them in this state?" Fair asked.

"No, there were others in other places," Mitchell continued, "Ohio, North Carolina, Virginia, and I think West Virginia as well. The first one was in Ohio."

Mitchell later elaborated about the Ohio murder, explaining that Crutchley's first victim had been a girl he dated at Defiance College.

He killed her in his dormitory and then burned up her body in the boiler of the dormitory's furnace.

"I can't deal with out of state cases," Fair said. "I can't make promises for them, but in all likelihood if you work out an agreement here, the other states won't pursue prosecution if he's serving multiple life sentences here in Florida."

"I want one life sentence," Mitchell stated.

"The Sheriff is not going to agree to that, and neither will the state attorney," Fair pointed out. "How about this, whatever the numbers are here in Florida, he takes that number of life sentences. If it's six, it's six life sentences. If it's ten, then it's ten." Mitchell thought for a moment.

"I can live with that," he said finally. "And he can live with that." "What will we get in return for a deal?" Fair asked.

"You'll get the burial locations, the body parts, and the trophies. He'll lead you to all twelve of the burial sites."

Mitchell said that one of the twelve was Patti Volanski, whose headless body Crutchley had concealed in the framed out foundation of a TGIFriday's restaurant. He buried the body where the concrete slab was ready to be poured for the building's vestibule. He thought it funny that people would be walking over her everyday without knowing it.

"Does he still have the trophies?"

"He removed some body parts from the house and property while out on bail," Mitchell said, "however, he still has access to the trophies. But time is short. I'll have him at your office tomorrow at 1:00. But he will confess to you and only to you."

About a half hour after arriving at Mitchell's house, Fair left with a plea deal agreed to in principle. He immediately called Chief Deputy Ron Clark of the Brevard County Sheriff's Office and filled him in about his discussion with Mitchell. Clark told him that the deal was a good one and that he should call Norm Wolfinger. After hanging up, Fair called Wolfinger, who was in Quantico, Virginia. Wolfinger was asleep when his phone rang, but he quickly woke up when he heard about the deal.

"Great job," Wolfinger said, "I'll be on a plane in the morning to fly back."

Fair's last call was to Bo Russell to arrange for him to be present for Crutchley's confession.

After a few hours of sleep, Fair arrived at the Sheriff's office and was greeted by the news that a meeting was going on "with all of the bigwigs." Wolfinger, Clark, the Sheriff, and Speedy Dewitt were behind closed doors in a conference room along with Leatherow and Joe Crosby.

Perplexed, but clearly not welcome in the meeting, Fair went up to his office on the second floor. Mitchell arrived shortly afterward.

"What's going on, Tom?"

"Hi Joe, I don't have a clue."

Then jail personnel brought Crutchley up in shackles.

"We'll be right in, John," Fair said as Crutchley was led into an interview room adjacent to his office.

"Ok, Tom," Crutchley replied.

A few minutes later, Speedy Dewitt came up the stairs. "Fair, I need to talk to you in your office," he said, "now!"

Dewitt had long harbored resentment toward Fair, stemming from Dewitt's removal as commander of the Sheriff's homicide unit. Dewitt had been removed after his chief subordinate had endorsed a competitor running against the Sheriff for reelection, and Fair had been the man who had taken Dewitt's place as homicide commander.

Now Dewitt leaned across Fair's desk and pointed his finger at him. "You and Russell are going on two week's leave. You went around me on this and I don't appreciate it. You know better. We're not going to give Crutchley anything. We're going to work for everything we get and we're not giving him anything."

"Speedy, that's a bad decision," Fair replied. "You need to hear this from me: This guy is a serial killer. He's willing to give up twelve bodies. The burial locations, body parts, trophies, and a full confession. Twelve times."

Without a moment's pause, as if he had not heard what Fair

said, Dewitt fired back, "You're on two week's suspension. You will turn in your equipment and leave the building immediately."

Just then, Crutchley stepped out of the interview room. "Mr. Fair, I'm waiting to talk to you."

"You won't be speaking to Lt. Fair," Dewitt interjected, "You'll be speaking to me."

"Fuck you, old man," Crutchley replied, "I've got nothing to say to you."

As a result of Dewitt's intervention and Fair's suspension, the plea deal died on the vine.

In addition to the Florida murders that Crutchley would have admitted, Mitchell confirmed that Crutchley would have also confessed to murders he committed out of state. Mitchell had supported Crutchley's idea of initiating plea bargain discussions because, based on what he had learned from investigators and from Crutchley himself, he believed that prosecutors would eventually build a strong murder case against his client.

Mitchell had attempted to resurrect the plea deal while in California in March 1986 to take the deposition of Christina Almah. After the deposition, he went to lunch with Norm Wolfinger. Wolfinger's very presence at the deposition spoke volumes to Mitchell, telling him in no uncertain terms that the state attorney considered it to be a big case. As a "quintessential politician," rather than a hands-on prosecutor, Wolfinger rarely attended depositions in person, usually sending one of his assistant state attorneys instead. In fact, Mitchell could not recall another time during his nearly three decades of practice that Wolfinger had attended a deposition in person.

During lunch, Mitchell asked Wolfinger if he would be receptive to a plea deal in exchange for the State Attorney agreeing to forego seeking the death penalty against him. Under the proposed plea, the Vampire Rapist would live out his days in prison and Brevard County investigators would be able to successfully close many of their unsolved homicide cases. After hearing the terms of Mitchell's proposal, Wolfinger told him that he would have to think about it and get back to him. But he never did.

Now nearing the end of his lengthy legal career, Mitchell remains saddened for the victims' families, for their lost chance to have closure, for their now permanent inability to properly bury their murdered mothers or daughters. When Crutchley died in prison without formally acknowledging responsibility for any murders, the families' opportunity for certainty and closure died with him. Now the bodies of Patti Volanski and unknown numbers of others may never be found, and the murders of Debbie Fitzjohn, Kimberly Walker, Miss Hollywood, and the two unidentified Palm Bay victims may never be solved.

But Mitchell does not blame investigators for not jumping at the chance to make a deal with his client, nor does he fault them for not searching Crutchley's house and property more thoroughly on the night of his arrest, the small window of time in which they could have found evidence linking him to multiple murders. After all, Crutchley did not look like a murderer, let alone a psychopathic serial killer.

"It's not law enforcement's fault that they only treated it like a rape," Mitchell explained. They had no idea what they were getting into."

The police could not have been expected to see beneath the polished surface image that Crutchley projected. They could not be faulted for failing to understand Crutchley's personality. Indeed, Mitchell himself never really understood Crutchley. He struggled to come to terms with how his client did not seem to think that he had really done anything wrong. As best he could tell, his client could not understand why society thought that what he had done was so reprehensible. It was largely Crutchley's sociopathic personality, his utter lack of remorse, his complete inability to feel sorry for what he had done, that caused Mitchell to decide that if murder charges were brought against Crutchley, he would not represent him. Mitchell had labored long enough defending murderers. He did not want to use whatever lawyering talents he still possessed representing someone who all signs pointed to as being a serial killer.

Asked to assess his representation of Crutchley, Mitchell is quick to mention that his former client liked to talk too much, particularly to the news media. He was overly fond of the attention and celebrity-like fame.

"I did the best I could with a very difficult client," Mitchell concludes.

Norm Wolfinger steadfastly maintained that the "very informal" plea negotiations with Mitchell broke down because the State Attorney's Office did not have sufficient evidence to connect Crutchley to any deaths.

"If we had anything to tie a charge to, we would have done it," Wolfinger insisted. "But we had nothing."

Unable to definitively link him to a single unsolved murder, prosecutors adopted the strategy of putting Crutchley in prison as quickly as possible so that the murder investigations could be continued with him behind bars and safely off the streets.

The lack of a confession troubled many who were involved in Crutchley's case, even though it was wholly consistent with his personality and psychological profile. Indeed, everything learned about Crutchley's background showed that he was an extremely secretive individual who preferred keeping things to himself, hiding them from everyone, even his wife. His soul housed two selves: the seemingly harmless public persona and the darker, depraved identity that he kept hidden deep within the caverns of his psyche. In the end, the only person who really knew John Crutchley, if anyone *really* did, was Crutchley himself.

———————

To this day, Joe Mitchell remains fascinated by his former client, an enigmatic man whose actions, he says, fell "beyond my understanding." Throughout his representation of Crutchley, his client never displayed any inclination toward aggressive or anti-social behavior. In fact, he seemed timid if anything. He certainly did not look like a rapist, let alone a malevolent, blood-sucking vampire or psychopathic serial killer. Mitchell remembers Crutchley as being extremely clever and calculating, and he had not been surprised to learn that Crutchley had an IQ of over 160. He recalls with a smile how Crutchley demonstrated such an incredible knowledge of computer systems that prison officials privately hoped he would not be released on parole simply because they wanted to be able to keep him working on their computers.

Mitchell estimates that he handled approximately 3,000 criminal cases during his twenty-two-year career as a criminal attorney. Crutchley's case left a lasting mark on his memory. The case of the Vampire Rapist went "absolutely beyond the most bizarre facts" of any other case he ever came across. It is a case that he still finds troubling today.

"It's amazing to me," Mitchell explains, referring to his former client's likely role in multiple murders and disappearances. "If he did all of this—and I'm satisfied that the evidence is overwhelming that he did—the question that I keep coming back to is '*why?*'"

THIRTY-FIVE

Some guy

I wasn't some guy hanging out in bars, or a bum. I wasn't a pervert in the sense that people look at somebody and say, 'I know there's something wrong with him.' I was a normal person. I had good friends. I led a normal life, except for this one small, but very potent and destructive segment that I kept very secret and close to myself

– Ted Bundy

The answer to why Crutchley took pleasure in killing young women is likely hidden among the puzzle pieces of his past, perhaps concealed somewhere in the forgotten shards of his child-hood. It may be that insight into that question can be gleaned from a psychological evaluation or profile of his enigmatic, innermost self. Perhaps, however, the most convincing evidence of his guilt can be pieced together from fragments found by persistent investigators following his trail, as well as from the words of the Vampire Rapist himself.

Shortly before entering his guilty plea in the Christina Almah case, Crutchley conferred with his attorney in his cell at the Brevard County Jail. During their meeting, his lawyer advised that it would just be a matter of time before investigators searched his house again. He asked Crutchley if the police might find anything incriminating on the property.

Crutchley stared down at the table for a few moments before shifting his gaze to the attorney, peering into his eyes as if examining his soul, evaluating his trustworthiness before deciding how truthful to be. His deliberations apparently satisfactorily completed, Crutchley answered without breaking eye contact.

"They might find a hacksaw," he said casually, as if engaging a friend in idle chitchat.

"Ok, what's so bad about that?" the attorney asked.

"There might be human flesh on it," Crutchley replied without blinking an eye.

Since no murder charge had been brought against his client, and therefore no defense to murder needed to be prepared, Crutchley's counsel did not question him further about the hacksaw. Instead, he cautioned his client not to share anything that could constitute incriminating information because he would be obligated, under the Rules of Professional Conduct governing attorneys in Florida, to tell the police if he received any such information. However, Crutchley was in a talkative mood. Perhaps he had decided that he could trust his attorney. Maybe he just needed to get something off his chest. Whatever the reason, Crutchley proceeded to tell his lawyer how someone could have abducted and murdered the women that he was suspected of killing, but he stopped short of a direct confession. Just as Ted Bundy "confessed" to writers Steve Michaud and Hugh Aynesworth in 1980 by detailing, in the third person, how his crimes were committed, Crutchley provided a third-person narrative about the killing of his victims and the disposal of their bodies.

"If someone wanted to kill these women and not get caught, here's how they'd do it," Crutchley began, as if presenting a lecture on the stalking secrets of serial killers. He described how the victims' trust could be gained so that they would drop their guard, how they could be subdued and sexually assaulted, and how their blood could be drained. He spoke of how the dead bodies could be dismembered with a hacksaw in the bathtub, and how the body parts could be taken to wooded or other undeveloped areas to be disposed of, discarded there so that animals and the elements would help destroy the evidence.

He also emphasized the importance of disposing of the body parts at different locations.

"The killer would never put them together in one place," he said.

Crutchley also gave his attorney the impression that when he was arrested for the abduction and rape of Christina Almah, a skull from one of the unsolved homicide victims had been buried in his yard.

Crutchley continued to speak in the third person throughout his monologue, just as Bundy had in his confession, careful to emphasize that he was not talking about himself, although it would have been clear to anyone who heard him that he was retracing his own steps, recounting his own morally depraved acts.

And the similarities with Bundy did not stop there. Like Bundy, who frequently feigned an injury to lure his victims into vulnerable positions, Crutchley liked to trick his prey. For prostitutes, he pretended to be a simple john looking for a date. For the women he came across along the roadside, such as Christina Almah, he played the part of the Good Samaritan offering to help by providing a much-needed ride. Like Bundy, Crutchley's preferred manner of killing was by strangulation, frequently during the act of rape. The two also shared the characteristic of using a hacksaw to behead or otherwise dismember the corpses of their victims for the dual purposes of impeding the identification of their bodies and enabling them to keep prized body parts as trophies. Both sexual predators were also highly mobile, killing in multiple states as they moved around the country. Bundy officially confessed to eleven murders in seven states, but many believe that he killed at least thirty women. Crutchley had been ready to confess to at least twelve murders in Florida, and according to an internal Sheriff's Office memorandum dated April 28, 1995, his multi-state victims may have numbered as many as thirty-two.

The similarities in motive and behavior were so close that Bundy's third-person narrative of one of the murders he committed could easily be attributed to Crutchley's explanation of what drove him to kill, as Bundy described a "need to totally possess [the victim], after she's passed out, as she lay there in a state somewhere between coma and sleep."

Sexual gratification had not been the primary driving force for Bundy's behavior. Instead, he killed for the sense of control, the psychological pleasure derived from being in a position of absolute power as he literally held his victim's life in his hands, slowly strangling her to death.

As Bundy described it, "You feel the last bit of breath leaving their body. You're looking into their eyes. A person in that situation is God! You then possess them and they shall forever be a part of you."

Crutchley undoubtedly shared Bundy's feeling of excitement at having total power over another human being, and he was driven by a similar need to have absolute possession and control of his victims.

Both men also harbored an aggressive narcissism that formed the core of their personality. Inseparable from this narcissistic nature was their lack of empathy for others and their deep-seated need for attention. Just as Bundy reveled in the spotlight, playing to the press and representing himself at trial, Crutchley basked in the limelight of press conferences and enjoyed the widespread attention of having his case covered by newspapers and television reporters.

Just as Bundy relied on a "whole bunch of little beasties who would, in effect, destroy every last shred of the victim," Crutchley counted on help from Mother Nature in the form of the hot, humid Florida climate, as well as scavenging birds and beasts of the woods. He had learned the effectiveness of that method of disposal when he dumped Debbie Fitzjohn's body in a densely wooded area of Northern Virginia. Later, he improved his method of limiting a means of identification by decapitating the bodies of most of his Brevard County victims before disposing of them.

Finally, the killing careers of Crutchley and Bundy ended in similar fashion as a result of uncharacteristically sloppy mistakes, almost as if they wanted to be caught. Bundy drove around at 1:00 a.m. in a stolen car. Crutchley left his relatively unsecured victim alone while he went to work. And following their arrests, both men blamed their deranged behavior on pornography.

Although they shared many similarities, Crutchley was in some ways smarter than Bundy, both in IQ level (Crutchley's was 160 or 168, Bundy's 124 or 140), and in carrying out the commission of his crimes. Most notably, after the close call he had with law enforcement following the Debbie Fitzjohn murder, Crutchley deliberately chose prostitutes, transients, and other social castaways as his victims because he knew that they would be less likely to be missed. Bundy, on the other hand, preyed primarily on middle-class women, and he thought nothing of abducting a young girl from school or attacking college girls in their sorority house on the campus of a state university.

THIRTY-SIX

A crack in the mirror

I f investigators' suspicions are correct, Crutchley should be counted among the deadliest serial killers in American history. Yet, during a killing career that appears to have spanned at least a decade, he was never charged with a single homicide. In the case having perhaps the most evidence arrayed against him, the Debbie Fitzjohn murder, the lead investigator and private detective working the case both believed that Crutchley had killed her, and yet no criminal charge or indictment ever issued.

Fitzjohn's father, Herman, maintained a conviction that more direct evidence of Crutchley's guilt could have been uncovered if the Fairfax County Police Department had ever bothered to conduct a search of his trailer. The lack of an arrest in his daughter's murder —in a case where all signs pointed to Crutchley as the perpetrator— incensed him.

"I'm blaming it all on the Fairfax County police," he said bitterly.

James Wilt agreed that the police should have at least sought a warrant to search Crutchley's trailer.

"I don't think they did a very good job," Wilt said in assessing the police department's efforts. Wilt also believes that the Commonwealth Attorney "made a terrible mistake" by not seeking an indictment of Crutchley after Debbie's Bible was found at Crutchley's house in Malabar.

The countless hours Wilt spent investigating Debbie Fitzjohn's disappearance and murder left no doubt as to who was responsible for her death.

"I feel sure in my mind that John Crutchley killed her," he says without hesitation.

Leatherow offered a similar assessment, deeming the Fairfax County Police Department's investigation of the case to be "really lax" for failing to move forward with an arrest of Crutchley for at least a lesser offense like manslaughter.

Joe Mitchell believes that Brevard County investigators missed a golden opportunity to get Crutchley to confess because they had the "wrong people" in the bones room with him. He maintains that his former client trusted Lieutenant Tom Fair, the officer who had overseen his arrest. Indeed, the first time Mitchell met Crutchley, his new client had boasted about some forgotten subject matter and then told him, "If you don't believe me, why don't you talk to my good friend, Tom Fair." Had Lt. Fair been in the bones room, Mitchell believes that his client would have confessed. As for why Fair was not there, Mitchell speculates that egos or internal politics may have gotten in the way.

"I love law enforcement, but their goal is not just to solve the homicide. Their goal is to solve it *and get the credit* for solving it."

Bob Carrisquillo is confident that Crutchley could have been linked to numerous unsolved murders well before the botched bones room experience. If an interrogation team had been ready to interview Crutchley when he was first caught, either the day of his arrest or shortly thereafter, Carrisquillo believes that he would have told the police everything. Crutchley would have been most vulnerable then, most in the dark as to what the police already knew, and did not know, about his history. But at the time there was nothing to suggest that Crutchley's criminal acts extended beyond those of a first-offense rapist, albeit one who exhibited a strange penchant for blood.

Carrisquillo's involvement in the investigation convinced him of Crutchley's guilt in numerous murders. The picture of Crutchley's lifestyle and personality that emerged from interviews with past girlfriends, coupled with his treatment of Christina Almah during her ordeal, led Carrisquillo to conclude that Crutchley had been a sexual deviant his entire life, and had likely been killing since he was a teenager. Carrisquillo is certain that Christina would have been killed in the bathtub if she had not escaped, a method he believes Crutchley employed to dispatch other victims.

Despite the passage of time, Michael Bross still regrets never having asked Crutchley about the unsolved homicides during his representation of the Vampire Rapist.

"If I had known that Crutchley would die in prison without ever revealing where the bodies of his victims were, I would have asked him about them to try to get closure for their families."

For the families of Crutchley's victims, the lack of a loved one's body formed a void and sense of emptiness that has never fully subsided. The family of Patti Volanski is not alone in wondering what happened during her final hours of life and what became of her mortal remains. Now the families of Crutchley's forgotten victims remain condemned to forever suffer from the uncertainty of the unknown.

After Crutchley was found asphyxiated in his prison cell, Wolfinger's office notified Patti's mother about his death.

"She was pleased this nightmare will have some closure," Wolfinger recalled, "but she will never have answers." Crutchley's death, he pointed out, "leaves a lot of unanswered questions."

In 2010, a forensic artist commissioned by the Brevard County Sheriff's Office completed a facial reconstruction of the only skull that was recovered among the four unidentified bodies of Crutchley's suspected Brevard County victims. Investigators hoped that the reconstructed face would generate new leads in determining the dead woman's identity, leads that might link Crutchley to her murder. However, the phones have stayed as silent as Crutchley himself.

"We normally get two or three calls on something like this," said homicide agent Carlos Reyes. "On this one, we did not."

The bodies of some unknown victims, those prostitutes, transients, or run-aways unfortunate enough to come across the Vampire Rapist's path, may never be found.

He refused to believe it at first, but over time George Hurley could no longer deny that his friend and former colleague at Harris Corporation was a serial killer. Now he beats himself up when thinks about how he used to go to lunch with Crutchley, sitting across the table from him sharing pleasant conversation, enjoying enthusiastic discussions about computers and motorcycles. He cringes when he recalls one particular conversation in which he told Crutchley how compliant and subject to suggestion his wife became whenever her blood sugar levels dropped.

Half-listening up to that point, Crutchley had immediately perked up, blurting out excitedly, "Oh, that could be kind of fun!"

Now Hurley is ashamed of his association with his former friend. He feels embarrassed that he exercised such poor judgment of character, trusting and confiding in someone who took pleasure in raping his victims and drinking their blood before ultimately choking them to death.

"That man," he now says, "was pure evil."

During his trial for multiple murders, serial killer Jeffrey Dahmer composed a letter to the presiding judge, revealing an acute awareness of the evil nature of his deeds. "I knew I was sick or evil or both,"

Dahmer wrote. "Now I believe I was sick."

If evil should be understood in absolute terms as the antithesis of that which is good, then perhaps John Crutchley may rightfully be deemed evil. While most individuals live counterfeit lives to some small extent of character, Crutchley's psychological makeup included a virtually limitless disposition for deceit and complete freedom from the constraints of conscience. Yet, irrespective of whether he personified evil, or instead suffered from a psychological sickness that he could not control, it is clear that Crutchley managed to successfully live two separate lives, employing deception to inhabit two very different worlds. In one world, he appeared as the successful computer engineer who worked on classified communications systems for the Navy, while holding a top-secret security clearance at the Pentagon. In that world, he projected the identity of a quiet family man with a genius IQ working a prestigious, high-income job at Harris Corporation.

Crutchley's other world revolved around bizarre sexual practices and cold-blooded manipulation of others, a world in which he found pleasure only when holding the life of another human being in his hands. Crutchley had deftly concealed this darker, ruthless side, letting it loose in an immoral world in which he murdered women for excitement in a never-ending search for something more stimulating, an incessant, insatiable quest for the ultimate high. The idea of "JB," the identity he conveyed to others, was illusory, an artificial image he projected to hide his true self. He became a master at compartmentalizing his life, maintaining a mask of sanity by working a white collar job, paying the bills, and running family errands, all while dispassionately planning a grisly fate for the subject of his next fantasy, the next prey to temporarily appease his dark hunger, the next victim of the monster hidden within.

THIRTY-SEVEN

Alive for evermore

Once I was dead,
But now I am alive forever and ever
I am he that liveth, and was dead;
And, behold, I am alive for evermore

- Revelations 1:18

Not long after closing out the Crutchley file, Bob Leatherow turned down the offer of a promotion in rank to major, and in doing so passed up the opportunity to oversee fifty to sixty detectives. The idea of a desk job and the corresponding administrative headaches that would accompany it held absolutely no appeal for him. He preferred to stay in the middle of the action doing a purer form of police work out on the streets.

That is where he was when he heard the news. Leatherow was on patrol in his squad car when he got word that John Crutchley had died in prison. It took a little while for the news to sink in, and he experienced mixed emotions about it. He felt some relief knowing that a serial killer would no longer pose a danger to the community, and justice had been served in the sense that Crutchley's conviction for the abduction and assault of Christina Almah put him in prison and ultimately kept him there, ensuring that he would never kill again. But at the same time, Leatherow felt an undeniable disappointment that the victims' families would never know what really happened to their loved ones, would never find out where their bodies were hidden, and would never be able to give them a proper burial. Crutchley had taken those secrets with him to the grave.

Yet, the full measure of Leatherow's disappointment ran deeper than that. On a personal and professional level, he knew that now he too would never have closure. It bothered him to the core of his being that he had not been able to put the Vampire Rapist on Death Row where he belonged. Leatherow had wanted to see Crutchley meet his end as Bundy had, strapped down to Florida's electric chair.

"He was a killer," Leatherow says without a trace of doubt, "but I couldn't prove it."

Neither could anyone else. Despite being the prime or sole suspect in so many homicides, Crutchley avoided being indicted and managed to sidestep a charge in a single one. Leatherow attributes that elusiveness to Crutchley's formidable intellect.

"He was smart and he was thorough. And he covered his tracks well."

Although Crutchley's death was officially ruled an accident by autoerotic asphyxiation, Leatherow still finds it hard to believe that Crutchley would have died in that fashion. He suspects that Crutchley may have been killed as a result of some prison lovers' spat.

Leatherow retired from the Brevard County Sheriff's Office on his birthday, August 22, 2007, having worked over fifty murder cases during a law enforcement career that spanned some thirty-eight years. After reflecting on the impressive length of his time in public service, he mentions that every cop looks for that one big case to come along during their career, the one that defines their life's work in law enforcement. The Vampire Rapist investigation had been Leatherow's defining case by a long shot.

"I worked a lot of murder cases," he says, "but this was way above everything else."

As the case agent and lead investigator, Leatherow quickly became a "superstar" at the Brevard County Sheriff's Office. He found himself thrust into center stage of the investigation, placed squarely within the media spotlight. He has no qualms now in admitting that he enjoyed the attention that came with working the infamous Vampire case, but more than that, Leatherow enjoyed the challenge of trying to tie Crutchley to the murders that he knew in his gut Crutchley had committed. Those who witnessed his work on the case described him as being "so passionate about it" and so "devoted" to proving Crutchley's guilt that he had become "consumed" by it.

All in all, it had been his "most fulfilling case," but it had also taken an irreversible toll.

"Murder cases live with you forever," he explains. "They're in your heart and become part of your soul. They live with you forever and haunt you."

Looking back on his years of involvement in the Crutchley case, through all of the highs and lows, the euphoria of discovering new evidence and the disappointment of promising leads that never panned out, Leatherow cannot help but feel some sense of regret. He cannot fully exorcise a feeling of incompleteness.

Over the years, Leatherow developed a personal friendship with Patti Volanski's mother, Alta Pratt. Pratt and her brother flew down from Michigan every year and visited Leatherow and his wife, and Leatherow always treated his visitors to dinner at a good restaurant. At the same time, Leatherow's son, a member of the Florida Highway Patrol, and Pratt's nephew, a member of the Michigan Highway Patrol, became pen pals and even traded badges. Then, during her latest visit, Pratt told Leatherow that she had been diagnosed with a serious medical condition. After that, he never saw or heard from her again.

"I always promised her that I'd find Patti," he recalls with a palpable feeling of regret. "But I never did...I feel sad about that," he says quietly.

Over the years, inmates told Leatherow that Crutchley had cut out Patti's heart and buried her head in his yard, but no trace of it or any other part of her body was ever found.

More than a decade after Crutchley's death, Leatherow remains convinced that Crutchley prowled the streets of Brevard County as a serial killer, murdering without reproach while hiding in plain sight. And the evidence supports Leatherow's belief, suggesting that Crutchley's victims numbered from six to more than two dozen.

"I believe that John Crutchley had other victims in his house and they didn't survive," Leatherow says, thinking back to Christina Almah's harrowing escape. "They died and he got rid of their bodies." Although crucial DNA technology and techniques did not exist in 1985 at the time of Crutchley's arrest, Leatherow insists that the homicide cases linked to Crutchley could have been solved if investigators had been allowed to be more aggressive in interrogating him. Moreover, he cannot shake the feeling that a mistake was made in not pursuing the plea deal proposed by Joe Mitchell early on in the case. Leatherow had wanted to accept the plea, but it was not his decision to make. The ultimate decision maker for the Sheriff's Office, Speedy Dewitt, who worked over 300 homicides in his career, wanted to roll the dice, confident that the investigative team could link Crutchley to the unsolved murders through their own police work, and then pursue a harsher punishment for him. Not wanting to set a precedent of "negotiating with killers," Dewitt decided that they should take their chances, and he persuaded Norm Wolfinger to decline the plea deal.

That gamble proved to be a costly one.

"That was a big decision," Leatherow remarks, the tone of disappointment clearly resonant in his voice.

Now John Crutchley's victims live on in Leatherow's memory, haunting him from beyond their undiscovered graves.

Driving by Crutchley's former house on a humid, summer afternoon, its brick-faced front still concealed behind thick, towering hedges, Leatherow becomes noticeably silent. Turning toward the house, his eyes scan the area, slowly, deliberately, as if he is searching for something that continues to elude him. Suddenly he stops, staring off into the distance, lost in thought.

"Did we do the right thing by not accepting that plea deal?" he asks quietly, his voice sinking almost to a whisper.

The question lingers for a while in the air, as if awaiting an answer.

The words that eventually follow break the silence, but bring little relief. Still staring into infinity, Leatherow lets out a tired, reluctant sigh.

"I don't know," he says finally, "I just don't know."

Every year on her birthday, Summer Walker Stiles, the little girl left motherless by Crutchley's psychopathic acts, battles personal demons. She is unable to dispel deep-seated feelings of guilt that Kimberly Walker would still be alive if she had not been trying to buy her a birthday present when she went missing. Raised by her grandparents, Summer did not learn the truth about her mother's death until her teenage years when she stumbled across old newspaper articles that her grandparents had saved. Now a nurse with three children of her own, she counts as one of her most treasured possessions the Easter basket that her mom gave her a few months before her murder, but she is still plagued by unanswered questions about her mother's death, and she remains tormented by a desire for justice that cannot be satisfied.

For years, Crutchley's sole surviving victim suffered symptoms of Post Traumatic Stress Disorder, bearing painful psychological wounds, forever scarred by the trauma of being repeatedly raped and nearly killed while her deranged tormenter drained and drank her blood. After the horrific events of November 1985, she lived with her parents for more than a decade due to a paralyzing fear of being alone.

She takes some solace in the knowledge that, by escaping from an unremarkable house on a mild November morning, she saved not only her own life, but the lives of untold numbers of other women who would have suffered the same fate as Debbie Fitzjohn, Kim Walker, Patti Volanski, and nameless others. Yet, even now, she cannot bear to speak about the events that transpired in an unassuming house in a quiet neighborhood of a small, tranquil, Florida town. Even now, she still feels the chills of the Vampire's presence.

Although she eventually married in 1996, she has never fully recovered from the abduction and assaults. She still wakes from vivid nightmares sweating and shaking. There are still times when she feels Crutchley's icy stare fixed on her from impenetrable shadows. There are still nights that she sees Crutchley's ashen face glaring at her from somewhere beyond the darkness. For Christina Almah, the Vampire Rapist will never really die.

———

Searching through Crutchley's cell, investigators found an untitled poem among his possessions. The poem provides a chilling reminder of his legacy.

Do not stand by my grave and weep
I am not there. I do not sleep
Do not stand by my grave and cry
I am not there. I did not die

Epilogue

Somewhere a well-dressed, attractive man stopped his car beside a pretty girl walking alone along the road. Though an older man, he looked much younger than his true age, a benefit no doubt derived from his unusual diet. The young woman did not normally accept rides from men she did not know, but she was tired and the handsome stranger seemed harmless enough. His voice held a hypnotic allure. It offered a soothing promise of reassurance. He reached across his seat, opened the passenger side door for her, and smiled.

The hunger was eternal.

Acknowledgments

Let the truth be known: nothing is created alone.

For his extensive assistance during the research phase of this novel, many thanks go to Robert Leatherow. This book would not be what it is without Bob's considerable help.

My deep appreciation to James Wilt for his willingness to walk me through his investigative process in the Debbie Fitzjohn case, as well as his generosity in providing me access to all of his materials regarding her case.

Thanks to Commander Doug Waller of the Brevard County Sheriff's Office for his courtesy in allowing me access to case files and evidence.

My deepest appreciation to those named in this book (some under fictitious names) who were willing to share their memories of the Vampire Rapist case, including Lisa Baker, George Hurley, Joe Mitchell, and Tom Fair, who provided insightful perspectives on relevant events.

Thanks to my dad for first introducing me to the case of the Vampire Rapist and sparking a two-year journey of many challenges, hurdles, and rewards. And much thanks to my mom for her unwavering support.

Thanks also to my favorite sister for her review and suggestions in connection with an earlier draft of the novel.

Of course, I owe much thanks and appreciation to my publisher and advisor, RJ Parker, who helped this book come to fruition and offered many valuable suggestions along the way.

Deb Hartwell deserves big kudos as well for seeing what I missed and for making the editing phase of this novel a pleasant process.

And last, but not least, many, many thank yous to my lovely wife for her ideas while reviewing the various incarnations of this account of the Vampire Rapist, and for allowing me to devote the necessary time to complete what became, at times, an all-consuming passion.

About the Author

JT Hunter is a true crime author with over fifteen years of experience as a lawyer, including criminal law and appeals. He also has significant training in criminal investigation techniques. When not working on his books, JT is a college professor and enjoys teaching fiction and nonfiction in his creative writing classes.

JT is the bestselling author of *Devil in the Darkness: The True Story of Serial Killer Israel Keyes*, *In Colder Blood: On the Trail of Dick Hickock and Perry Smith*, *and A Monster of All Time: The True Story of Danny Rolling - The Gainesville Ripper*

You can learn more about JT and his other books at www.jthunter.org

A Note From The Author

Thank you for reading *The Vampire Next Door*. Your support means a lot to me!

If you've enjoyed this book, I would be very grateful if you'd take a few minutes to write a brief review on whatever platform you purchased it from.

Reviews are one of the most powerful tools when it comes to book ranking, exposure, and future sales. I have some loyal readers, and honest reviews of my books help bring them to the attention of new readers.

Thank you so much,
JT

Also by J.T. Hunter

Don't miss some of JT Hunter's other True Crime Accounts!

DEVIL IN THE DARKNESS: The True Story of Serial Killer
Israel Keyes

He was a hard-working small business owner, an Army veteran, an
attentive lover, and a doting father. But he was also something more,
something sinister. A master of deception, he was a rapist, arsonist, bank

robber, and a new breed of serial killer, one who studied other killers to perfect his craft. In multiple states, he methodically buried kill-kits containing his tools of murder years before returning and putting them to use. Viewing the entire country as his hunting grounds, he often flew to distant locations where he rented cars and randomly selected his victims. Such were the methods and madness of serial killer Israel Keyes. Such were the demands of the "Devil in the Darkness."

This book is the first detailed account ever published about Israel Keyes. It contains exclusive personal information about this frightening serial killer gleaned from extensive interviews with his former fiancee.

Optioned May 2018 by a Major Production company to be made into a motion picture.

IN COLDER BLOOD: On the Trail of Dick Hickock and Perry Smith

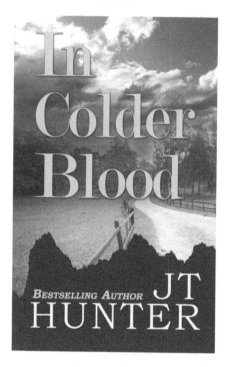

Two families, mysteriously murdered under similar circumstances, just a month apart. One was memorialized in Truman Capote's classic novel, *In Cold Blood*. The other was all but forgotten.

Dick Hickock and Perry Smith confessed to the first: the November 15, 1959 murder of a family of four in Holcomb, Kansas. Despite remarkable coincidences between the two crimes, they denied committing the second: the December 19 murder of a family of four in Osprey, Florida.

Over half a century later, a determined Florida detective undertakes exceptional efforts to try to bring closure to the long-cold case.

A MONSTER OF ALL TIME: The True Story of Danny Rolling
- the Gainesville Ripper

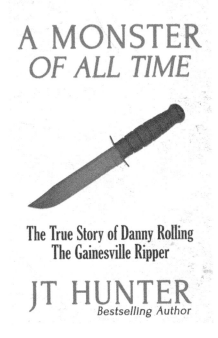

A MONSTER
OF ALL TIME

The True Story of Danny Rolling
The Gainesville Ripper

JT HUNTER
Bestselling Author

Ambitious, attractive, and full of potential, five young college students prepared for the new semester. They dreamed of beginning careers and starting families. They had a lifetime of experiences in front of them. But death came without warning in the dark of the night. Brutally ending five promising lives, leaving behind three gruesome crime scenes, the Gainesville Ripper terrorized the University of Florida, casting an ominous shadow across a frightened college town.

What evil lurked inside him? What demons drove him to kill? What made him "A Monster of All Time"?

Made in United States
Cleveland, OH
03 September 2025

20049989R00256